THE HEART'S AWAKENING

Praise for *The Heart's Awakening: 108 Steps to a Life of Love*

Bodhipaksa's book is a warm, accessible, and practical roadmap to the surprisingly complex territory of loving-kindness. It is also a robust challenge to think, to feel, and ultimately to live differently.
— **Will Buckingham**, author of *Hello, Stranger: Stories of Connection in a Divided World*

It takes a lifetime of practice to change, and a lifetime of trying to love well to know just how hard that is. In his beautifully rendered 108 reflections on kindness, Bodhipaksa exemplifies exactly why this Dharma work matters and can transform our very experience of being alive. This is a deeply felt, brilliantly researched, quietly revolutionary book on profound teachings. Bodhipaksa's gift here is to make them seem as fresh as they must have been thousands of years ago when they first woke up the hearts of seekers after truth and peace in a world that has always needed kindness as much as it does today. – **Candradasa**, founder of Free Buddhist Audio and The Buddhist Centre Online

Buddhist scholar Bodhipaksa gives those of us who are living in the modern world very simple steps to reawaken our hearts to the kindness and compassion that have always been there. He leads us to experience the true love and joy that reside in our hearts, alongside the realities of grief and despair. And he does so with an obviously clear understanding that it's very easy and *human* to lose our way to our hearts. No judgment.

Including exercises that are simple to practice, so that we don't become overwhelmed, this book is a delightful and insightful roadmap back to our heart's path of love, so that we can reclaim our joy and shine our light into this world, a world that really needs our light right now. – **Dr Mara Karpel**, clinical psychologist, speaker, radio show host, and author of *The Passionate Life: Creating Vitality & Joy at Any Age*

This book will not only tell you how to use the ancient Buddhist practice of metta bhavana or lovingkindness in your life but will give you many means of cultivating a compassionate attitude as you go about your day. The world has always needed compassion, but today we are more aware of that need than ever. Bodhipaksa brings his lifetime's interest in, and practice of, metta bhavana to this work. It's often said that you need to practice and not just read about metta bhavana in guides like this, and that's true. However, the quality of this book means that just reading it will make you a more compassionate person, more at peace with the world. – **Padraig O'Morain**, author of *Kindfulness: Be a True Friend to Yourself – with Mindful Self-Compassion*

What I love most about Bodhipaksa's writing is that he includes himself as an ordinary human being. Just like us, he also sometimes gets irritable, makes mistakes, and struggles to be happy. From this place he offers us the fruit of his decades of meditation and self-compassion. He writes in plain language with practical advice about how we can also access more kindness towards ourselves and others. – **Satya Robyn**, author of *Coming Home: Refuge in Pureland Buddhism*

With his clear insights and heartfelt approach, Bodhipaksa offers an antidote to the fears, struggles, and stresses inherent in this human experience. His latest book is a sincere and accessible step-by-step guide to opening the heart to all aspects of our lives. – **Sharon Salzberg**, author of *Lovingkindness* and *Real Life*

This book offers the meditator an imaginative and practical approach to cultivating kindness. Bodhipaksa offers personal insights from his life and teaching, creating an engaging and valuable resource for both teachers and practitioners alike. – **Suryagupta**, Chair of the London Buddhist Centre

THE HEART'S AWAKENING

108 STEPS TO A LIFE OF LOVE

BODHIPAKSA

Windhorse Publications
38 Newmarket Road
Cambridge CB5 8DT
info@windhorsepublications.com
windhorsepublications.com

© Bodhipaksa 2025

The right of Bodhipaksa to be identified as the author of this work has been asserted by him in accordance with the Copyright, Designs and Patents Act 1988.

No portion of this book may be utilised in any form for the training, development, enhancement, or operation of any artificial intelligence technologies. This prohibition includes all forms of AI, including generative models, neural networks, and any other types of computational intelligence. This restriction extends to all methods of obtaining or utilising data, including but not limited to data scraping, data mining, direct or indirect observation, manual entry, or any innovative data sourcing techniques that might be developed in the future.

Cover design by Katarzyna Manecka

Typesetting by Tarajyoti

British Library Cataloguing in Publication Data:
A catalogue record for this book is available from the British Library.

ISBN 978-1-915342-49-2

Excerpts from *A Guide to the Bodhisattva Way of Life by Śāntideva*, translated by Vesna A. Wallace and B. Alan Wallace. Copyright © 1997 by Vesna A. Wallace and B. Alan Wallace. Reprinted by arrangement with The Permissions Company, LLC on behalf of Shambhala Publications Inc., Boulder, CO, shambhala.com.

Galway Kinnell, "Saint Francis and the Sow" from *Mortal Acts Mortal Words*. Copyright © 1980, renewed 2008 by Galway Kinnell. Reprinted with the permission of HarperCollins Publishers.

Leonard Cohen, "Anthem", words and music by Leonard Cohen © 1992. Reprinted with the permission of SonyMusic Publishing Ltd, London N1C 4DB

Photograph of Chana Klos published by permission of the National Archives of Belgium. (Foreigners' file number 1407091.)

Photograph of Feliks Guliński used by permission of the Auschwitz-Birkenau State Museum Archives in Oświęcim.

Photograph of Henri Latowicz published by permission of Le Mémorial de la Shoah, Paris.

Photograph of Sura Brombart published by permission of the National Archives of Belgium. (Foreigners' file number A257448.)

Sean Thomas Dougherty, "Why Bother?" from *The Second O of Sorrow*. Copyright © 2018 by Sean Thomas Dougherty. Reprinted with the permission of The Permissions Company, LLC on behalf of BOA Editions Ltd., boaeditions.org.

Contents

	About the Author	viii
	Publisher's Acknowledgments	ix
	Audio Recordings	x
	Introduction	1
Part I	**Kindness**	10
Part II	**Compassion**	90
Part III	**Joyful Appreciation**	174
Part IV	**Overcoming Obstacles to Love**	258
	Conclusion	355
	Notes	357

About the Author

Bodhipaksa is a Buddhist teacher and author. He has been practicing meditation since 1982, and has been a member of the Triratna Buddhist Order since 1993. He is the founder of Wildmind: an online meditation resource, publisher of guided meditations, and meditation center offering online instruction. He is the author of *Wildmind: A Step-by-Step Guide to Meditation* (2010), *Vegetarianism: A Buddhist View* (2009), *I Can't Believe It's Not Buddha!* (2018), and *This Difficult Thing of Being Human* (2019).

Publisher's Acknowledgments

We would like to thank the individuals who donated through our "Sponsor-a-book" campaign. You can find out more about it at https://www.windhorsepublications.com/sponsor-a-book/.

Windhorse Publications wish to gratefully acknowledge a grant from Future Dharma and the Triratna European Chairs' Assembly Fund towards the production of this book.

FUTURE DHARMA

Audio Recordings

The Heart's Awakening has been produced with accompanying guided meditations by the author.

These can be streamed directly from the web.

Please go to https://tinyurl.com/THA-audio

Introduction

I remember the first time I realized that lovingkindness meditation could profoundly change my emotions. I was a student at veterinary school, sharing a Victorian apartment in Glasgow with three other students. Classes were over, and three of us were sitting in an ancient Mini Cooper, waiting for a fourth person to join us so that we could go home. I was in a horrible mood. I don't remember why; I was probably just tired. Liz and Sue sat chatting in the front seats, talking about this and that. Small talk wasn't my thing. I was an earnest young man who took himself very seriously. I rarely smiled when being photographed. I listened to classical music. I read world literature. I was interested in philosophy. When the girls started comparing notes on the ties their fathers wore, I became infuriated by the triviality of their conversation.

I was prone to irritability, so getting angry was nothing new. This time, though, something different happened. I realized I was suffering. And, because I'd recently started attending meditation classes in a shabby Buddhist community in the West End, I knew that I could do something about it. So I closed my eyes, and began to recite: "May I be well. May I be happy. May I be free from suffering." I said these words over and over in my mind. Although the phrases continued to roll on, I wasn't entirely paying attention to them; largely I said them on automatic pilot, with the bulk of my attention taken up by distractions. Yet "May I be well. May I be happy. May I be free from suffering" continued, unceasingly.

You might not expect such a half-hearted practice to achieve anything, but after a while I found I was happy. This amazed me. In the space of perhaps five minutes, I'd gone from bitterness to joy. I remember having been struck, as I was introduced to lovingkindness meditation, at how radical the idea was that we can shape our emotions rather than have them simply happen to us. I'd found it calming. Never, though, had it brought about such a dramatic shift in how I felt.

I certainly needed to become a kinder person. I'd grown up in a culture steeped in cynicism and sarcasm, where people judged your worth by how clever your put-downs were. I didn't have many role models of kindness, and there was little emotional warmth, encouragement, or nurturing around me. I wasn't happy, and I could be difficult to be around. Things have changed a lot since then. Cultivating *metta* or kindness has helped me become kinder, more compassionate, and happier.

Since you've already picked up this book, I'm assuming you're familiar with lovingkindness meditation, and that you're looking for ways to take that practice deeper. You don't need to have had experience of the other three meditation practices we'll be exploring together. If you have, you might find my approach different in some ways from what you're used to. Different in enriching and helpful ways, I hope.

They say that the best way to learn something is to teach it. Explaining something to others forces you to clarify what you do and how you do it. And, when you're dealing with people whose well-being you care about, there's an ever-present

Introduction

imperative: *how can I make this more helpful for them?* I've often had to ask myself: *am I teaching things just because I was taught them, or because they're genuinely helpful?*

One of the things I've found helpful is to call metta "kindness" rather than the more common "lovingkindness."[1] The first time I encountered the word "lovingkindness" was at a meditation class. I assumed that, because I was hearing a new word, I was supposed to experience an emotion I'd never known before. This impression was heightened when I heard teachers referring to "universal lovingkindness," which sounded impossibly exalted. I picked up that we were supposed to be able to love all beings – not just in the world, but in the entire universe. That's a daunting challenge. In contrast, "being kind to everyone you meet" and "meeting everyone you think of with a mind of kindness" seem both inspiring and practicable. I'll talk later about this word choice and what it implies, but I wanted to get it out of the way now, so that when I talk about kindness you'll know that I mean (so-called) lovingkindness.

The four practices we're exploring here are collectively known as the *brahma viharas*. This is often translated as "divine abidings" or something similar. Brahma is the name of an Indian god, and when we experience states of love we can sometimes feel an almost god-like sense of benevolence. In a Buddhist context, though, the term *brahma* often indicates "ideal, best, very great,"[2] and *vihara* often indicates a way of being or living.[3] I don't reject the association between the brahma viharas and the deity, Brahma, but the practices could be rendered simply as "the best ways of living." Using a different translation can help us to see things in new ways.

3

Introduction

In this case it reminds us that the best way to live is to be kind, compassionate, and appreciative. Perhaps that's a more helpful way to approach practice than the idea that we're striving for divine states of being. Talking about them as the four best ways to live our lives also reminds us that we're aiming to be helpful to the world, rather than to retreat into states of bliss, and that these are not just meditation practices, but practices to be cultivated in daily living. The brahma viharas are also known as the "immeasurables" (Pali *appamanna*; Sanskrit *apramana*), although calling them "the four boundless (or limitless) qualities" is easier on the ear. They are boundless or limitless in the sense that we can be kind, compassionate, and appreciative toward anyone we may encounter.

The brahma viharas predate the Buddha, and he acknowledged that he was putting his own spin on them. They're found in Jain teachings, Jainism being a slightly older tradition than Buddhism. In the Jain *Tattvartha Sutra* there is a mention of four right attitudes. These have slightly different names from those in the Buddhist tradition and are in a different order:

1. *Maitri*, or benevolence toward all living beings.
2. *Pramoda*, or joy at the sight of the virtuous.
3. *Karunya*, or compassion for the afflicted.
4. *Madhyastha*, which literally means "standing in balance" or "standing in the middle," and which means having tolerance toward those who mistreat us.

Most contemporary teachings on the Buddhist brahma viharas are based on a fifth-century Indian manual called

The Path of Purification.[4] This was written by Buddhaghosa, who is generally treated as if he was a meditation master. In reality, Buddhaghosa probably never meditated in his life. He was a scholar, and even wrote extensively about how it was impossible for monks like him to meditate because the monasteries they lived in were bustling places, more like college-cum-administrative centers than retreat centers. Moreover, there are records that his monastery, the Mahavihara, had abandoned the practice of meditation several centuries before he lived there. I suggest we regard Buddhaghosa as a non-meditator writing about meditation, and treat his works with due skepticism.

I've found it liberating to stop treating Buddhaghosa as infallible. He did us an invaluable service by compiling, expanding, and trying to make sense of earlier teachings on Buddhist practice, but his writings are sometimes confused or even contradict what the Buddha taught. I've also found it helpful to refer to a meditation commentary written about 400 years earlier by a monk called Upatissa. It's called *The Path of Freedom*.[5] Buddhaghosa seems to have incorporated some of Upatissa's work into *The Path of Purification* – including some of the teachings on the brahma viharas – but, because they were from rival schools, he doesn't directly acknowledge this.

Upatissa lived much closer than Buddhaghosa to the time of the Buddha, and was more likely to have been in touch with actual meditators. Some of what Upatissa says about the brahma viharas has added clarity to my own practice, and later I'll explain those shifts of understanding and their significance. By way of a preview, here is an overview of my current understanding of the brahma viharas. These descriptions may not be what you're used to. You've probably seen *mudita* translated as "empathetic joy," for example, and *upekkha* as "equanimity." The shifts in terminology below reflect fundamental changes in how I understand these practices.

- *Metta* is kindness. It's an empathetic recognition that others' feelings are as real to them, their joys just as welcome, and their sufferings just as unwanted, as our own are to us. Knowing this, we naturally think of others supportively, talk to them in ways that make them feel valued, and act in ways that put them at ease and contribute to their long-term happiness and well-being.
- *Karuna* is compassion. When we support someone's long-term happiness and well-being – that is, when we're kind – and we come to know that they are suffering, we naturally want to help them as best we can. Compassion is not merely a feeling but is a desire to relieve suffering.
- *Mudita* is joyful appreciation. It is not "being happy because others are happy." Much as the Jain *pramoda* is joy at the sight of the virtuous, mudita is a joyful recognition of the skillful qualities beings have that bring them joy and peace. But we don't simply see those qualities and feel gladdened by them. Rather, we aspire to practice them in our own lives and encourage them in others.
- *Upekkha* is the practice of using wisdom to remove obstacles to the first three brahma viharas.

Introduction

> Cultivating wisdom is a necessary step in purifying our kindness, compassion, and appreciation, because, no matter how much we work on changing our emotional habits, there remains an untouched core of delusion within us. This makes us act selfishly and unkindly, and creates suffering for ourselves and others. Upekkha uproots greed, hatred, and delusion, which obstruct our capacity to love. Upekkha is about seeing what obstructs love, and removing those obstructions.

This book is in four sections: one for each brahma vihara. Each contains twenty-seven brief chapters. The first few chapters in each section will introduce the practice in general, while the rest are roughly structured around the five stages of each meditation practice. You'll find suggestions for enriching your meditation practice here, as well as a link on page ix to guided meditations I've recorded to accompany this book. However, this book is not just about meditation. The brahma viharas are to be practiced in daily life as well as on the cushion. In fact, I see daily life, which occupies most of our time and frequently brings us into contact with others, as a more important arena for practice than our formal sitting practice.

Twenty-seven chapters, times four brahma viharas, equals 108. That's the number of beads on a meditation mala, or Buddhist rosary, and I hope that reading this book will in some way be a kind of meditation practice for you. You will gather, as you read, that I don't regard myself as an "expert" on kindness. I'm someone who struggles to be kind and who

Introduction

simply wants to share what he has found helpful. I like to think of it as an offering made humbly, not as something completely understood, but as a work in progress that I hope might help you in your own spiritual explorations. You'll find here what's helped me be a little kinder. Maybe it will help you, too.

Finally, a few acknowledgments. There are many people from whom I've learned about kindness. In a way, they are the ones who wrote this book. I think of the wonderful men of Dhanakosa Retreat Center in the Scottish Highlands, each of them an incomparable gift to the world. Thank you, Smritiratna, the jewel of mindfulness, Nayaka, the guide and leader, Amoghavira of unobstructed heroism, and the sadly missed Mahacitta, the great-hearted. I think of Shelly, Elizabethe, and above all Teresa, who have helped me understand on a deeper level what love is, and who have compassionately helped me become a better person. I think of my children, Maia and Malkias; it's a privilege to have witnessed you unfold beautifully, day by day, into this not-always-kind world. I look forward to seeing where your journeys take you, and the contributions you make to the world. And great thanks to my editor, Dhammamegha, for having more confidence in my writing than I do, and for offering gentle and helpful advice, and to Dhatvisvari, for her meticulous copyediting and kindness.

Part I
KINDNESS

The essentials of metta

Metta (Sanskrit *maitri*) is kindness. It is the desire, based on empathy, that beings, ourselves included, be well and happy. Kindness actively supports others through kind thoughts, kind speech, and kind actions. We can cultivate it both in daily life and in meditation.

Other translations
Lovingkindness, love, goodwill, friendliness.

The stages of the meditation
We cultivate kindness toward:
- Ourselves.
- A good friend.
- A relative stranger.
- A person we have difficulty with.
- All beings.

Suggested phrases
- May you be well.
- May you be at peace.
- May you be kind to yourself and others.

One crucial thing to know
Kindness is a quality you already have. You know it intimately. If you simply let yourself be kind, you are already developing and strengthening it within yourself.

1

What is kindness?

Kindness begins with empathy. When I recognize that you are, just like me, a *feeling being*, who experiences happiness and suffering, and who prefers happiness, I naturally want to act in ways that support your well-being.[6] Knowing that your joy is just as real to you as my own is to me, and that your suffering is just as vividly painful, why would I want to cause you suffering? Why would I be anything other than kind? To have empathy for another being is to recognize that they are in the most fundamental way just the same as us.

If we don't empathize with ourselves, it's unlikely we'll be able to empathize with others. So, to be kind to others, we first need to cultivate self-empathy. Empathizing with ourselves means recognizing that, just like anyone else, we are feeling beings. Our feelings are important to our well-being, and we prefer to be happy rather than to suffer. Strangely, we often forget this. We might, for example, think of ourselves as *doing* beings rather than as *feeling* beings. We push ourselves too hard, causing ourselves suffering. We also might think of ourselves primarily as *thinking* beings rather than *feeling* beings. We get so caught up in our thoughts that we forget to pay attention to the heart. So you need to keep reminding yourself: I am a feeling being.

We empathize with ourselves also as beings who are doing a difficult thing in being human.[7] We recognize that life is not

What is kindness?

easy, that happiness is rarer than we want, and that suffering crops up in our lives all too often. Knowing these things, we naturally want to offer ourselves support. We talk to ourselves kindly, let go of habits of harsh self-criticism when we notice them arising, forgive ourselves our errors, and take care of our own needs. This is kindness.

Once we have empathized with and begun to be more kind to ourselves, we are well placed to empathize with and be kind to others. When we recognize that they are just like us – feeling beings doing a difficult thing in being human – we naturally want to offer them support, too. When we are kind to someone, our actions let them know they are valued, cared for, and respected. We talk to them in a kind tone of voice, and we say things that are encouraging and helpful. Our body language is supportive. The body is likely to be relaxed and open, rather than stiff and closed off. We might smile or look concerned, show kindness with our eyes, or nod attentively so that they know they're being heard.

Kindness is something we all know. We know what it's like to be with someone who is kind to us – to be looked at with kindness and be spoken to kindly. We also know how to be kind to others ourselves, even if we sometimes forget to do so. Remembering to be kind can be the hardest part. The Pali word for "remembering" is one you know well: it's *sati*, or mindfulness. Mindfulness is remembering to be present and kind. As a reminder to be empathetic and kind, the Buddha emphasized that we should set the following intention:

We will develop and cultivate the liberation of mind by kindness, make it a habit, practice it thoroughly, make it stable, get to know it thoroughly, and undertake it completely.[8]

The best way of living our lives is to remember to be kind.

It's very hard to cultivate kindness if we haven't connected with ourselves empathetically. It's like trying to start a fire with wet wood. Beginning our lovingkindness practice with empathy is undoubtedly the most significant and effective change that's taken place in my metta practice since I first learned it. It's relatively easy to establish empathy, and, once we've done so, kindness flows naturally.

Exercise

Starting now, keep reminding yourself, "I'm a feeling being." Keep bringing your attention back to your heart as you do this. Notice experiences of happiness and suffering. Notice which you prefer. Remind yourself that life is a challenge, in which we often suffer. As you see others, keep reminding yourself that they too are feeling beings, doing a difficult thing in being human. Notice how this changes the way you respond to them.

2

Three kinds of empathy

In a well-known statement, the Buddha said: "All fear violence; all love life. Treating others like yourself, don't kill or cause to kill."[9] In a less well-known one he said, "The thing that is disliked by me is also disliked by others. Since I dislike this thing, how can I inflict it on someone else?"[10] That kindness is based on empathy is implicit in both these statements. The word "empathy" can mean many different things, however. I won't attempt to survey them all, but there are three meanings I'd like to highlight as being particularly useful to understand when we're cultivating kindness and the other best ways of living our lives.

1. Understanding how someone feels

When we talk about empathy, it's usually in terms of knowing how someone is feeling. As you tell me about some difficult situation you've experienced, I understand how you felt at that time and how you're feeling now. If I can't do that, I can't be genuinely kind to you; the best I could do would be to be "nice."

To empathize with you, I don't have to experience what you felt. In fact, that is often unhelpful. If someone is feeling desperate and hopeless and you end up feeling crushed too, you won't be able to help them. To be supportive, it's enough just to understand how someone is feeling. If you're feeling hopeless, I can know how unpleasant that is without having to fully experience it too. After all, I've been there before.

2. Understanding *that* someone feels

We might not always know how someone is feeling – for example if we've only just met them – but we can still be sensitive to them as feeling beings, and behave in a considerate and kind way. You meet a stranger, and recognize that they are just like you, and that their feelings of pleasure and pain, happiness and unhappiness, are just as real and vivid to them as yours are to you. Recognizing this commonality, you naturally want to act in ways that help them feel happy and at ease. This is the form of empathy illustrated in the two scriptural quotes above.

Before you begin to cultivate kindness for yourself in meditation, reflect on the fact that you are a feeling being. Recall experiences of happiness and suffering, and recognize the natural preference you have for one of these over the other. We need to recognize ourselves as feeling beings before we can be truly kind to ourselves. We need to be empathetic and kind toward ourselves before we can be kind to others.

3. Understanding that life is a difficult thing

Life is challenging for us all. When we or others are struggling, it's common to make the mistake of thinking of

Three kinds of empathy

life as an easy thing we're doing badly, and end up making harsh judgments. My experience of life, however, is that it's extremely complicated. Despite what some people say, happiness is not a choice. Sometimes we do things believing that happiness will result, but we suffer instead. Being human is not an easy thing we're doing badly. It's a difficult thing that we're doing as best we can, given our limited and imperfect resources. Recognizing that life is a challenge, frequently filled with unexpected and unwanted suffering, is another form of empathy. Seeing this, we're less likely to judge, and more likely to be supportive, reassuring, and encouraging.

I remind myself at the start of each stage of the metta bhavana practice that, since I'm a feeling being, struggling my way through life, I need support. So I offer it to myself by saying, "May you be well. May you be at peace. May you be kind to yourself and others." These phrases are not a way of manufacturing kindness. They are a way of *expressing* the kindness that naturally arises from the empathetic perspective of recognizing that life is a challenge. Recognizing this as the purpose of the lovingkindness phrases was another important turning point in my practice.

When I call to mind someone else – a friend, relative stranger, or someone I find challenging – I remind myself that they too are struggling. They too go through life seeking happiness and often not finding it, hoping to avoid suffering yet encountering it more often than they would like. Knowing this, I want to support them. And so I say, "May you be well. May you be at peace. May you be kind to yourself and others." Once again, these words are not a way to generate kindness. They are an expression of kindness toward other beings who are, just like me, doing this difficult thing of being human.

Exercise

Notice shifts in the way you empathize. Sometimes empathy will take the form of knowing *what* another person is feeling, and your kindness will respond specifically to that. Other times you might be aware only *that* they feel, with no access to their inner world, and you can treat them with respect and kindness. And sometimes you might be aware that life is hard. This, too, can make us kinder and more sympathetic. Notice times you don't feel empathetic; does recollecting these three forms of empathy help you find your way back to kindness?

3

Soft eyes, gentle heart

These days I always suggest letting the eyes soften at the beginning of meditation. This means letting the muscles around the eyes be at ease and allowing the focus within the eyes to be soft. You can try that right now, with the eyes open, although it might be best to look away from this book. As you let the eyes be lightly focused and at rest, you'll probably notice a few things:

- You can effortlessly take in the entirety of your visual field, rather than being narrowly focused on the central portion of it.
- The mind becomes quieter.
- Your breathing slows and deepens.
- The body softens and lets go of tensions.
- Your inner field of awareness, like your visual self, is now more open, receptive, and expansive.
- You can be aware of sensations of the breathing from all over the body.

Now, usually in our lives we carry tension in the eyes, and we focus tightly. We tend to focus on one small part of our visual field – for example when we're reading, or watching a screen, or looking at the triangle made by the eyes and the mouth on someone's face as we're talking with them. When we sit down to meditate, we bring this narrowness with us, and focus on just one small area of the breathing. Because there's not much sensation in that area, the mind looks elsewhere for stimulation, and we become repeatedly distracted.

Bringing soft eyes into our meditation practice, by contrast, opens us up to the richness of our experience. We begin to sense the breathing as a body-wide phenomenon, with soft waves of movement and sensation sweeping through the entire body. We may experience this richness and connectedness as fascinating, so that we become immersed in the breathing. We find that we're much less likely to become distracted than we usually are. All of this is helpful, but right now I want to emphasize one thing: with soft eyes comes a gentler heart. With soft eyes, the mind becomes more accepting, more patient, and kinder.

So, I encourage you to experiment with letting the eyes soften during meditation, and see what happens. Notice the gentling of the heart.

Soft eyes, gentle heart

Exercise

When it's safe to do so, keep bringing your attention back to the eyes throughout the day. Let them soften. Let the focus of your gaze rest lightly on the world, rather than fixing onto it in the probing way it so often does. If you can, let your soft eyes gently close, and notice how the whole body, the mind, and your feelings come more fully into your awareness. Notice how the mind becomes quieter and the heart gentler.

GUIDED MEDITATION: Soft eyes

4

Kind eyes

I'd like to share a kindness practice that I learned from Jan Chozen Bays, who describes it in her book, *How to Train a Wild Elephant*.[11] She calls the exercise "Loving eyes." I call it "Kind eyes," but it's the same thing. The practice is very simple. All we do is recall the experience of looking with love and notice the sensations of softening, warmth, and tenderness that arise around the eyes. What we find is that these loving qualities become part of the way we're paying attention to anything – ourselves or another person. We see ourselves or others with kind eyes, meaning that we care for them and want them to be happy and protected.

You can call to mind any memory that reconnects you with the experience of looking with love. Often I recall watching my children sleeping when they were young. This inevitably brings about, in and around my eyes, a strong sense of caring, appreciation, and tenderness. You might instead remember looking at a dear friend, a lover, or even a pet. All that's important is that the experience you're recalling is one of looking with love. Traditional teachings on cultivating metta usually warn against recalling children, lovers, partners, and so on. The early commentators on metta practice would no doubt have considered the very idea of doing this with an animal to be outrageous. But it really does not matter, as long as it evokes loving feelings.

Kind eyes

This is a simple and effective way to help us connect with our innate kindness. Many of my meditation students have told me that this is the single most effective tool they have found for bringing their lovingkindness practice to life. Although we begin with the eyes, this practice is really about the *quality of our attention*. We're evoking a warm, kind, appreciative, cherishing field of attention. Once you have evoked a warm, loving field of attention, you can turn it upon anything, including yourself. As you notice your body, your breathing, or your thoughts, you can regard them with a loving inner gaze.

The practices of soft eyes and kind eyes flow into one another. Often I'll begin with soft eyes, which helps to calm the mind and anchor my attention in the body. Then I'll return my focus to the eyes, this time accompanied by a recollection that evokes love or kindness. Now, with my mind imbued with warmth and empathy, anything I turn my awareness to is met supportively and with tenderness.

Notice that we don't *make anything happen* at any time. We don't make the eyes soften; we simply allow them to come to rest. We don't make kindness appear; we simply recall what it's like to look with love, and kindness manifests. It's all very gentle and organic. The best way to kindness is through kindness. By contrast, habits we've picked up of "trying" to make lovingkindness happen seem unkind.

You can have kind eyes both in meditation and in daily life. You can do it right now, as your eyes scan the words in front of you. Remember that, when you're reading words, you're connecting with the person behind them. In reading kindly, you can regard yourself and the author kindly. You can let the eyes be kind as you walk down the street, as you drive, or as you sit looking out of the window. You can let the eyes be kind in meditation, even if the practice is not the metta bhavana. My mindfulness of breathing has become "kindfulness" of breathing.

Kindness is a natural part of your being, and you can allow it to arise anytime.

Exercise

As you move from meditation on to your next activity, see if you let the experience of kind eyes remain. Throughout your day, keep regarding yourself and others with kind eyes.

GUIDED MEDITATION: Kind eyes

5

Sitting with kindness

To sit with kindness is to embody kindness. It's to regard the body with warmth and appreciation, and to sit in a way that promotes our well-being.

The Buddha said we should keep asking ourselves, "What kind of action will lead to my lasting welfare and happiness?"[12] Since kindness is the desire to support someone's *long-term* happiness and well-being, including our own, the key to the spiritual path is being kind toward ourselves. Yet, unwisely, we often do things that feel good now, or that we think will make us feel good, but that don't help us in the long term.

It's unkind to sit in a way that's forced and uncomfortable, and yet this is what people sometimes do, perhaps wanting to impress others or to do things "perfectly." So please don't hold your body rigidly or in a way that's going to cause unnecessary discomfort. To sit with kindness, we need to find a posture that's open, upright, and that allows us to breathe freely – as well as being comfortable.

Let the body be at ease. If you notice parts of the body that are tense, it's kind to let them soften, perhaps imagining the breath flowing through and around them. At the same time, it's not kind to completely let go and let the body slump. For a while, slumping might feel good, but in the long term it's not good for us. It inhibits our breathing, promotes depressive thinking, and makes it hard for us to sustain our attention. Finding a balance of openness and ease may take some experimentation, and you might need some help from experienced meditation teachers.

Give your body permission to adjust itself. As you observe the body with soft, kind eyes, notice how, as you breathe in, the spine becomes taller and straighter, and the chest more open. You'll also notice how the body settles and softens every time you breathe out. You might be tempted to *make* those things happen, but just let the body be soft, and you'll notice that these changes happen on their own. If you trust the body, it will find its way into a posture that supports your long-term welfare and happiness. You don't need to do anything except observe the body with soft, kind eyes.

With kind eyes, we meet even pain with kindness. Often, when a part of the body is in pain, we think it's betraying us. But this aversive attitude is unkind. Aversion makes us tense up around pain, leading to even more discomfort. We also suffer mentally because, regarding ourselves as being stuck with something unwanted, we feel distress. Regarding pain with kind eyes, we don't see it as an enemy. Instead, we recognize it as a struggling part of ourselves – as a part of us that needs our support. As we meet discomfort with a kindly gaze, the unnecessary tensions that have gathered around it begin to soften, reducing our suffering. And we begin to let go of the mental distress that comes from feeling we're stuck with an unwanted experience.

Even when there's no discomfort present, the body likes being seen with warmth and acceptance. When we regard the body with kind eyes it begins to soften, often releasing

Sitting with kindness

sensations of tingling, aliveness, and pleasure. Be kind to the body, and the body will be kind back to you.

Exercise

I encourage you to keep bringing a kindly gaze into the body. Keep looking for a balance of ease and openness in the way you sit. Meet everything with warmth – especially parts of the body that are in discomfort.

GUIDED MEDITATION: Sitting with kindness

# 6

The words we say

When I was first taught lovingkindness meditation, the phrases I was taught were, "May I be well. May I be happy. May I be free from suffering." The "I" became "you" in the next three stages, and "all beings" in the final stage. I was told that I was free to use other words, but these were the only ones I ever heard, so they were the only ones I ever used. Over the years, I've experimented with variations on the phrasing, and for several years now I've settled on the following:

- May you be well.
- May you be at ease.
- May you be kind to yourself and others.

The first two phrases are general expressions of kindness. To wish myself well refers mainly to physical health. In effect I'm saying, "Bodhipaksa, may you, as a feeling, struggling being, be free from physical ailments and pain, and feel healthy and alive." That's not the only way to interpret those words, but that's what I have in mind.

To wish myself ease is more social and emotional. In saying "May you be at ease," I mean something like, "Bodhipaksa, as you do this difficult thing of being human, may you be free from stress, and, even if you do experience stressful situations, pain, or illness, may you maintain emotional balance and a

The words we say

sense of peace." The word "ease" also implies physical ease. Every time I say it to myself, it reminds me to let the body be soft and responsive rather than stiff and controlled.

The third phrase, "May you be kind to yourself and others," reminds me that the purpose of the practice is to become kinder. It's surprisingly easy for us to forget that the metta bhavana is about kindness. If we've taken on the idea that "lovingkindness" is some magnificent and rare emotion, and that the phrases in the practice are the mechanism by which we crank it out, then we need such reminders, because those attitudes are unhelpful and unkind.

You probably noticed that I don't use the first-person singular pronoun, "I." I don't say "May *I* be well," and so on. Saying "May I be happy" can feel like you're striving to attain something for yourself. Saying "May *you* be happy" feels like you're offering yourself something. Grasping isn't kind, while giving is. For me, this shift in language is also a recognition that there are parts within me that need support and encouragement, and parts that are capable of offering support and encouragement. In saying "May you be well. May you be at ease," one of those parts is talking to the other. Many people who struggle with self-metta find that talking to themselves as "you" makes this stage of the practice easier. We talk to ourselves in the same way as we talk to a friend, a stranger, or someone we have difficulties with. We're not singling ourselves out as special in any way. When we get to the final stage, we can say, "May we be kind to ourselves and each other" or "May all beings be kind to themselves and each other."

I encourage you to experiment with these phrases, and to consider them as expressions of kindness, rather than as ways to manufacture kindness. When we try to make kindness happen, we treat ourselves almost like machines. So start with kind, soft eyes, empathize with yourself as a feeling, struggling being, letting kindness arise naturally. And then let the phrases you say be expressions of and reminders of kindness. Above all, be kind, right here and now.

Exercise

Notice moments of suffering in your daily life. See if you can adopt the perspective that this is a part of you that needs support, and consider that there is also a part of you that can offer that support.

7
It's all about kindness

One of the phrases I was taught when I first learned lovingkindness meditation was, "May I be happy."[13] I mistakenly took from this that the point of the practice was, well, to be happy. The practice, however, is about becoming kinder, not happier. If we believe we're trying to attain happiness – and I think that's a common misperception – then we might spend our time thinking about or visualizing things that bring pleasure. We hope that this will make us happy, and sometimes it will. But, depending on our motivation, it might not make us *kinder*, meaning that we've missed the whole point of the practice.

There's nothing wrong with thinking about things that make you happy, including in lovingkindness meditation. But doing this should be an expression of kindness, since that's what the practice is about. If you're being kind to someone, you want them to be at ease. You want them to be happy. In the first stage, the person we're being kind to is ourselves. So you might say, "May I be happy" to show yourself kindness. If you then think about things that bring pleasure, it's as if you're saying, "Hi there! I care about you, and I want you to be happy. Here's something beautiful I'd like to offer you, as an expression of love." Just remember, you do this as an act of kindness, not to try to be happy. If happiness happens, that's fine. If it doesn't, that's just how things are, so that's fine too.

Wanting to be happy can make us unhappy, if it involves grasping. We can become frustrated when happiness doesn't arrive fast enough, or disappointed when it ends. Often, we grasp after happiness because we're unable to accept unpleasant feelings that are present. Grasping not only causes suffering, but also arises from suffering. If we notice a grasping tendency, the kindest thing is to let go of chasing happiness, and instead to accept whatever we're feeling. Accepting unhappiness is a surer route to happiness than directly aiming to be happy.

If we believe that the goal of the first stage is to become happier, we'll assume we're failing when we're not happy. But the times that we're sad, or lonely, or afflicted with grief are those when we especially need to be kind to ourselves. We can meet our suffering with empathy and kindness, knowing that we're doing a difficult thing in being human. We can regard ourselves with kind eyes. We can express our kindness with supportive words, such as "May you be well. May you be at ease. May you be kind to yourself and others." The very reason I use the word "ease" is to remind myself to accept whatever feelings are arising.

Sometimes, when we're going through a hard time, happiness will be distant. But, as soon as you begin softening the eyes or letting the body be more at ease, you're already being kind, even if you're not happy. Kindness is never distant. It's right here, right now, waiting for you to connect with it. Happiness and unhappiness will always come and go. But, however you're feeling, you can be kind. Take care of kindness, and your happiness will take care of itself. Just keep checking in with yourself, asking, "Am I being kind right

It's all about kindness

now?" And if you aren't, ask yourself, "How, can I meet this moment with kindness and gentleness?"

Exercise

Remember in your lovingkindness practice and in life that, whether you are happy or unhappy, you can be kind. Remember that kindness is what the practice is about.

GUIDED MEDITATION: Self-kindness

8

Strengthening kindness toward a friend

We've seen how we can empathize and be kind to ourselves. Now we extend our empathy and kindness to a friend. A friend (*mitta*) is someone for whom our kindness (metta) arises readily; the similarity between those two Pali words is not coincidental. We already empathize with friends and care about their well-being. When they are unhappy, it troubles us; when they are happy, we are glad. We want them to be well and at ease, and don't want them to suffer.

Although we naturally have kindness toward friends, we can nevertheless strengthen that kindness. This is part of the training where we make kindness a habit, practice it thoroughly, make it stable, get to know it thoroughly, and undertake it completely.

Just as we regarded ourselves with soft, kind eyes, we can call a friend to mind and regard them, too, with soft, kind eyes. And we can empathize with them, as we did with ourselves, by reflecting:

1. They want to be happy.
2. They do not want to suffer.
3. Happiness is often much more elusive than they expect.
4. Suffering is something that they experience much more than they want to.

Strengthening kindness toward a friend

You might notice that I often bring a little compassion – the desire to relieve suffering – into the lovingkindness practice. Reminding yourself that your friend suffers will sometimes evoke a little heartache, and that's a good thing. It reminds us that we care for them and motivates us to support them. It can be grounding to bring into the lovingkindness practice a gentle reminder that we suffer. Again, it's a reminder that the practice is about becoming kinder, not about being happy.

Having reflected on your friend as a feeling being who is doing a difficult thing in being human, you naturally want to support them. And you can express that support in the same way as you did for yourself, by saying:

- May you be well.
- May you be at ease.
- May you be kind to yourself and others.

This is all very simple. It's just you, as a feeling, struggling being, reminding yourself that someone you care about is also a feeling, struggling being. And, in doing so, you find that your care and kindness for them deepen.

Exercise

Right now, or anytime you want, you can do the reflections numbered above. Take a couple of minutes and dwell on each in turn. Give them time to sink in. Notice how this changes how you feel about your friend.

GUIDED MEDITATION: Supporting a friend, in kindness

9

Being a guardian angel

We are all familiar with the idea of guardian angels, but we usually think in terms of having one. I find it helpful to think in terms of being one.

In lovingkindness meditation, the act of calling other people to mind – like the friend in the second stage – can be awkward. You might imagine your friend sitting opposite you, and that can feel stilted and unnatural in the same way as sitting directly opposite someone on the subway can be.

To get around this, I started imagining the other person not as sitting still, opposite me, but as going about their daily business. I simply imagine what they might be doing right now. I might visualize a friend working at their computer, cooking, practicing the piano, or doing some gardening.

When I do this, I feel like I am an invisible, benevolent presence. I am their guardian angel, protecting them, supporting them, and wishing them well. I say, "May you be well. May you be at ease. May you be kind to yourself and others." Sometimes I imagine that I am offering them a loving touch, and I imagine that there is warmth and light streaming from my body into theirs as I repeat the phrases. I offer them strength, calm, peace. This seems more intimate and natural than simply imagining them sitting with me.

I see them, as they go through their day, having experiences that are challenging, and I support them in that. I imagine them having pleasant experiences, and share their joy. I envision times when their experience is neutral – perhaps when they're deeply absorbed in their work – and am present with and supportive toward them then, too. I am simply a kind presence, supporting them with everything they do in life. I might imagine, too, that they feel my invisible loving presence, so that they experience an unaccountable glow of joy. Most of all, I wish not just that they be happy and at ease, but that they be kind to themselves, and that they share that kindness with others, too.

This approach brings an almost mythic dimension to the practice. It reminds us that we're doing something significant in wishing another person well. The lovingkindness practice becomes an act of bestowing blessings upon the other person. We become like bodhisattvas. But, most of all, we become more loving toward our friends, and more likely to support them when we next meet.

Exercise

Amid your daily activities, imagine that you have your own guardian angel. Let yourself feel a benevolent force near you. Feel the warmth, energy, and tender concern of that presence. Let yourself feel loved, so that you, in turn, can be more loving to others.

GUIDED MEDITATION: Being a guardian angel

10

Don't just feel kindness, do kindness

When I lead guided meditations I no longer talk, as I used to do, in terms of "bringing the practice to a close." Talking about meditations ending inadvertently suggests that we stop practicing when the bell rings – that when we get up from our meditation cushion we leave behind any qualities of kindness or mindfulness that have arisen. So nowadays I talk instead about "bringing whatever qualities we've cultivated more fully into the world." This reminds us that meditation can carry over into our daily activities, so that any mindfulness and kindness we've cultivated can make their way into our everyday interactions.

Since we're currently talking about strengthening kindness toward friends, I invite you to think what you could do today to show kindness to a friend. Maybe you could pick up the phone, or send a text message or email. You could then:

- Tell them you appreciate them and why.
- Send a link to some music they might enjoy.
- Find a photograph of them, or of the two of you, and send it to them with your reminiscences.
- Suggest getting together for coffee or to watch a movie.
- Offer to babysit so that they can get out.

Don't just feel kindness, do kindness

Or perhaps you could go "old school" and send them a card, or think of a book they might like and order it for them. Or you could look ahead to dates that are significant to them (birthdays, anniversaries, and so on) and make a note to make a personal gesture when those dates come around.

Also, the next time you see a friend, give them a hug (assuming they like hugs), take even more of an interest in their life than usual, or in some way move toward deepening the friendship you have.

Exercise

This chapter is all about practical things you can do. Why not try doing some of them?

11

Self-kindness and self-care breaks

Many of us, including me, have difficulty practicing self-care. We treat ourselves as "doing beings" rather than feeling beings. We become obsessed with accomplishing things. We drive ourselves too hard at work, not taking enough breaks, and denying our bodies the opportunity to move and stretch. Often we'll eat lunch at our desks, continuing to work around quick bites of food. Half of us work on our vacations. We see taking care of ourselves as the enemy of productivity.

If a friend were doing these things we'd encourage them to be gentle on themselves, to take breaks during the workday, and to have time away from work altogether. If we want to be kinder to ourselves, we should listen to the advice we would give that friend.

The ironic thing is that taking breaks is good for our productivity. According to an article by author Tony Schwartz, Professor Nathaniel Kleitman found that the brain has a regular cycle of alertness and tiredness. We can only remain alert for around ninety minutes at a time; after that, we become fatigued, and our efficiency drops off sharply. A ten-minute break for rest and renewal restores our ability to think clearly and stay focused. Taking breaks in this way, we become more productive in the long term. Schwartz says that Professor K. Anders Eriksson at Florida State University studied the habits of elite performers in fields as diverse as sports, music, and chess, and found that the most outstanding performers in these fields were those who interspersed periods of practice with breaks.[14]

To be effective, breaks should be real breaks. Switching from working on spreadsheets to scrolling through social media on your computer doesn't give your body and brain a chance to recharge. It's better to get up, move around, go into a different room and have a cup of coffee, or, best of all, get outside for a complete change of scenery.

Taking self-care breaks is an expression of kindness, but breaks can also be opportunities for cultivating kindness. When you take a break, let your eyes be soft and kind. Connect with yourself and others empathetically and with warmth. Let your eyes be kind and soft as you get up and stretch your legs, or as you make that cup of coffee. You can even repeat lovingkindness phrases, saying to yourself "May all beings be well. May all beings be at ease." That way our breaks are self-kindness not just in the sense that we are taking care of our needs for rest; they become a way of bringing more kindness into our lives.

You can take breaks more frequently than once every ninety minutes. Maybe it's because I'm getting old, but I find that forty minutes is often the longest I want to work without a break. Beyond that, I tend to hit a wall of resistance where it becomes hard to focus. So that's often how long I work between breaks. A hybrid model I've found helpful is to set a thirty-minute timer, after which I spend a minute or two disconnecting from work, with my eyes closed, connecting with myself kindly. I then repeat this. After a third thirty-minute stint of working, I take a longer break of fifteen to twenty minutes.

Some of this might sound like advice on "getting more done," and as suggestions that you treat yourself as a "doing being," but that's not my intention. Treat yourself kindly; as a feeling being, you deserve it. Taking breaks is an expression of kindness. We often don't do these things because we fear we won't get enough done. As it happens, though, that fear is misplaced. We can get stuff done while being kind to ourselves.

Exercise

As suggested, set a thirty-minute recurring reminder on your phone or watch. On the first two, take brief meditation breaks. On the third, take a ten- to twenty-minute break. Let your eyes be soft and kind.

12

The spiritual importance of friendship

Friends can bring out the best or the worst in us. If we're around people who are dishonest, cynical, or hateful, we may well acquire their habits, or we waste our time and energy managing the chaos they bring into our lives. Having friends who are kind, supportive, and honest, by contrast, encourages those same qualities to emerge within us. The latter is what the Buddha called *kalyana-mittata* (*kalyana-mitrata* in Sanskrit), which means beautiful or virtuous friendship. The Buddhist concept of the virtuous friend is similar to the *anam cara*, or "soul friend" in the Celtic tradition. As the Irish philosopher John O'Donohue wrote, "With the *anam cara* you could share your inner-most self, your mind and your heart. This friendship was an act of recognition and belonging."[15]

The ancient Buddhist and Celtic traditions typically thought of these virtuous friendships as involving mentorship, with one party being wiser than the other, but all friendships include mutual guidance. Friends always learn from each other and are influenced by each other's skillful qualities. Any true friendship is a virtuous (kalyana) friendship. Any real friendship is a soul-friendship.

The Buddha said that spiritual life *requires* friendship:

This entire spiritual life depends on virtuous friendship, virtuous companionship, virtuous comradeship. When a practitioner has a virtuous friend, a virtuous companion, a virtuous comrade, it is to be expected that they will develop and cultivate the noble eightfold path.[16]

You might sometimes think of practice as substantially a solitary affair; you meditate on your own and your ethical practice rests on values that exist within your mind. But where did the *idea* of meditating come from? You picked it up from someone else. How did you learn to meditate? Someone taught you. How do you refine your practice? You learn from others. Where do your ideas of what is ethical and what is unethical come from? From others. The longer I practice, the more I realize that I would have no practice were it not for others.

Real friendship – virtuous friendship, soul-friendship – helps us grow. When we're with friends, we're able to be more fully ourselves. There is no need for social masks, and we can be relaxed and at ease, and be understood. Friends don't just see us; they give us the blessing of being witnessed. With friends, we can be vulnerable and reveal our struggles. Friends help us to clarify what's most important to us, what our key values are, and how we might live them.

Friends rejoice with us, without envy or jealousy. They often celebrate good qualities that we fail to see in ourselves, reflecting our own unacknowledged goodness back to us. Friends act as mirrors, too, for what is unworthy of us. We might not see how out of place an unethical action is in our lives, yet a friend, out of love, reflects these lapses so that we can recognize them as unbecoming. Sometimes, friends support us by challenging us. They don't let us settle with murky ethical evasions. Instead, they nudge us toward acting more wholesomely, so that we will decrease the amount of suffering in the world rather than add to it. Friends give us a space to heal. They surround us with acceptance and kindness. When we reveal our pain and sorrow and feel that we might fall apart, we know there's someone there to hold us together.

Friendship arises from mutual kindness, or *sampiya*, which is an important word in the early scriptures. Just as our friend helps us, we help them. Through our kindness toward our good friends, we become a dispenser of blessings as well as a recipient of them. Any friendship is an ongoing act of mutual giving and receiving. This is what we are building when we cultivate a deeper kindness for our friends.

Exercise

Spend some time reflecting on your friendships. Often there's pressure, due to time and geography, to neglect these precious connections. Take time to bolster your faith in friendship. Cherish your friendships, and then reflect on what you can do to sustain them and take them deeper.

13

Seeing your deep kinship with strangers

The third stage of the lovingkindness practice is where we cultivate kindness for a so-called neutral person, or what I call a relative stranger. The world is almost entirely made up of strangers, which means we have many opportunities to train in kindness, making it a habit, practicing it thoroughly, making it stable, getting to know it thoroughly, and undertaking it completely.

Strangers are everywhere: driving cars, walking by, making deliveries, in advertisements, living in nearby buildings. What are their names? What are their regrets and dreams? You don't know, and perhaps you never will. But you do know something crucial about them. It's the deepest and most essential thing, which is this: just as you feel, so do they. Just like you, they prefer joy, happiness, and peace to misery, sadness, and turmoil. Their joys are just as real and as welcome to them as yours are to you. Their sufferings are as vivid, painful, and unwelcome to them as your own are to you. Just like you, they're doing this difficult thing of being human.

Everyone in the world has these things in common with you. They are the basis of our deep kinship. When you recognize this kinship with anyone, even if you don't know them at all, you'll feel supportive of them. This empathetic awareness allows us to treat anyone, and ideally everyone we

Seeing your deep kinship with strangers

encounter, with kindness. That we can feel kindness toward someone we know nothing about is something that we should marvel at.

In our meditation practice we call to mind just one relative stranger – perhaps someone who works in a shop or post office, or who makes deliveries, or a neighbor we don't know. We empathize with them. We regard them with loving eyes, and we offer them kind and encouraging words:

- May you be well.
- May you be at ease.
- May you be kind to yourself and others.

Perhaps, as you do this, you can imagine you're with them while they go about their day, as their guardian angel – an invisible presence, offering warmth and support. Do whatever works to sense your deep kinship, and to bring more love and kindness into your life, and into the world.

Exercise

Meditation is not enough; bring the practice into your daily life. Whenever you see strangers – driving past your house, walking past you on the street, on your television screen, in the supermarket – remind yourself: "This person's feelings are as real to them as mine are to me." And then wish them well, using the lovingkindness phrases I've suggested, or any other words that work for you.

GUIDED MEDITATION: Kinship

14

Kindness versus "being nice"

Once I'd stumbled upon the idea of connecting empathetically with myself and others as feeling, struggling beings, I realized that in the past I'd often focused more on being nice than on being kind.

Being nice is similar to when my daughter was three years old and would say, "Daddy, I love you!" Then after a slight pause would follow, "Can I have some candy?" Being nice is transactional. It's what you do when you want something. Often the thing we want is to be liked. You do it because you hope they'll be nice back to you. Niceness may contain an element of kindness (my daughter did love me!), but it's also appeasing or manipulating. These are things you don't do when you're being kind.

Whether you're being nice or being kind, you'll probably smile, talk in a friendly tone of voice, try to put the other person at their ease, and so on. So the two might look similar. And in both cases you might want to make the other person feel good. But the intention is different. Being nice arises from fear or grasping, while being kind arises from empathy. When you're kind, you know that another person is a human being just like yourself, and you know that suffering is unpleasant, and you want neither of you to suffer. So you behave in ways that are supportive both to them and to you. People on the receiving end might sometimes not notice

Kindness versus "being nice"

the difference, but niceness often comes across as fake.

In being nice, we often subjugate our own needs and preferences in favor of the other person's. We fear that they won't like us if we say what we want, so we pretend we don't have preferences. Ironically, our attempts to please others in this way are often annoying for other people. They want to know if we'd prefer tea or coffee, and we keep saying "It doesn't matter," shifting the burden of that decision onto them. Even if you don't have a strong preference – not just with respect to beverages, but in other areas too – it's often better to say what you'd prefer just to get out of the habit of niceness and appeasement.

When you're being nice, it's hard to say no because you fear rejection. You say, "Yes, I can do that favor!" even though you don't have the time. Being nice, we open ourselves to exploitation. Or perhaps we're exploiting others by trying to make them feel good. When you're being kind, you don't mind saying no, especially if someone asks you to do something that will harm them or yourself. If you don't have the time, you just politely and kindly say you can't. When we're being nice, we can't risk challenging people if they're doing something unethical, because they might stop liking us. We co-dependently encourage them to go ahead with actions that aren't in anyone's best interests. When we're kind, we can afford to be brave, because we care enough to say, "Is that really a good idea?"

Many of the fears people have about practicing kindness, such as concerns about being exploited, are really about niceness. With self-empathy and self-kindness, we protect ourselves while also being helpful to others.

Exercise

When you notice you're afraid of rejection, recognize this as a normal part of being human. Offer yourself support, warmth, and encouragement through kind eyes and kind self-talk. Recognize, too, that the other person needs support, warmth, and encouragement. Then, as best you can, act with both their and your long-term happiness and well-being in mind.

15

Walking with kindness

I often turn a solitary walk into a period of lovingkindness practice. There are many ways to do this, but here is my approach.

I walk with soft, kind eyes. My field of attention – both visual and auditory – is warm and open, restfully aware of the space around me. My awareness is imbued with kindness, and, since it also fills the space around me, my well-wishing touches the world. As I walk, I say to myself, "May all beings be well. May all beings be at ease. May all beings be kind to themselves and each other." These phrases naturally match the rhythm of my movements and my breathing.

If there are no beings to be seen, then I simply continue walking, repeating the phrases, letting my kindness radiate into the world around me, as if my attention were a lamp, shining in all directions. I'm aware there are many beings I don't see: birds in bushes, people in houses, ants in their tunnels. If I see a person or animal, I direct my attention toward them, as if it were a spotlight, and wish them well, specifically. At these times the words change to, "May *you* be well. May *you* be at ease. May *you* be kind to yourself and others." I hear a train in the distance, and the spotlight turns toward it. I wish the staff and passengers well. A car goes by, and my attention lovingly tracks the driver.

When there are lots of living beings around, having my

spotlight dashing around would not be conducive to calmness, so I return to a lamp-like field of kindness extending around me, knowing that it touches all who pass through my awareness. As part of my practice of kindness, I interact with others, and I'll greet them as we pass. These greetings are part of the meditation, not interruptions to it.

The *Karaniya Metta Sutta*, one of the key Buddhist teachings on lovingkindness, mentions walking as an opportunity to cultivate kindness:

> *Let them radiate boundless love towards the entire world – above, below, and across – unhindered, without ill will, without enmity. Standing, walking, sitting or reclining, as long as they are awake, let them develop this mindfulness.*[17]

You can take any walking you already do as an opportunity to cultivate kindness – even walking around the supermarket. A period of walking lovingkindness practice adds to whatever sitting practice you're already doing, increasing the amount of time you're devoting to consciously developing kindness.

Exercise

Try practicing lovingkindness meditation while you walk. You can go for an unguided walk or listen to a guided meditation.

16
Driving with kindness

If you don't drive, some of what you read here can be adapted for when you ride on public transport or when you're cycling.

There were no cars in the Buddha's day, but people did drive carts, carriages, and chariots. However, driving with kindness is not something the Buddha is recorded as having talked about. If he were alive today, though, I'm sure he'd talk about it a lot. Driving is a stressful activity. It can be irritating to be in traffic jams, to be cut off by a reckless driver, or to be stuck at traffic lights. The nature of driving means we're cut off from one another in our mobile boxes, unable to speak to each other or see each other's body language and facial expressions. Not seeing each other's humanity, people are more inclined to behave aggressively.

Practicing kindness while driving can remind us that those we share the road with are, just like us, doing a difficult thing in being human. It can help us calm down when anger arises. It can help us be more considerate, which reduces the possibility of conflict arising in the first place.

As in walking lovingkindness, when it's safe to do so, I let my eyes be soft and kind. Be careful as you experiment with this. There are times while driving when we need to be laser-focused and times we can have a more relaxed form of attention. Let your mode of awareness be appropriate for the conditions you find yourself in.

With kind eyes, I imbue my field of awareness with warmth. As with walking lovingkindness practice, I sometimes have an open, lamp-like field of loving attention where everyone I see is touched by my kindness. Other times it's more appropriate to focus my attention like a flashlight on an individual vehicle. As I drive, I'll say, "May you be well. May you be at peace. May you be kind to yourself and others." The lovingkindness phrases help prevent the mind from wandering. And, because we are less prone to getting lost in thought, this helps us drive more safely.

Red traffic lights give us an opportunity to pause, be mindful, and connect with our hearts. Take a breath when you pause at them, wishing yourself and others well. As you're approaching green lights, remember that these are the color of Amoghasiddhi, the buddha of fearlessness. Drop any fears that the lights will change before you reach them. That fear is a source of stress, and it's unkind and unhelpful.

Be forgiving of drivers who try to cut into a queue of vehicles. We sometimes want to punish others for their bad behavior, but forgiveness allows us to be happier and more at ease. If you see someone driving dangerously, rather than cursing them, try saying, "May you be safe, and may those around you be safe." Look for opportunities to show kindness. Be gently vigilant as you approach pedestrian crossings, so that you can let people cross the road if they need to. When drivers need to merge, let them slip in if possible. Above all, enjoy being kind.

Driving with kindness

Exercise

If you drive, try the suggestions above. If you commute on public transport, enjoy the ride as you wish others well.

17

Be present with strangers

"Attention is the rarest and purest form of generosity," Simone Weil wrote to a friend.[18] Being attentively present with someone is one of the most effective ways of letting them know that they matter. It's one of the simplest and most powerful ways to be kind.

While you're having your groceries scanned, instead of daydreaming or looking at your phone, notice the person who is serving you. Let your eyes be soft and kind. While you're waiting, regard them as a feeling being, and silently recite the lovingkindness phrases. Take an interest in them, and ask how their day is going. Keep your attention on your heart as well as on the other person, so that there is a field of awareness embracing self and other. Let your heart be open, tender, and responsive.

The Buddha talked about *pema*, which means "liking" people. Pema can include being drawn toward people we find attractive or people we feel comfortable with. This is not necessarily sexual or romantic, although sometimes that comes into it. It's often to do with whether we think we will be comfortable with them. Pema, or liking, makes us "nice," which as we've seen is not at all the same as being kind, even though they might at times look similar. Previously I talked about "being nice" as a way of seeking approval, but it can also involve trying to get pleasant feelings from our interaction with someone. Often, we're looking for validation. Kindness is about being sensitive to how the other person feels. Being nice is about how they make us feel.

When we walk into a room full of strangers, we immediately identify those we want to move toward, those we want to avoid, and those we have no feelings about either way and would tend to ignore. It's an interesting practice to choose to interact with someone we're not immediately drawn to. They may simply seem boring, or perhaps there's something about them that's off-putting.[19] I suggest that, among the vast number of so-called neutral people in the world, it's worth paying attention to those we are not immediately drawn to. You might think of them as the "super-neutral" – those strangers we don't even notice. When we do this, we give ourselves the gift of connecting through empathy rather than through liking, because liking is not why we were drawn to them. We give ourselves the gift of breaking from our usual habits, which limit who we meet. And we give the other person the gift of being acknowledged as a fellow feeling being.

Be sensitive to the other person's needs. They don't exist as your special lovingkindness project. They may not want or be able to chat, and might prefer to just get on with their job. They may interpret your kindness as intrusive "niceness." If so, give them the space they need. It's not personal. It's not about us. We're not trying to get a particular response from them. We're not trying to change their life or even their day. We're simply aiming to be present with them for a moment as the currents of our lives carry us past one another.

Exercise

I love the concept of committing Random Acts of Kindness. If you search for that phrase online you can find lots of suggestions, some of them very inventive, for ways to express kindness to strangers.

18

The far enemy of kindness

In the fourth stage of the lovingkindness meditation, we connect empathetically with a person we have difficulty with and cultivate kindness for them. This stage uproots ill will in all its forms. A millennium or so after the Buddha, the Buddhist tradition came to call ill will the "far enemy" of kindness, which means its directly opposing emotional quality. While kindness is the desire to support someone's well-being, ill will is the desire to hurt them.

The term "ill will" encompasses a variety of emotional attitudes:

- *Irritability* is often defensive. We're unhappy, and our prickliness is a signal telling others to avoid us or to be careful around us. We ignore their well-being and cause them pain in turn.
- *Anger* is often an attempt to forcefully break through a barrier in communication. Trying to make someone take what we're saying seriously, we raise our voice and express ourselves in strong terms. We don't necessarily want to hurt them, but often we do, because when we're angry we use hurtful words, and the insistent quality of our communication may alarm them.

- *Resentment* is an ongoing state of bitterness for past hurts that we haven't forgiven. Mentally, we keep returning to the "scene of the crime" in a way that arouses anger and prevents us from resolving our feelings of hurt. We may do all of this in the privacy of our own thoughts, bring up our resentment with the other person as a form of punishment, or share it with others as a way of finding support. Resentment and the two previous forms of ill will often manifest toward people we otherwise love.
- *Hatred* is when we harbor an intense, entrenched dislike for someone. We come to see them as intrinsically and perhaps irredeemably bad. We want to hurt them because we think they deserve it. We may snub them, say unkind things, try to rally others against them, or do other things that make their lives difficult. We cannot love someone we hate.
- *Contempt*, unlike the hot emotions above, is cold. Contempt is a species of disgust. These days contempt is often political: we see our political opponents as so stupid or evil that there is no point in even trying to change their minds. When we have contempt for someone, we think they are unworthy of love.

Cultivating kindness for ourselves and for those we have difficulties with can help us weaken and uproot these forms of ill will, and any others I haven't mentioned.

The person we call to mind in the fourth stage of the practice is traditionally called the "enemy." Many of us feel uncomfortable with that language, however, because it seems to suggest that there's a permanent state of ill will between us, and that the other person is at fault. These days we're more likely to say something like "the person we have difficulty with," which suggests a less permanent state of affairs, and reminds us that the ill will we're seeking to uproot is our own. It's helpful to focus mostly on people we know personally, as opposed to, say, politicians we're unlikely to ever meet. We can certainly cultivate kindness for the latter sort of person, but kindness is most urgently needed closer to home.

I've often heard people say that they don't have any enemies, in the sense of someone they hate. And that may well be true. But, unless you're a saint, there are almost certainly people you find fault with, or get irritated or angry with. Failing that, think of the things that irritate you about the people you love.

Whoever we choose to focus on, what we do in this stage is the same as in the previous ones. We reflect that this person is, just like us, a feeling being – that their joys and sorrows are as real to them as ours are to us. Moreover, they, just like us, are doing a difficult thing in being human. They need support as they go through life, experiencing as they do more suffering and less happiness than they would like. Having connected empathetically with them, we can offer them support: "May you be well. May you be at ease. May you be kind to yourself and others."

In this way we cultivate attitudes of kindness that undermine and displace our ill will, with the aim of transforming our own minds, our relationships, and even our lives.

Exercise

Notice ill will, in whatever form it might manifest in your life. Practice connecting empathetically, and then cultivate kindness: "May you be well. May you be at ease. May you be kind to yourself and others."

19

Look close to home

You almost certainly have relationships, such as those with partners, children, parents, siblings, that are primarily loving, yet into which ill will, in its various forms, keeps intruding. We can get upset, for example, when those close to us go against our advice, don't meet our needs for affection, ignore us, or have habits we dislike. Even our most loving relationships can become tainted by resentment, anger, and irritability.

This doesn't make us bad – it just makes us human. Living closely with others always brings challenges. So I suggest that in your meditation practice, when you're calling to mind someone you have difficulty with, you sometimes look close to home. I also suggest, when you call a loved one to mind, you focus specifically on the difficult areas of your life together. Clearly recall the things they do that drive you crazy – not to make yourself resentful, but so that you can practice bringing more patience and kindness into these areas of your relationship. Learn to keep loving your partner even when they stack the dishwasher badly, strew clothes around the bedroom floor, or leave clumps of hair in the shower drain. Treat these meditations as a rehearsal, so that bringing love into your memories of these situations makes it more likely that you'll respond lovingly in real life.

Sometimes people assume that putting someone in the fourth stage of their lovingkindness practice is a sort of punishment or judgment, and they don't want to do that with people they love. But putting someone in the fourth stage is just a practical matter of recognizing a difficulty and working with it. Doing this shows not just that we care, but that we want to get better at caring.

I was told early on not to add romantic partners in the second stage – the friend stage – of the practice. This was to avoid confusing romantic or sexual feelings with real kindness. We were also warned not to add children or parents, in case some of the emotions unique to those relationships be confused with kindness. And for beginners that's fair enough. But we can neglect entirely to cultivate kindness toward those we're most intimately connected with, which is surely a mistake. We especially need to work on bringing more kindness into those relationships.

Don't hesitate to bring those you're closest to into the fourth stage. You're not saying that they're your enemies. You're saying that you care for them enough that you want to remove anything that obstructs your love for them.

Exercise

As you notice ill will arising in the context of intimate relationships, remind yourself that both you and your dear one are feeling beings. Remember that you both want to be happy and in harmony. From a state of tenderness, wish them well by repeating the lovingkindness phrases. If apologies are necessary, feel free to make them.

20

When you are your own enemy

One time when I was suffering from self-loathing, I devised a new approach to lovingkindness meditation where I applied the middle three stages of the practice to myself. That may sound selfish, but it wasn't. The pain of my self-hatred had been spilling out as intolerance, irritability, and arrogance, causing pain to others too. I needed to address this.

1. The first stage remained the same – I wished myself well. I didn't at that time know how to practice self-empathy in the way I've been teaching here, but that's what I would do now.
2. Where we normally cultivate lovingkindness for a friend, I called to mind the parts of myself that I liked. I'd name these qualities and wish them well. For example, adapting the lovingkindness phrases I'd been taught, I'd repeat, "May the intelligent part of me be well. May it be happy. May it be free from suffering." I'd cycle through a few different qualities, devoting some time to each in turn.
3. Where we would normally wish a neutral person well, I'd cultivate kindness toward qualities that I hadn't yet developed. Just like relative strangers, these were parts of myself that I hadn't yet got to know. I would say, "May the confident part of me be well. May it

The Heart's Awakening

be happy. May it be free from suffering." If I felt I needed to develop an aspect of myself much more than it was developed already, then I would include it here. Sometimes I'd name qualities other people had appreciated, but which I didn't appreciate myself. People would tell me that I was friendly, for example, while that wasn't the way I thought of myself.

4. In the fourth stage I'd call to mind parts of myself that I didn't like or that were unskillful. I'd say things like, "May the self-critical part of me be well. May it be happy. May it be free from suffering." Those qualities were my inner "difficult people." There was no shortage of these. I found it helpful to do this. I started to recognize that these unhelpful traits were attempts to protect myself. They weren't bad, just misguided.

5. Finally, I'd conclude the meditation in the usual way by taking my well-wishing into the world. It was important that the practice not be all about me.

In the middle three stages I related to different parts of myself as if they were other people – those I cared for, those that were strangers to me, and those I clashed with. This brought more kindness and harmony into my inner life. It also broke up the notion of my "self" being a monolith. I could see myself as a mixture of skillful and unskillful traits, rather than being one thing that I could like or dislike.

I offer up this modified approach to lovingkindness meditation in the hope that some will find it useful.

Exercise

When you find yourself being self-critical, see if you can recognize this as a misguided attempt to protect yourself. Let your eyes become soft and kind, place a hand on your heart, and invite a wiser, kinder response to arise. You might say, for example, "Let me protect myself with kindness rather than ill will. Let me care for myself tenderly. Let me be gentle with myself."

GUIDED MEDITATION: Self-hatred metta bhavana

21

Lovingkindness meditation as rehearsal

When you call to mind someone you have difficulty with, how do you see them? I was encouraged early on to see them happy and smiling, and, while there's nothing wrong with that, I now take a different approach. I now imagine them doing the very thing that makes me feel hurt or angry. My intention in doing this is to become better at maintaining kindness in the face of provocation.

After developing this approach, I discovered that members of the US Civil Rights Movement of the 1950s and 1960s had also used rehearsal as a way of learning to be at peace while they were surrounded by hatred. The civil rights marchers faced, without retaliation or hate, racist white policemen who set dogs on them and beat them viciously. They were able to maintain an attitude of love in these circumstances *because they had trained to do so*. They had rehearsed being insulted and beaten while keeping love in their hearts, seeing their enemies not as inherently bad, but as potential allies who were currently misguided. Rehearsals can never fully simulate the experience of being assaulted, but it was enough to make a profound difference.

Imagining your enemy happy and smiling as you cultivate love for them can be a way of bypassing the difficulty you have with them. It's depriving you of the opportunity to work

Lovingkindness meditation as rehearsal

with your own reactivity. We need to learn to be loving in circumstances where normally we would get angry. In my own life, those circumstances are trivial in comparison to what the civil rights marchers endured, but that's good; my task is much simpler than theirs.

So what really irritates you about the person you hate or tend to get angry with? As you imagine those things clearly, uncomfortable feelings will arise in the body – perhaps around the heart or gut. Remember that these sensations are simply unpleasant, not bad. Surround them with kindness. Regard them with loving eyes, as a part of you that needs support and kindness. Talk kindly to them: "May you be at peace. May you be at ease." When angry thoughts and impulses arise, don't indulge in them. Simply let them fall away. Once you've taken care of your hurt, it'll be easier to respond to the other person kindly. Imagine responding to them in real life, warmly, kindly, seeing them as a feeling, struggling human being.

In this way, you rehearse for real-life encounters. You forge new pathways in the brain, helping you to respond in future with love rather than ill will. Rehearsing in this way won't be the same as experiencing real-life challenges, but it's enough to make a difference.

Exercise

Try this form of rehearsal outside of meditation as well. In quiet moments, imagine things that typically make you angry, and practice being at peace with them.

GUIDED MEDITATION: Rehearsing with difficult situations

22

The anatomy of kindness (and unkindness)

In the Buddha's teachings on conditionality there is a key sequence of factors that goes: contact, feeling, craving, grasping.[20] Each of these arises in dependence on the one before. Understanding how these factors arise within us can help us be kinder.

Contact is our perception of things in the world and in the mind. Contact is not just raw sensory impressions of color, shape, sound, etc. By the time it reaches conscious awareness, anything we perceive has already gone through mental filters that help us to understand what it is and what its significance is to us. Contact is our *interpreted* experience of the world. It's the world as we understand it.

When I look at you, I don't just see a collection of colors and shapes. My brain makes assumptions about your age, gender, status, what your facial expressions and body language mean for me, and so on. Much of this interpretation concerns whether you can potentially benefit me, are a threat, or are irrelevant to my well-being. This filtering happens in ancient parts of the brain that work unconsciously and rapidly, outside of conscious awareness.

As an example, perhaps my mind interprets your demeanor and words as communicating that you see yourself as superior to me.

The anatomy of kindness (and unkindness)

Feeling arises in dependence upon contact. Feeling is pleasant or unpleasant sensation produced within the body. Feelings are things we receive rather than things we do. They are generated unconsciously, automatically, and rapidly. If my brain interprets your actions and demeanor as beneficial, I might feel a warm glow, softening, or excitement.

I don't like being looked down on, and my brain has interpreted you as a threat to my sense of well-being, so this leads to an unpleasant feeling arising. I might sense a tight knot of indignation in the solar plexus, and my limbs tensing, as if for a fight.

Craving arises in dependence upon feeling. Craving is a volition, which is to say, a desire, urge, or emotion. We desire to move either toward things that are pleasant or away from things that are unpleasant, so the term "craving" covers both craving *and* aversion. If I am aversive to your judgments, that's because I crave being approved of.

I perceived your actions as a threat, and that perception gave rise to an unpleasant feeling. Since I judge that you're asserting superiority, I might be motivated to defend myself, angrily.

Grasping arises in dependence upon craving. Grasping represents the acting out of our emotions, in thought, word, and physical deed. It's us reaching, in the world, for what we want. What happens here is that our volitions give rise to actions.

I've interpreted you as asserting superiority; that feels unpleasant, which gives rise to the angry desire to defend myself, and that emotion may manifest as my uttering a withering comeback as I grasp for a restored sense of equality or superiority.

Uttering a put-down isn't the end of the chain of conditions, since my actions themselves have consequences such as the argument I've just provoked, and future resentment about the situation, all of which lead to further suffering. I might still be painfully obsessing about our encounter years later.

What I've outlined is the anatomy of a reactive, unkind act, which takes much longer to explain than it does to unfold in real life. This is the kind of thing that happens when we operate habitually and unmindfully.

But what about the anatomy of an act of kindness? How could things have gone differently?

Contact is unchanged. I still interpret you as acting in a superior manner. This happens automatically, because my mind has been conditioned to react in this way.

Feeling too is produced involuntarily, and so my feelings are hurt in the same way as before.

Volition is where things change. When I'm more mindful, I recognize that my feelings are hurt. I understand that I'm suffering. I may sense anger beginning to arise, but, knowing that it leads to further conflict and pain, I let go of it. I know that I can respond instead with kindness. I arouse empathy, remembering that the person I'm talking to is a feeling being. I feel hurt, but I don't want to hurt them in response. I let the volition of kindness arise.

Actions are shaped by that kind volition. Rather than turn away from the other person or try to push them away, I can connect with them, as one human being to another. My body language, the words I say, and how I say them can all be kind. I can, for example, communicate, in as friendly a way as I can manage, that I felt hurt in response to whatever they did. There's no guarantee that the other person won't be upset by this and try to escalate, but I'm more at peace now. I haven't done anything I'll later regret and obsess about, and so I'll avoid that future suffering as well.

The connection between feeling and emotional responses is the axis upon which our being turns either toward suffering or toward freedom from suffering. An unpleasant feeling is saying, in the inarticulate speech of the body's sensations, *here is a threat! Deal with it! Do something!* It's a cry for help. Meeting pain with mindfulness and kindness gives it the support and reassurance it needs, but in a healthy way. Liberated from the reactivity of anger, we're now free to direct our kindness outward, to the other person. If we do not find our feelings to be so difficult, we do not find others to be so difficult. Ultimately, self-kindness makes kindness for others possible.

Exercise

If we practice observing our feelings, we can learn to react to them less. To help with this, try what I call the "look and feel meditation." This is an exercise in mindfulness of feelings. Find somewhere you can relax and look around you. It could be outdoors or in a familiar room. Let your eyes roam, alighting on one thing after another. As you see various things, note whether the feelings that arise are pleasant or unpleasant. Where do they manifest in the body? Don't try to change anything; just observe.

23

Breaking the bounds

The fifth stage of lovingkindness meditation is about permeating the world with kindness. Traditionally this is "breaking the bounds," which means moving beyond the one-to-one relationships of the previous stages into a more open and expansive state of well-wishing.

We've seen that we can either direct our kindly attention toward a single individual, like a flashlight, or let our kindly awareness permeate the world, like a lamp. This "unbounded" approach is often more relaxed, open, and restful than the more directed approach. In the early scriptures the directional approach was called "the expansive release of the heart," but the non-directional approach was "the limitless release of the heart."[21]

At the beginning of the fifth stage, before we extend our attention into the world, we're often encouraged to recall all four individuals who have been in the practice so far, so that we can practice regarding us all with equal kindness. I don't always include this part of the practice, but, when I do, this is my approach:

- With my eyes soft and kind, I pervade my entire field of attention with a kind, empathetic awareness.
- I remind myself again that all beings are feeling beings, just as I am. They are doing this difficult

thing of being human, just as I am, and they need support and encouragement, just as I do.
- I recall that all beings are equally deserving of kindness because they are feeling, struggling beings.
- Now, when I call to mind all four people, my awareness, permeated with kindness, meets us all equally. There is no "beam" of awareness moving from person to person. A narrow beam of attention cannot be applied equally, because it can only illuminate one person at a time. Instead, all four are within one field of attention, met equally by its kindness.
- There is no bias toward self over others, others over self, or the friend over anyone else. All four individuals are simply met with an open, expansive mind of kindness. The bounds have been broken.
- I say something like "May we be well. May we be at peace. May we be kind to ourselves and others."

If you try this approach, you can now sense the space around you, allowing it to be filled with your empathetic attention, recalling that all beings are feeling beings. All within that space are embraced by love. The mind being another kind of space that is already permeated by kindness, anyone you imagine or remember will also be embraced by love.

If you want, you can simply rest here, feeling that your kindness is radiating in all directions, including inwards. Or, as some of the traditional instructions suggest, you can call to mind wider and wider circles around you, wishing all beings well. You can, if you wish, direct your kindly attention in the cardinal directions – or in front, behind, to the left and right, above and below – as far as your mind will reach. However you approach this, kindness pervades the mind, and the mind pervades the world, and so your kindness pervades the world. Let this be restful, without striving. Whoever appears in the space of your awareness is simply met with kindness. Express that kindness by saying, "May all beings be well. May all beings be at ease. May all beings be kind to themselves and each other."

Exercise

As often as you can amid your daily activities, take short breaks. Let your eyes be kind and soft, and let your entire field of attention permeate the world around you, filling it with kindness. Say to yourself, "May we all be well. May we all be at peace."

GUIDED MEDITATION: Breaking the bounds

24

Kindness is contagious

You may have noticed that, when someone does you a favor, such as holding a door open, this creates a sense of magnanimity so that soon afterward you do a favor for someone else. When people are kind to you, you pass it on.

Never underestimate the power of a kind action. Studies have shown that, when people see an act of kindness, they become kinder too. Then they influence others in turn, so that an act of kindness ripples out into the world. When we bring more kindness into our lives, we become advocates for kindness, emissaries of empathy.

Jamil Zaki, a professor of psychology at Stanford, speculates on why kindness is contagious:

We've found that when individuals learn that their own opinions match those of a group, they engage brain regions associated with the experience of reward, and that this brain activity tracks their later efforts to line up with a group. As such, when people learn that others act kindly, they might come to value kindness more themselves.[22]

I'm more inclined to think it's less to do with conformity, and just that we need to be reminded sometimes that kindness is possible. We get very caught up in our own "stuff," and someone doing a kind act for us reminds us that there's another way of being. We realize that it's pleasant to have a favor done for us, and we remember that it's also pleasant to do a favor for someone else.

Whatever the cause, the contagiousness of kindness might sound too good to be true. If my kindness sparks your kindness, and your kindness sparks kindness in others, you'd think that a kindness cascade would eventually engulf the entire world. This doesn't happen, because unskillful emotions are contagious too. In fact unskillful emotions are even more contagious than kindness. A study by the US-based Pew Research Center showed that posts on Facebook showing "indignant disagreement" received more likes, shares, and comments than other types of content.[23]

This is something to think about before you click the like or share buttons on social media. No matter how much you agree with a post, if it's characterized by indignant disagreement or other forms of anger, consider whether you want to boost those emotions into the world. Also, be mindful of what you expose yourself to on social media. Consider unfollowing people who build audiences by "moral grandstanding" – that is, publicly performing anger, denouncement, and shaming as a way of growing their following. Often these accounts are highly popular. These angry performances can be very entertaining, but they make the world angrier and more polarized. Consider instead following those who are quietly thoughtful and reasonable, even if they are less stimulating. Don't we owe it to ourselves to protect our minds from outrage, and to guard our precious capacity for kindness?

Exercise

In daily life, bear in mind that kindness is contagious. Take encouragement from knowing that any kind words or actions – including attentiveness and curiosity – ripple outward. Notice when you're in the presence of angry, outraged communication. How can you minimize this?

25

Living with love for all sentient beings

The Buddha said that someone living ethically thinks like this:

I want to live and don't want to die; I want to be happy, and recoil from pain. Since this is so, if someone were to take my life, I wouldn't like that. But others also want to live and don't want to die; they want to be happy and recoil from pain. So if I were to take the life of someone else, they wouldn't like that either. The thing that is disliked by me is also disliked by others. Since I dislike this thing, how can I inflict it on someone else?[24]

The Buddha said these words in an exposition of the first ethical precept in Buddhism. This precept is: "I undertake the path of training of abstaining from harming living beings." These are words that many of us chant daily in Pali as *Panatipata veramani sikkhapadam samadiyami*. The quote above makes it clear that this precept is about living with empathy.

Elsewhere, the Buddha was clear that the first precept was about living with kindness and compassion:

A certain person, abandoning the taking of life, abstains from the taking of life. He dwells with his rod laid down, his

> *knife laid down, scrupulous, merciful, compassionate for the welfare of all living beings.*[25]

He was also clear that we can't absolve ourselves from the consequences of our actions by outsourcing our violence to others. Getting others to kill on our behalf does nothing to reduce the amount of suffering in the world.

A phrase I've used a lot, "this difficult thing of being human," reminds us to practice empathy, but it focuses our attention purely on our own species. When it comes to the final stage of the lovingkindness practice, we're encouraged to cultivate kindness toward all feeling beings, including animals. So I invite you to consider what you eat. It's true that all human activity kills living things. Plowing a field of grain will kill insects and worms, for example. But we can reduce the amount of suffering caused by our diet by giving up eating animals.

In talking about this difficult thing of being human, the Buddha acknowledged animals' suffering, saying, "Life as a human is like a cow being slaughtered. It's brief and fleeting, full of suffering and distress. Be thoughtful and wake up!"[26] He also talked about the reality of animals' suffering when he explained to his physician, Jivaka, why it was unethical for people to slaughter animals for him and his monks. He talked not only about the unhealthy volitions involved in killing, but also of the pain and distress experienced by the animal on its way to slaughter and as it was being killed.[27] Are we prepared to consider that animals' suffering is as real to them as ours is to us? And are we willing to abandon the view that our gratification is more important than their desire to live? These are things I invite you to consider.

It's not easy to change habits, and suggestions to do so are often met with resistance. This is especially true when the suggestion is that we give up things we find pleasant. It involves work; it takes effort to change what ingredients we buy and the recipes we use. It's all challenging. If you encounter resistance, I suggest meeting it with kindness. When we resist, part of us is afraid and in need of support. So offer it warmth. Be supportive. And then see if you can feel free to do what's kindest, rather than what's easiest.

Exercise

If you eat products derived from animals, I invite you to acknowledge the suffering this causes. Consider what would be the first and easiest step in changing that habit. Please do this with as much kindness toward yourself as possible. If you already don't eat meat, you can reflect on whether there are further changes you could make, such as cutting out dairy and eggs, or eliminating other animal products from your life. The aim isn't perfection, which is unattainable, but simply a reduction in the amount of suffering entailed by our dietary choices.

26

Lovingkindness as a path to awakening

The Buddha said:

A mindful one who develops
limitless love
weakens the fetters,
seeing the ending of attachments.[28]

The fetters mentioned here are ten mental habits that hold us back from enlightenment. Since kindness wears away these fetters, the Buddha is saying that lovingkindness practice directly helps us move toward enlightenment.

I think of all Buddhist practice as being about "unselfing." We "self" all the time, the word "selfing" being a rendering of *ahamkara*, which literally means "I-making." If you watch your mind, you'll see that it's continually pushing and pulling. In craving, we're trying to pull something in toward *us*. In aversion, we're trying to push something away from *us*. It's this pushing and pulling that create and reinforce our sense of self. Frustratingly, no matter how much we push and pull, we never get things the way we want them to be. Or not for long.

Kindness helps us to unself – to weaken this constant, sometimes exhausting emphasis on *I, me, mine*. When kindness is present, the unskillful volitions of ill will and craving are

Lovingkindness as a path to awakening

absent. Pushing and pulling become subtler, or are temporarily absent. Ill will and craving, which are two of the ten fetters, are exercised less and become weaker. And the sense of there being a self that they surround and defend becomes weaker too. Kindness unselfs.

Empathy unselfs too, because it expands our circle of concern to include others. It's the "limitless" (unbounded) part of the quote above. The self we assume is at the center of pushing and pulling seems like the most important part of the world. Other people are outside, mattering less than our own concerns. But, when we recognize that others' joys and sorrows are as real to them as ours are to us, the world is no longer centered on us. We expand our circle of concern to encompass others. Instead of seeing ourselves as the uniquely important center of our world, we begin to recognize that we are living in a world that is multicentered, or even centerless.

Reducing our craving and ill will, taking others' well-being into account, expanding and attenuating our sense of self – all of these are aspects of unselfing, and they bring contentment, well-being, and joy. We can come to recognize more and more clearly how unsatisfactory our preoccupation with self has been, and how rewarding it is to release it. Kindness gives us insight into the unsatisfactory nature of the reactive patterns our minds are addicted to.

Kindness is not a basic practice. It's a deep and liberating practice. The more we cultivate kindness, the less selfing there is in our lives. And, in a classic positive feedback loop, the less selfing there is, the easier it is for us to dwell in kindness. Kindness leads us into a spiral of beneficial growth. Kindness is not the be-all and end-all of the practice of love – there are three other brahma viharas, after all – but it can take us all the way to enlightenment.

Exercise

In daily life and in your meditation practice, observe selfing and unselfing, and ask: which of these ways of relating to the world brings happiness, and which brings suffering? When kindness arises, notice how it's accompanied by a softening and opening of our sense of self.

GUIDED MEDITATION: Observing selfing and unselfing

27
A kindness prayer

Many years ago, I did a translation of the famous *Karaniya Metta Sutta*. I had not long finished studying Pali at university, and I hoped to get a better understanding of the teaching. I also included it in my first book on meditation.[29] In this final chapter on kindness, I offer a version of that translation that's designed to be recited as a prayer. I hope you find it helpful.

The metta prayer

In order that I may be skilled
In discerning what is good
In order that I may understand the path to peace,
Let me be able, upright, and straightforward,
Of good speech, gentle, and free from pride;
Let me be contented, easily satisfied, having few duties,
Living simply, with controlled senses, prudent,
Without pride, and without attachment
To nation, race, or other groups.
Let me not do the slightest thing
For which the wise might rebuke me.
Instead let me think:

> May all beings be well and safe. May they be at ease.
> Whatever living beings there may be,
> Whether moving or standing still, without exception,

Whether large, great, middling, or small
Whether tiny or substantial,
Whether seen or unseen,
Living near or far,
Born or unborn;
May all beings be happy.
Let none deceive or despise another anywhere.
Let none wish harm to another, in anger or in hate.
Just as a mother would guard her child,
Her only child, with her own life,
Even so let me cultivate a boundless mind
For all beings in the world.
Let me cultivate a boundless love
For all beings in the world,
Above, below, and across,
Unhindered, without ill will or enmity.
Standing, walking, seated, or lying down,
Free from torpor, let me as far as possible
Keep my mind on this recollection.
This, they say,
Is the divine life right here.

Exercise

I suggest you try reciting this prayer before or after periods of lovingkindness meditation.

GUIDED MEDITATION: Metta bhavana

Part II
COMPASSION

The essentials of karuna

Karuna (Pali and Sanskrit) is the desire, based on empathy, that beings, ourselves included, be free from suffering so that they may have long-term happiness and well-being. Through compassionate thoughts, compassionate speech, and compassionate actions, we actively support and help others as they face difficulties.

Other translations
Pity, mercy (usually in older translations).

The stages of the meditation
We cultivate compassion toward:
- Ourselves.
- A person who is suffering.[30]
- A relative stranger.
- A person we have difficulty with.
- All beings.

Suggested phrases
- May you be free from suffering.
- May you find peace.
- May you be compassionate to yourself and others.

One crucial thing to know
Compassion does not involve taking on others' suffering. It involves knowing that the other person is suffering, recognizing that this is difficult for them, and offering them support. This support can take many forms, but most often what people need is simply to know that someone cares, and to be able to share their experience.

1
Cultivating compassion

Compassion is what happens when kindness – the desire for beings to be at ease – meets suffering. When this happens, we want beings to be free from pain or distress. To be compassionate, we recognize ourselves and others not just as feeling beings, but also as *suffering beings* – meaning that suffering inevitably arises in our lives.

The Path of Freedom describes compassion like this:

> *As parents, who on seeing the suffering of their dear and only child, feel compassion for them, saying, "Oh, how they suffer!" so one feels compassion for all beings. This is compassion.*[31]

This analogy of parents responding to a child's suffering reminds us that compassion is an emotion that we all have. This image also reminds us that compassion is a desire to help, and not simply a feeling. When you see your child suffering you don't just experience heartache: you do what you can to comfort and help them. That the word for compassion, *karuna*, comes from the verb *karoti*, "to do," is another reminder that compassion is an active quality.

We all naturally experience compassion in our lives, and your lovingkindness meditation will inevitably have included an element of compassion. There are bound to have been times

Cultivating compassion

you've cultivated kindness for someone and been aware they were suffering. So this is something you have some familiarity with. In fact, in discussing the practice of developing kindness, I often mentioned the fact that we are all doing a difficult thing in being human. We go through life seeking happiness, and yet often suffer instead.

Compassion, like kindness, rests on a foundation of empathy. If you look at your own experience, you'll see that episodes of suffering often arise – often mild, and sometimes more extreme. All this suffering is unwanted, and given a choice we'd rather be happy and at ease instead. When we reflect on others' experience, we see it's just the same for them. All have their suffering. Some have more, and some less, but all want to be free from suffering in just the same way as we do. And, just as we want to be free from suffering, they too want to be free from suffering. Compassion is supporting them in that desire. At the very least it involves caring about beings' suffering, but sometimes, when it's possible, we can help them directly.

The karuna bhavana meditation helps us to cultivate a deeper awareness of beings as suffering beings, and to strengthen the desire to help and support them. There are five stages, beginning with cultivating kindness or compassion for ourselves. We'll see how we need to be able to have compassion for our own suffering in order to have compassion for others. If we can't support ourselves, how can we support anyone else? We'll also see that compassion meditation can be tenderly joyful, rather than depressing. In discussing lovingkindness practice, I said that an awareness of suffering can be grounding. That's true of compassion, which is ennobling, bringing a deeper sense of meaning into our lives.

Because compassion is an active quality and involves doing what we can to alleviate suffering, it's not enough just to generate warm, tender feelings on the cushion. We come across ample suffering in our everyday lives, sometimes at a distance and sometimes up close. So we will explore how we can cultivate compassion in daily life as well as in meditation.

Exercise

Today, carry around an attitude of well-wishing as best you can. As you encounter others, or even just think of them, be aware of them as suffering beings – that is, as beings prone to suffering.

2

What is suffering?

The essence of compassion is wishing that beings be free from suffering. But what do we mean by suffering? We often think of it in grand terms: the person with a severe illness, the refugee, the starving child in a drought zone. Looked at this way, suffering is a rare event. It may even seem that you don't really suffer. But you do, every day. All beings do. You are suffering when you're worrying what people think about you, when you feel resentful, impatient, embarrassed, self-doubting, irritable, sad, flat, frustrated, lonely, jealous, bored, or regretful. As you observe your experience, you'll probably notice that you spend a lot of time dipping in and out of various forms of suffering. You might even suffer most of the time. If you observe those around you, you'll see it's just the same for them. For some of course it's much worse.

The first of the Buddha's four noble truths is not, as many people say, that "life is suffering" (something the Buddha never said) but simply that suffering exists in our lives. And this suffering, the Buddha says, should be *understood*. We often suffer without understanding that that's what's happening. Think what happens when you're frustrated by your computer running slowly. You probably say, "This damned computer is too slow!" rather than "I am suffering – let me have compassion for myself." You might think the computer is making you feel bad, and yet the frustration is not arising in the computer and moving into your mind. It's created entirely within you. So you *understand* neither that you are suffering, nor the process of suffering.

We also frequently don't understand others' suffering. When you are with someone who is in a bad mood, how often do you think, "This person is suffering. What can I do to ease their pain?" You probably think, "Jeez, they got out of bed on the wrong side this morning! I'd better steer clear." Not understanding that this person is suffering, you might be brusque with them, adding to their distress.

And sometimes, when we do see that someone is suffering, we don't understand that suffering is common to us both. Instead, we judge them, seeing their suffering as a sign of failure, or almost as a personality defect. We arrogantly assume that we're perfect and above such things. And yet we are *all* prone to suffering. To be vulnerable to suffering is a universal phenomenon. It's something that affects all living beings. This is yet another way we can fail to understand suffering.

Our first task is simply to understand when we and others are suffering. Until that happens, there can be no compassion.

Exercise

Let's work on understanding suffering, by recognizing it in ourselves and others. Don't just notice that you're anxious, for example; understand instead that this is a moment of suffering. Don't just notice that someone is grumpy; understand that they're suffering. Understand also that suffering people need support.

3
Self-compassion as self-support

One day I was walking to work. It had rained all night, and the wet sidewalk was covered with worms. Because the sun had come out, many of them were going to die. I had made a promise many years before that I would not walk past a worm without moving it to safety. I just don't like the way I feel when I ignore another's suffering, even if the other is a slimy invertebrate. So every few steps I would stoop, scoop up a worm, and move it to a grassy area.

There were a lot of worms, and I was doing a lot of stooping, scooping, and moving. As I carried one worm to safety, I'd pass several more. So I'd go back and rescue them, too. I realized this was going to take a long time, and I was going to be late for work. I could have decided to abandon Operation Worm Rescue, but I wanted to stick to my promise. So, as I continued ferrying worms, I practiced self-compassion in the following way:

- I recognized that my impatience and anxiety were forms of suffering: "Just as they are suffering, you are suffering."
- I kept letting go of thoughts such as, "I'm late, I have to get to work!"

The Heart's Awakening

- I turned my attention instead to the body, and felt my suffering as a knot in the belly.
- I accepted that it's okay to suffer.
- I wished my suffering well and regarded it with kind eyes.

Considering the suffering of another naturally induces a sense of discomfort. That discomfort might take the form of an ache in the heart or an uncomfortable feeling in the belly. It's right and normal to feel this discomfort. It's empathy.

So accept your discomfort. But don't wallow. Wallowing is when the mind creates more suffering by telling stories about how awful this is, how inadequate we are, how we can't bear these feelings another moment, and so on. Let go of those thoughts, over and over. The uncomfortable feeling is just a sensation in the body. It can't hurt you. Offer it your love with kind eyes, reassuring touch, and supportive speech.

All of this can be applied in the first stage of compassion meditation, where we cultivate compassion for ourselves. We can remind ourselves that we are feeling beings and suffering beings. Even if we're not suffering at that time, we can remember that it's something we're prone to. If this recollection triggers heartache, so be it. We know how to deal with that. We regard it with kind eyes, accept it, and offer it kind and supportive words, such as: "May you be free from suffering. May you find peace. May you be compassionate to yourself and others."

Compassion for self and compassion for others go hand in hand. Because having compassion for a suffering being can activate discomfort, we need to be able to offer ourselves

Self-compassion as self-support

emotional support. It's self-compassion that makes compassion for others doable. This is why we begin the practice of compassion with ourselves.

Exercise

Notice your suffering and understand it as suffering, then try responding compassionately to it. Once you've done that, notice anything else that changes, such as your compassion becoming more available to others.

GUIDED MEDITATION: Supporting yourself with compassion

4

Don't try to like yourself. Just be kind to yourself

It's painful when we hate ourselves. Often, wanting to be free from this pain, we wish we could like ourselves instead. But the solution to self-hatred is not to like ourselves; it's being kind and compassionate to ourselves.

Liking something means that you respond to it with pleasure. The people you like are those it's pleasurable to be with, for example. But we all contain unskillful habits such as selfishness and cruelty, and you're never going to find those things pleasurable. You're never going to like them. You *can* offer kindness and understanding, however, to the hateful, angry, cruel, and deluded parts of yourself. Practicing self-kindness and self-compassion is how we learn to be at ease with who we are, despite our many imperfections.

Hatred has evolved to help us. When we hate others, we hope that this will prompt them to avoid us, which means we don't have to confront the things we don't like about them. Or perhaps we hope that, faced with our disapproval, they'll change. We may also, through expressing hatred, hope to get emotional support from others who dislike the same thing or person. Sometimes these strategies work, to an extent, but, like all unskillful emotions, hatred is counterproductive; aiming to make us happier, it creates more suffering than it relieves us from. When we express hatred to others, we usually receive

Don't try to like yourself. Just be kind to yourself

hatred in return. Hatefulness can make us hard to be around and cause others to avoid us, thereby increasing our woes. The very act of hating is painful, too: as the Buddha said, "association with the disliked is suffering."[32]

Hating ourselves is even more counterproductive than hating others. We might drive away someone we hate, but we can't drive away the things that we dislike about ourselves. They are a part of us. They're not going to change just because we hate them. We're stuck with them, and with the pain they cause us. When we hate unskillful aspects of ourselves, all we're doing is adding another unskillful emotion to the mix.

Hatred is only ever ended by love. To cultivate love, or kindness, toward things in yourself that you dislike, you can:

1. Understand that having destructive emotions and making mistakes is not a personal failing. These things are part of the human condition. You are not alone.
2. Regard unhelpful habits and the pain they cause with loving eyes. Having a kindly gaze helps you to feel more at ease with yourself.
3. Place a hand where any painful feeling is manifesting in the body, and let it rest there tenderly, offering kindness and reassurance. The more primitive parts of your being respond to loving touch in much the same way as a frightened animal does.
4. Talk kindly to yourself, saying things like, "It's okay to be imperfect. We all mess up. I know you're suffering, and I wish you well. I just want you to know that I love you and want you to be happy."

These actions constitute a powerful practice of self-kindness, especially when we combine them.

Being kind toward parts of ourselves that are unskillful doesn't mean that we approve of them. It just means recognizing that hating parts of ourselves is pointless and painful. We can still know that our destructive tendencies need to be changed, and work, kindly and self-compassionately, to change them. When we practice self-kindness, we discover that there is no part of us that is unworthy of compassion and kindness.

Self-kindness and self-compassion help us accept that it's okay to be imperfect. They give us the freedom to be patient with ourselves. As we learn to relate kindly to what is difficult in ourselves, we become more skillful in relating to what we find difficult in others, too. Being kind to ourselves helps us to be kinder to everyone.

Exercise

When you understand that you are suffering, practice loving eyes, kind and compassionate self-touch, and supportive and empathetic communication with the suffering part of yourself. Notice how this changes your relationship with yourself, and with others.

5

Self-care and self-compassion

Self-compassion is where we support ourselves through difficulties by giving ourselves emotional support and reassurance. As we've seen, this can involve regarding ourselves with kind eyes, talking to ourselves in a gentle and comforting way, and reassuringly touching the parts of the body where painful feelings are most prominent.

Self-care is where we look after our own needs so that we will be healthier, happier, and experience less suffering in the first place. It includes, as we've seen, breaks from work, but also exercising, eating healthily, getting enough sleep, and maintaining friendships.[33] If we don't meet those needs, we cause ourselves unnecessary suffering. Self-compassion helps us support ourselves when we're in pain, but it's even better if we practice self-care and prevent that unnecessary suffering from happening.

Having had to support myself through some extremely challenging circumstances in my life, I'm good at practicing self-compassion, but find self-care much harder. I take care of my needs for healthy food and getting sufficient sleep, but I often neglect to exercise and stretch, and I've had some painful injuries as a result. If I stretch and exercise, I don't experience as much physical pain. So self-care is like a form of self-compassion that anticipates and heads off future suffering.

The Heart's Awakening

Some people are the opposite of me. They're good at self-care but not emotionally self-supportive. They might exercise religiously, for example, but it might be more like self-punishment than self-compassion. If this describes you, then you're already learning self-compassion here. But if you need to translate self-compassion into self-care, here are some suggestions:

1. Think of one thing you could do to take better care of yourself, for example, getting enough sleep, eating more healthily, or exercising regularly.
2. Recall the suffering that arises from that lack of self-care – for example, feelings of exhaustion, the bloated feeling of bingeing on unhealthy food, or the physical discomfort of being stiff or injured. Remember what that suffering is like.
3. Surround it with compassion. Regard it with kind eyes. Place a hand tenderly on the place where the discomfort is most prominent. Offer it reassurance: "I'm sorry you suffer this way. I love you and I want you to be at ease."
4. Express the intention to do things differently in the future. Let your pain know that you will seek to be kinder, practicing acts of kindness and self-care. It's okay to feel and express regret, if it's done out of love: "I'm sorry I haven't looked after you the way you need. I want to take better care of you."

Now, having established that intention to practice self-care, set a goal for manifesting it.

The goal should be small and easily doable. It's better to aim for a brisk five-minute walk every day and succeed than to aim for a thirty-minute run and fail. You can expand the goal later. Make your goal specific. Don't aim to eat more healthily; aim to eat a piece of fruit for a snack instead of a chocolate bar, for example. Don't just aim to get to bed earlier; aim to be in bed by a specific time.

With my tendency to forget to stretch, my goal is to spend five minutes stretching before my morning meditation. My goal is not over-ambitious, it makes a difference, and it's specific (I'm not vaguely aiming to "stretch more").

I know I lose track of the time when I'm busy, so I've set a recurring reminder on my phone. You may also need something like that. My reminder currently says, "Out of love and self-care, I choose to stretch my body." If my reminder comes across as an order, I'm likely to resist it, because I don't like following orders. So I've phrased my reminder to express kindness and compassion. Whatever reminder you set, phrase it in a way that works for you.

Exercise

Try out the numbered suggestions above. I suggest spending just a few moments at the start of your new habit connecting with yourself with kindness and compassion, with kind eyes, reassuring touch, and warm and supportive words. Make sure that your self-care is a genuine expression of self-compassion.

6

Understanding three forms of suffering

The Buddha said that the noble truth of suffering was to be "understood." We've already seen the need to understand that we're suffering when we're suffering. Another way we can understand suffering is to know that it has three different forms, which are:

1. the suffering of pain (*dukkha-dukkhata*);
2. fabricated suffering (*sankhara-dukkhata*);
3. the suffering of reversal (*viparinama-dukkhata*).

Some of you will be familiar with this list but with the second and third items switched. The order here, however, is what's found in the scriptures.[34] Also, what I've called "fabricated suffering" is usually described as "the suffering of the conditioned" – meaning that nothing that's conditioned (nothing that's impermanent, in other words) can give true satisfaction. It's true that things that are conditioned don't last, and therefore can't give lasting satisfaction, but that's not what this form of suffering is about. "Fabricated suffering" (sankhara-dukkhata) is the suffering we make for ourselves.

I arrived at this interpretation by comparing three teachings. As well as the list above, the Buddha elaborates elsewhere on these three forms of suffering, showing us how they work together. In a third discourse he gives three concrete examples of these three kinds of suffering. Put these teachings together, and it becomes clear what these different kinds of suffering are.

Three forms of suffering – three arrows

There is a well-known teaching, the *Salla Sutta*, where the Buddha says that suffering is like two arrows.[35] First we have ordinary physical pain, which is dukkha-dukkhata. When we think about physical pain, what may come to mind is having a headache, a sore back, or the aches and pains of having the flu. But painful feelings should also come under this category. Think what it's like when your feelings are hurt. You literally experience this as pain in the body. The Buddha said this kind of suffering is like being shot by an arrow.

Then there's the second arrow. We often react to the pain of the first arrow with what the Buddha called "sorrow, wailing, and lamentation," also known as self-pity. Our self-pity shows up as thoughts like, "This is awful. Why me? I wish it would stop!" Each of those thoughts, the Buddha says, is like being shot with a second arrow in response to the first. Resistance constructs or "fabricates" a secondary layer of unnecessary suffering. The Pali word for "fabricated" is *sankhara*, and so "fabricated suffering" is sankhara-dukkhata.

Then we have the "third arrow." True, there are only two images involving arrows in this discourse, but in the *Salla Sutta* the Buddha describes a third form of suffering, which is when we pursue pleasure so we can escape the pain of the first and second arrows. Usually it's not that we replace pain with pleasure; it's the pursuit itself that is the distraction. We might overeat, binge-watch Netflix, drown our sorrows in alcohol, or flirt with someone we probably shouldn't flirt with. We might end up numb rather than in a state of pleasure, but our distraction always ends, doesn't fundamentally address our initial suffering, and often brings its own unpleasant consequences.

The Buddha didn't offer an arrow simile for this third form of suffering, but I'll have a "stab" at it. This form of suffering is like shooting ourselves with an arrow dipped in a narcotic drug. For a while, doped up, we ignore the pain of the first or second arrow. But there's a reversal when the drug wears off, and we experience the pain we were trying to avoid, *plus* the hangover effect from the narcotic. The word for "reversal" is *viparinama*, and so this form of suffering is viparinama-dukkhata, or the suffering that arises from reversal.

The third discourse also contains the same three forms of suffering in the same order, and has helpful examples. The Buddha, talking to his fellow countryman Mahanama, gives three examples of how suffering arises from work:[36]

1. There are physical pains that come from working. This is the first arrow. It's dukkha-dukkhata, or the first arrow.
2. Business might not go well, and then you "sorrow and pine and lament, beating your breast" (or experience self-pity). This is the second arrow. It's the suffering we fabricate for ourselves, or sankhara-dukkhata.

Understanding three forms of suffering

3. If we make money, we then lose it or fear losing it. That's the pain of reversal. This is viparinama-dukkhata, which I've called the third arrow.

This isn't just an interesting intellectual exercise. The Buddha didn't just want us to know that there are three forms of suffering. He wanted us to *understand* suffering, how it arises, and how we can free ourselves from it.

- When you recognize initial suffering, as painful sensation or feeling in the body, practice non-reactive acceptance, or equanimity. That pain will pass in time.
- When you realize you've been fabricating suffering through resistance, drop those resistant thoughts, again turning with equanimity toward your initial pain. Because you're no longer creating an extra layer of suffering for yourself, you will suffer less.
- And when you find you're trying to distract yourself from pain, you can compassionately remind yourself that this is unwise, and instead practice self-care. Try resting, talking to a friend, or going for a walk. In whatever healthy and skillful ways you can, look after yourself, kindly and wisely.

Understanding these three forms of suffering helps us to suffer less.

Exercise

Notice the three forms of suffering in your own experience, and practice accepting the pain of the first arrow, dropping the reactive thinking of the second arrow, and turning to self-care as a way of responding to what I've called the third arrow.

7

Don't ignore your suffering

People often have concerns that self-compassion is selfish, especially when they consider that others' sufferings may be greater. We shouldn't underestimate, however, the effect of supposedly minor things like worrying about whether people like us, feeling lonely, or being irritable. These sufferings can wear us down, making it harder for us to be compassionate to others. Practicing self-compassion frees us from this self-preoccupation. Having acknowledged our suffering and having offered it support, we can move on. Our empathy and compassion become aroused and are available to support and help others.

Now it's true that there are always people who are suffering more than we are, and sometimes we're asked, as a spiritual practice, to consider this. But the point of these reflections is not to show us that our suffering doesn't matter. All suffering matters. We make these comparisons to help us abandon the self-pity of "sorrow, wailing, and lamentation." When we think that our suffering isn't important or isn't "real" compared to what others are going through, or when we think we've been uniquely singled out for punishment by the universe, we need to recognize that this kind of thinking is just another example of the second arrow. These assumptions make us feel alone in our suffering. And that leads to self-pity, which makes our energies unavailable for others.

Considering instead that suffering is universal tells us that suffering is not a sign of failure, that we're not being singled out, that we are not alone but are participating in that most universal of things – human suffering. We realize that we're all in this together. This prevents self-pity, leaving us free to take an interest in others.

Noticing our suffering and offering it support isn't complicated and usually doesn't take long:

1. Notice you're suffering.
2. Let go of self-pitying thoughts.
3. Locate the painful feeling in your body.
4. Regard it with kind eyes, offering it support and warmth.
5. Talk to it kindly and supportively.

With your pain acknowledged and soothed, your energy and attention become freed up, so that you can have empathy and compassion for others. Sometimes this takes seconds. In contrast, self-pity can continue for a lifetime.

When we turn toward the painful feelings in our body – which might show up as pangs of disappointment, hurt, loneliness, or flutters of anxiety – they're often surprisingly mild compared to the turbulence and pain stirred up by our reactivity toward them. It's strange how such mild and fleeting sensations can provoke such enormous emotional convulsions, plunging us into the torment of self-pity. If we don't shoot the second arrow of reactivity, the pain of the first arrow usually passes very quickly.

Don't ignore your suffering

There are times, though, when we can't easily move on. Grief is the longest-lived feeling, often because the experience that generates it, such as a bereavement or a disrupted relationship, is by nature long-term. We may need to deal with wave after wave of grief for weeks or months until things settle down. But, even here, freeing ourselves from our reactivity also frees up our attention for others, so that we can at least be a little more empathetic toward them. An important part of our self-compassion practice can consist in us realizing, "I'm going through grief. It's going to be with me for a while. That's just how things are."

Self-compassion is not selfish. In fact, it's what frees us from selfishness. Failing to meet your pain with compassion leads to the self-indulgence of "sorrow, wailing, and lamentation." So remember: your suffering matters. All of it. And so do you. Ask yourself, "If a dear friend was suffering in the way I am, would I ignore it, or would I want to support them?" Treat yourself as you would treat that friend. Give yourself compassionate attention so that you can move on from it and be of greater use to our suffering world.

Exercise

No matter how minor an episode of suffering is, practice the steps in the numbered list above. Once you've offered yourself compassion, observe what happens. Especially notice how your compassion becomes available for others.

GUIDED MEDITATION: Supporting a friend, compassionately

8

Calling to mind a suffering person

In the first stage of the practice, you connect with yourself empathetically. You recognize you are a suffering being, like all other beings, and recognize that you need support as you do this difficult thing of being human. You offer yourself that support, regarding yourself with loving eyes and offering yourself reassuring and compassionate messages. You awaken your empathy and your compassion. And now you're ready to do the same for someone else.

In the second stage of compassion meditation, recall someone who's suffering. We all suffer every day, but this should be someone who's going through a particularly hard time. It might be someone you know, but it could be someone you've heard about on the news. Perhaps they are sick, depressed, anxious, struggling in a relationship, having a hard time at work, or doubting themselves.

Be aware of what this person is going through. Understand that their suffering is real, and painful, and that they don't want it. Just as suffering is something you don't want to experience, it's something they don't want to experience. Just remembering these things will usually awaken the desire that their suffering be alleviated. This is compassion.

What we are *not* trying to do is to feel this person's pain. This is what's known as "empathic distress," and it leaves us

Calling to mind a suffering person

feeling drained and in need of help ourselves. We go from being the helper to being helpless. The Buddha referred to this very problem when he said, "If someone going down into a river, swollen and swiftly flowing, is carried away by the current – how can they help others across?"[37]

It's enough to know that this person is suffering, and that they would rather not. You know this because anyone in the same situation, yourself included, would want to be free from suffering. Yes, as you recognize the other person's suffering, you will likely experience some heartache. This is good and healthy. This is not empathic distress. It's not disabling. It's just empathy. Hold this heartache lightly, and offer it support. Regard it with kind eyes. If you need to, say a few warm and encouraging words. Support yourself. Then support the other person. Stand strong on the bank; don't dive into the river.

Offering support, you can regard the suffering person with kind eyes, and you can, as a guardian angel, offer them the comfort of human touch. And you can express your kindness by saying, "May you be free from suffering. May you find peace. May you be compassionate to yourself and others."

Again, these words are not attempts to create compassion. They're expressions of compassion. If you first connect with yourself kindly and empathetically, and then connect with a suffering person in the same way, compassionate support will arise naturally. You don't have to make that happen. Expressing your compassion helps strengthen what is already within you.

Exercise

Notice people suffering. Look for the suffering under their anger, frustration, craving, and so on. Seeing their suffering, let yourself feel supportive of them. If you feel moved to do so, and if it's appropriate, let yourself act compassionately toward them. Compassion is to be done as well as felt.

GUIDED MEDITATION: Supporting a suffering person

9

The near enemy of compassion

The Path of Purification says that the near enemy of compassion is grief,[38] and that compassion "fails when it produces sorrow." Both of these things refer to the "sorrow, wailing, and lamentation" of the *Salla Sutta*, to self-pity, and to the empathic distress I've mentioned, where we take on others' sufferings and feel overwhelmed by them. They are all ways of talking about the second arrow. And they are near enemies because we might confuse them with compassion itself.[39]

We compound this confusion when we believe that sharing someone's suffering is the point of compassion practice. We may try to vividly imagine the suffering that another person is going through, and experience overwhelming empathic distress. This isn't helpful. When a child falls and skins a knee, they are often extremely distressed. They wail and cry because of the pain and the disturbing sight of their own blood. From the child's perspective, something has gone horribly wrong. If a parent were to experience the suffering that the child is going through, they would be unable to help. Now a parent must have empathy. They need to know and care that the child is suffering. But what the child needs is a calm, empathetic, reassuring, and helpful presence, not a fellow sufferer. When we engulf ourselves in sorrow, we're unable to be of help to anyone.

Another way we can turn compassion practice into a wallowfest is by thinking we have to fix problems it's not in our power to fix. If someone has a terminal illness, for example, we might become distressed at the seeming pointlessness of wishing them well. The second arrow here manifests as helplessness.

How can our saying "May you be free from suffering" cure someone's illness? Well, it can't. But, although compassion is not meant as a miracle cure, it can give people emotional support while they're going through a hard time. It can let a suffering person know that they are cared for, that they are not alone, and that they matter. This is a precious gift to offer another human being. Even if we can't communicate directly with them, having compassion for them helps us with our own distress, lessening our feelings of helplessness and despair. We feel useful.

When the Buddha talked to one of his followers who was terminally ill, he advised them to practice with the intention, "Though my body is ailing, my mind will be healthy."[40] The Buddha knew that his own compassion couldn't heal someone physically, but he knew that he could help them be at peace. Sometimes that's all you can do. And if you're doing all you can do, you're doing enough.

Exercise

When sorrow arises, which is bound to happen, recognize that part of you is suffering, and offer it support. Often in the wake of this, wiser perspectives arise that will allow you to return to a state of peace, contentment, and love.

10

Compassion can be joyful

One time, when I was doing lovingkindness meditation every day for a month, sometimes practicing more than once a day, my sits became filled with joy. Outside meditation I felt cocooned in happiness. Then I switched to a month of compassion practice, and it seemed like my joy had been snatched away. The practice wasn't depressing, but it felt sober. However, after about a week of continuing with compassion meditation, the joy, to my surprise, began to return.

Interesting things happen when you turn toward discomfort with openness and acceptance. When you first look at a feeling, it can seem solid and weighty, but, if you keep on looking, you find that layers of fear, aversion, and tension – all those second arrows – begin to drop away, and the experience becomes lighter and less substantial. Often the primary heartache that comes from calling someone's suffering to mind is nothing more than a pang or ache. And it's bearable. It can even be beautiful.

Compassion can be joyful because it is love, and love is a joyful thing. Compassion meets our deep need for connection with others, which is rich and rewarding. Compassion also connects us with a deeper purpose, which brings about a deep and stable kind of contentment. And so, even with our hearts wide open to suffering, we can be joyful and at peace.

The Heart's Awakening

I think about times like my sister's and my mother's funerals. We all felt a painful loss, but there was joy as well. There was the joy of seeing one another again ("It's a shame it's always at funerals" was a common lament). There was the joy of supporting each other, the joy of giving support; the joy of knowing others care enough to support us. There was the joy of celebrating those we'd loved and of recalling the precious time we had together.

Within me I felt a painful ache, but that ache was surrounded by a field of loving attention. Sometimes, especially when talking with others, waves of sorrow would sweep through me. I'd let that happen, and in their wake I felt peace, knowing that the pain was bearable.

We all experienced that heightened sense of meaning that comes when we're together because of a death, none of us knowing when the next death would be, or whose it would be. Death reminds us that life is precious and that love is one of the things that makes it that way. At those two funerals there was pain, but there was also joy, and love, and sometimes laughter.

There is no point thinking that people shouldn't die or that life is unfair, or that suffering should not exist. This is our old friend, the second arrow, once again. People get sick. People die. These things will happen to us all. The best we can do is to choose to be there for each other. As a quote attributed to Ram Dass says, "We're all just walking each other home."[41] Compassion can be an act of defiance in the face of sickness, old age, and death's inevitability. It keeps alive a space for joy to flourish amid the suffering.

If you find compassion to be joyful, nothing is wrong. This does not mean you're lacking in compassion or empathy. It's just a normal human experience. Don't try to block or suppress the joy of compassion; embrace it. Compassion, joy, and even pain can go hand in hand.

Exercise

You might have assumed compassion meditation to be heavy and serious. But there's no reason why it can't, at times, be playful and joyful. Watch for these assumptions and any others that may suppress joy.

11

Taking compassion off the cushion

If our compassion only happens on the cushion, it's not of much use to the world. We cultivate compassion in meditation so that we can be more compassionate in daily life. From a practical viewpoint, I see three categories of compassionate activity: major undertakings, short-term practical help, and offering moral support.[42]

Usually we need to think carefully about taking on major commitments. I was fortunate in my twenties to have abundant resources of time and energy. I taught literacy to adults, helped a teenager from an underprivileged background with his schoolwork, supported classes at my local Dharma center, and volunteered in an adventure playground for children with learning disabilities – more or less simultaneously. I am no longer that person. I'm older and tire more easily. I have work commitments, a relationship with my partner to sustain, two children to chauffeur, and three dogs to take care of.

My children are adopted. Adopting them was the result of a strong desire on the part of my ex-wife and I to provide a home and parenting for children who lacked those things. My dogs are adopted as well, and this too was a decision of the same sort; we wanted to provide love and shelter for abandoned animals. These were major undertakings we committed to after much deliberation, knowing that they would have a big impact on our lives. Even then, I found after adopting our first child that I could no longer sustain some of my other responsibilities. I had to stop teaching in prison – which I'd been doing for years – and no longer had the time to teach at my local Buddhist center. Major undertakings often turn out to be more major than you'd anticipated. I'm not trying to talk you out of them; I'm just suggesting that they require careful thought. I'll probably have to wait until retirement, and my kids going off to college, before I can get back into volunteering on a regular basis.

Many of our acts of compassion, however, will not involve ongoing commitments. Everyone needs help from time to time, and sometimes we can provide it, even if it's just offering to pick up someone's groceries or walk their dog when they're sick. This doesn't solve all their problems, but it gives them support and lets them know that they matter. I'd suggest that we might train ourselves, when we hear someone's sick, not just to think, "That's a shame" but to get in touch and ask, "Do you need any help?"

In many cases, though, people who are struggling don't need practical help – they need to share. One of the worst things about suffering is the feeling of being alone with it. We can help alleviate a great deal of others' suffering just by taking an interest in them. Probably most of the help we can offer in our lives is of this sort. We can see a coworker or family member looking unhappy and ask what's happening. We can see a cashier looking stressed and reassure them that we're not in a hurry and to take their time. "What's going on?" and "Are you okay?" are simple but powerful questions that can let someone know that they are worthy of being cared about. Watch for opportunities to bring a little warmth and tenderness into the world.

Giving people your attention often helps; giving them advice often doesn't. One of the least compassionate things we can do is to see ourselves as a savior who is there to tell the other person what to do to sort out their life. The "Well, you just need to do such-and-such!" type of advice usually comes from a place of feeling superior. One of the most helpful forms of compassion is instead to listen actively, asking clarifying questions, and giving the other person space to share how they feel. Giving someone your attention in this way helps them, while feeling supported, to think through their problems on their terms. If you have advice to offer them, ask if they're open to it. If they are, offer it knowing that you can never know all the complexities of their situation.

Also, don't use someone else's difficulties as an excuse to unload your own. Much of the time we have a mild desperation to talk about ourselves. In chitchat with a friend, that's fine. In a conversation where someone needs support, talking about ourselves negates their need to be heard. If you feel an urge to divert the conversation back to yourself, acknowledge the painful feelings that accompany that, and offer yourself some compassion. Connecting with yourself compassionately will help you stay compassionately connected with the other person.

Simply being present with others is one of the highest acts of compassion.

Taking compassion off the cushion

Exercise

I suggest especially being aware of opportunities to listen to what's going on with another person without judging or trying to fix things.

12

Avoid idiot compassion

When discussing lovingkindness, I talked about not confusing "being nice" with "being kind." Here we return to a similar topic: how not to practice what Chögyam Trungpa called "idiot compassion."[43] Idiot compassion involves avoiding conflict, letting people walk all over you, and not giving people a hard time when that's what they need. It's not compassion at all. It's a source of pain, both to ourselves and to those we think we're helping.

As with being nice, idiot compassion is about wanting to be liked. It lacks courage, because we're afraid to do anything that might make us unpopular. It lacks wisdom, because it sets out to help but achieves the opposite. If someone cheats you, and you "compassionately" decide to trust them again, you're not helping either them or yourself. The person who cheats you is unlikely to have a sudden conversion to honesty, and any promise they make to change their ways is likely to be just another form of cheating. Letting them off the hook, you enable their dysfunctional behavior, which will only cause them more suffering. And you'll regret being duped, so you'll end up suffering as well. Sometimes the most compassionate thing we can say to a cheat is, "I'm sorry, but you've given up the right to be trusted. You're going to have to earn my trust back, and that might take a long time." The cheat will try to manipulate you by saying you're not being compassionate.

Avoid idiot compassion

Their idea of you being compassionate is that you help them harm themselves and others.

True compassion doesn't shy away from causing pain when necessary. The Buddha discussed this with a prince named Abhaya. Abhaya was the follower of a rival teacher, and he had been sent to entrap the Buddha by asking whether he would say words that were disagreeable to others. If the Buddha said he would, then he would be accused of acting just like unenlightened people who hurt others. If he said he wouldn't, then it would be pointed out that his words had indeed caused others to be upset. This was described as a "two-pronged question." "When you put this dilemma to him," Abhaya is told by his teacher, "the Buddha won't be able to either spit it out or swallow it down."[44]

The Buddha however turns this metaphor to his advantage. A baby boy happened to be lying on the prince's lap, and the Buddha asked, "What do you think, prince? If [...] your boy were to put a stick or stone in his mouth, what would you do?"

Abhaya replied:

I'd try to take it out, sir. If that didn't work, I'd cradle his head with my left hand and take it out using a hooked finger of my right hand, even if it drew blood. Why is that? Because I have sympathy for the boy, sir.

The Buddha had led Abhaya to recognize that it's acceptable to cause pain in the short term if you want to keep someone from long-term harm. He goes on to say, "The Realized One knows the right time to speak so as to explain what he knows to be true, correct, and beneficial, but which is disliked by others."

Those are the only circumstances under which the Buddha would say something that he knew to be disagreeable. This is a tough example to follow. What you say must not be just your biased opinion – it must be objectively true. This requires a great deal of mental clarity. For what you say to be beneficial, you must have a good understanding of psychology and of the spiritual path. You might need to know the person you're talking to well. And you need to know if it's the right time for the other person to receive what you say, which requires empathy.

We can't wait until we've attained a near-superhuman state of wisdom to start practicing honest but critical communication. All we can do is communicate with as much courage, honesty, kindness, and wisdom as we can muster, and see how it works out. We mess up, we apologize, and we learn from our mistakes. Keep supporting yourself with self-compassion as you do this.

Eventually this ability to communicate sensitively, wisely, and courageously becomes an unconscious skill. Once the Buddha has explained the nature of skillful speech to Abhaya, he talks about the spontaneous nature of his communication. He doesn't plan what to say; he simply sees beings' needs, and lets his inner compassion and wisdom speak. Be wary of "trying to be compassionate." The more you do this, the more likely it is that you're not being compassionate at all.

Exercise

If you find that you sometimes avoid truthful, necessary, kind communication because you're afraid it might make you unliked, try noticing your fear, and talk to it in a compassionate way, offering yourself support and encouragement to do the right thing.

13

Compassion is inherent

We can develop compassion for anyone, including complete strangers. Philosopher and neuroscientist Josh Greene says that, although we may think of morality as being handed down from on high, written in scriptures, or carved on stone tablets, moral emotions are to a much greater extent handed up from below, inscribed in our DNA.[45] The late primatologist Frans de Waal observed chimpanzees taking care of each other, for example by bringing water to individuals with disabilities.[46] Even rats show the capacity for empathy, and will try to help each other escape traps.[47]

The capacity for compassion is there all the time, even if we temporarily lose touch with it. If you observe what happens when a homeless person asks you for money or you see a stranger in need of assistance, you'll see that your first instinct is to help. The reluctance to help comes later, in the form of fears of being exploited, or judged, or making ourselves late. Compassion is instinctual, while our fears about responding compassionately are learned.

The language of "cultivating" or "developing" compassion can mislead us into thinking that we're creating something that doesn't yet exist. However, the words "cultivate" and "develop" are meant to imply that we already have compassion. When we cultivate a garden, we don't start with nothing. We take already existing seeds and give them what they need to grow. Perhaps we should translate *karuna bhavana* as "strengthening compassion" instead.

The reflections I've suggested for compassion meditation are intended to help us reconnect with our innate compassion. As I'm beginning the practice of cultivating compassion, I recognize the truth of the following:

- My feelings are important to me.
- I don't want to suffer and want to be happy.
- But suffering is hard to avoid.
- Therefore, I need support and encouragement as I go through life.

As you read those words, they may have no discernible effect. The left brain understands them as information, but perhaps wasn't touched by them. But sit with them and let them sink in, and the emotional brain begins to connect. We start to understand in a deeper, primal way, in the gut, rather than just the head. So read these phrases again, meditatively. Hold each one in your heart, and see what happens. When we do this, we don't make a response appear. We issue an invitation, and a response is handed up from below. Sometimes that response takes the form of heartache. This tender vulnerability, as I've said, is not something to avoid; we need to accept and surround it with kindness. It's the stirring of self-empathy and compassion within the heart, making us want to offer ourselves support.

We can employ the same reflections for others, including strangers. They are just like us. They don't want to suffer, and yet they do. They too are doing this difficult thing of being human (or being a chimpanzee, rat, or other lifeform). As we realize this, the same empathetic ache arises. And the compassionate part of us awakens and reveals itself, and we want to support them. Through repeatedly evoking compassion in this way, we create a channel through which it can emerge more easily in the future. As we exercise compassion, it increases in strength, and we feel it more readily. Through practice, it manifests with greater wisdom. But we're not creating anything from scratch. We're waking up to what had been there all along.

Exercise

When you notice that you're inhibiting a compassionate response, recognize that this is just another moment of suffering. Let it be an opportunity for self-compassion, so that you offer yourself support. You might say to yourself, "It's okay to be compassionate. It's okay to help." And just see what happens.

GUIDED MEDITATION: Compassion for a stranger

14

Compassion out and about

We can cultivate compassion while driving, walking, shopping, standing in line, and so on. The main difficulty with this is often remembering, so I suggest that you try keeping the words "suffering beings" in mind as you go about your activities. Not all beings are suffering all the time, but all feeling beings suffer. Anyone may be secretly suffering in the moment you encounter them. It's therefore wise to go through life treating others as if their hearts are tender and vulnerable. Repeating "suffering beings" helps us remember this.

Having reminded yourself that others are prone to suffering, you can bring into daily life whatever compassion phrases resonate with you. You can say things like:

- May you be well.
- May you be free from suffering.
- May your pain and sorrow be eased.
- May you be at peace.
- May you be protected from harm.
- May you be safe.
- May you be kind and compassionate to yourself and others.

Be aware that there are many more feeling, suffering beings around you than you can see. There are people and animals inside houses. There are wild creatures who live in the earth or who hide from you. So even if you aren't directly aware of other living things, you can keep repeating these phrases.

Notice your biases: it might be easier to have compassion for those who look sad and downtrodden, and harder to have compassion for those who look angry or behave in ways you find annoying. Even those who look happy need compassion: often people experience profound depression or anxiety while on the surface they look cheerful. You can never know.

Remember that compassion is not something that needs to be earned. Pain requires and deserves a compassionate response, no matter who it manifests in. And it manifests in everyone.

Exercise

Try setting reminders to take brief compassion breaks. Perhaps your phone or watch can remind you to pause every hour to connect compassionately first to yourself and then to others. Brief breaks taken repeatedly can nudge the mind into a more ongoing state of compassion.

15

Compassion and emulation

In some versions of lovingkindness meditation we start by calling to mind someone who has been kind to us – a benefactor. This reminds us what kindness is like. We remember what it's like to be looked at with kind eyes, to hear kind words spoken in a kind tone of voice, to see kind body language, and to be on the receiving end of kind actions. This makes the qualities of kindness more real for us, so that we can become kinder ourselves.

Sometimes we just don't know how to act compassionately, and so we're in need of examples. Like many Scots growing up in the 1960s, I didn't witness many examples of kindness and compassion around me. Instead I saw a lot of criticism and harshness, and suffering was often dismissed as unimportant. Often it was even ridiculed as a sign of weakness. These patterns were impressed deep into the substrate of my developing brain, just as they'd been impressed into my parents' brains, and into the brains of their parents. I'm not blaming anyone. The emotional culture of 1960s Scotland was formed by grueling work in fields and factories, through going to war and losing those who had gone to war, and through enduring the grinding poverty of the Depression. Toughness and unsentimentality were what people needed to survive. We're all working with what we've inherited, with whatever tools, if any, we've been handed down.

I'm faced with the task of unlearning habits of harshness. Those who have had the blessing of a genuinely empathetic and compassionate upbringing have vastly different patterns imprinted in their neural pathways. They know what compassion looks like, sounds like, and feels like. They know how to behave when faced with someone's suffering. The rest of us have to seek out and dwell upon instances of these things. It's a precious and heart-expanding privilege to witness compassion.

This brings to mind the importance of spiritual community and friendship. Spiritual development – transcending the limitations of our conditioning – is a team sport. We're never going to figure out compassion all by ourselves. Much of our learning is likely to come from observation. Our learning might come from a book, course, or video, or perhaps from seeing examples of compassion in action. When we've witnessed instances of forgiveness, understanding, and patience, we can call those memories to mind, imprinting compassion on our neural pathways, and retraining our brains.

Compassion spreads slowly, virally, from mind to mind: from parent to child, child to parent, teacher to student, or friend to friend. This is why the world has been becoming a better place overall over the last few millennia.[48] Compassion has been "infecting" our minds in a beneficial way. And we too can provide examples of compassion that influence others, and make them realize, *Wow! It's possible for someone to behave like that? Maybe I can do that too!*

Exercise

Spend some time remembering compassionate actions that you've witnessed. Let the details – facial expression, tone of voice, the actual words spoken – register. You might want to do this repeatedly, so that you imprint on your mind what compassion in action is like.

16

The benefits of compassion

As a proud science geek, I thought I'd pause and look at some of the things that science says about compassion – and especially about its benefits.

1. We're compassionate from the start

Researchers at the Max Planck Institute for Evolutionary Anthropology observed how eighteen-month-olds reacted to seeing an adult having trouble picking up an object they'd dropped. In response to seeing the adult's predicament, the children's pupil size increased, which is a sign of concern. Their distress decreased if they were allowed to help – and ten out of twelve children did so – or if another adult stepped in. Not being able to help increased their distress.[49] Even toddlers demonstrate compassion.

2. Selfishness is calculated

Researchers found that the less time people had to think about the decision to give, the more generous they were. These studies suggest that people have an initial impulse to behave cooperatively, and that selfishness is a more deliberate, secondary, and socially learned phenomenon.[50]

3. Compassion makes us cool

Psychologist Kristin Layous of the University of California, Riverside, asked nine- to eleven-year-olds either to perform three acts of kindness – like sharing their lunch or giving their mom a hug when she felt stressed – or to keep track of three enjoyable places they visited each week. Both groups of students improved in well-being, but the students who performed kind acts also became significantly more popular than the others. As the authors noted, "Increasing peer acceptance [...] is related to a variety of important academic and social outcomes, including reduced likelihood of being bullied."[51]

4. Compassion keeps us healthy

Compassion meditation helps protect our health. A study at Emory University School of Medicine found that those who did most compassion meditation showed the least distress when subjected to stress tests, and had a reduced level of Interleukin-6, which is a chemical linked to stress, heart disease, arthritis, osteoporosis, type-2 diabetes, and certain cancers.[52] A study at the University of North Carolina, Chapel Hill, found that compassion meditation increased a measure called vagal tone, which is the degree of healthy activity in the vagus nerve. If your vagal tone is greater, you're less at risk of heart disease.[53]

5. Compassion makes us happy

Elizabeth Dunn of the University of British Columbia gave money to participants, and asked half to spend the money on themselves, and the other half to spend the money on others. Those who treated others felt significantly happier than those who treated themselves.[54] This is true for children as well. Another study found that toddlers showed greater happiness when giving treats to their friends than when they received treats themselves. The more they gave, the happier they became.[55]

Entire political ideologies and economic models are founded on the assumption that we're motivated primarily or entirely by self-interest. And yet compassion is clearly an inherent part of our nature, and exercising it enhances our health and enriches our emotional well-being.

Exercise

Pay attention to any benefits you experience from thoughts, words, or acts of compassion. And perhaps try bearing in mind the Buddha's saying, "Looking after others, you look after yourself."[56]

17

Compassion without status

Because of our evolutionary history as social animals, we tend to see many human relationships in terms of status, with one person being superior to the other. We might assume that the person who offers compassion is in some way superior to the person they have compassion for. We need to unlearn this habit of assigning status. Buddhism calls a concern with status "conceit," or *mana*. We usually think that conceit is about feeling superior, but from a Buddhist point of view it concerns thinking of oneself as higher, lower, or even being equal to others.

The Buddha said of those who are awakened:

Not as higher, lower, nor equal
do they refer to themselves.[57]

The awakened don't think in terms of status at all. They just do what needs to be done, with no thought about hierarchies and where they stand in them. They have opted out of the hierarchy game. They simply let their compassion respond spontaneously to suffering, with no thought of their or the other person's status. This is why the Buddha, without hesitation, tenderly cleaned up a sick monk who was covered in diarrhea. He didn't think it was beneath him. Neither did he think that he was gaining status by doing something good. He simply saw suffering, and his compassion arose to meet it.

This is the ideal, at least. To completely opt out of the status game is something only the very spiritually advanced can do completely, but we can start moving toward this status-free way of being right now.

We begin to abandon status when we embrace the realization that we're all in it together. We might find ourselves suffering or supporting at any time, and to believe we're either superior or inferior to others is uncompassionate. If you feel that you're looking down on people when you're cultivating compassion for them, remember that you too suffer. It's just not your turn yet. Or, more likely, you simply don't understand that you're suffering in that very moment, and your assumed superiority is an attempt to deal with your suffering.

If you feel hesitant to reveal that you're struggling, remember that it's a sign of strength to ask for help. It's something everyone must do at one time or another. Someone who offers support may *seem* like they have it all figured out, but they have their struggles too. You can even consider that you're compassionately giving them an opportunity to exercise compassion. Every act of compassion is a collaboration, involving mutual giving.

Exercise

Reflect on status, and what it would be like to not care about it. Perhaps that sometimes already happens, when you're in the flow of communication. How does it change things?

18

Cruelty, the far enemy of compassion

Compassion is caring about others and wanting to relieve their suffering. The opposite of this – the "far enemy" – is cruelty, which is not caring about others and wanting to inflict suffering. We might not want to think we're ever cruel, but we all sometimes want to hurt others. And we can all be indifferent to suffering, which is another kind of cruelty.

Some cruelty stems from our belief that punishment – the infliction of suffering in order to modify behavior – is necessary to get people to change. The most effective animal trainers, however, show us that punishment is counterproductive to getting the behavior you desire. They find that nurturing the behaviors they want is more effective.[58] The same is true for everyday human-to-human interactions, where a reward can be a simple "Good job!" or "Thank you, I appreciate what you just did." Yet all too often we cling to a punishment mindset.

We need instead to embrace a culture of nurturance. Here are some suggestions for doing that:

- Listen to your thoughts and words, and see how often you blame others for things that have gone wrong. See if you can address mistakes without blame.

The Heart's Awakening

- Listen to the jokes and put-downs you make, and any teasing you do at others' expense. Consider building people up instead.
- Notice the desire to rain on someone's parade when they're excited about something. Celebrate with them instead.
- Notice when you feel judgmental when someone's suffering, and instead accept that we all suffer.
- Observe any tendency to ignore those who are close to you when they're asking for your attention. Take a breath, and value these opportunities to be with them.

The fourth stage of compassion meditation is another opportunity to unlearn the punishment mindset, as we call to mind someone we have conflict with, and might in moments of unmindfulness want to see suffer. Instead, we recognize them as a suffering being, like any other. We see not a person we dislike, but the suffering within them. And we allow our compassion to connect with that suffering, offering its bearer our support.

We need to train ourselves, over and over again, to move from cruelty to nurturance. An important part of this training is to catch ourselves being harsh toward others, apologize, and then try again with more kindness. Don't punish yourself for these mistakes. We all slip up. Instead, practice nurturance and self-kindness by forgiving and reassuring yourself. Recognize that your cruelty comes from an inability to deal with your own suffering, and offer yourself compassion.

Cruelty, the far enemy of compassion

How might our behaviors change if we regarded others' hearts as being like injured places that needed to be treated with great tenderness? Because that is what they are. Let your eyes be soft and kind as you go through life. Keep lovingkindness or compassion phrases ("May you be well; may you be free from suffering") running through your mind. Keep reminding yourself that we're all feeling beings, struggling beings.

Keep bringing your awareness to your own heart, too. Make sure that you're not unkind to yourself as you become more aware of the small cruelties embedded in the way you behave, speak, and think. Be compassionate to yourself, for the most common target of our cruelty is usually ourselves, and when we're unkind to ourselves we're inevitably cruel to others too.

Exercise

Reflect on what nurturance culture would look like in your life. Visualize nurturing, affirming speech and actions. Try them on for size. Discover how they work out in real life. Fine-tune them. Notice others being affirming and nurturing, and learn from them.

GUIDED MEDITATION: Compassion for a person we struggle with

19

Forgiveness and compassion

We do not, as many believe, store emotions in the subconscious, from where they venture forth from time to time. This idea reflects a view of emotion that we now know to be incorrect. What really happens is that, every time you call a painful memory to mind, the feeling of hurt is new.[59] Every time your hurt gives rise to anger, the emotion is a new one.

Being cruel to others out of resentment is a habit we share with other species. Crows, for instance, harbor grudges toward researchers who have previously caged and banded them. They can hold on to these grievances for years, showing their anger with scolding calls, wing-flicking, and physical attacks. Resentment is part of our own genetic inheritance, too. We don't choose to have resentment as part of our emotional makeup, and we suffer needlessly if we blame ourselves for being prone to it.

Resentment says, "This person hurt you, betrayed you, failed to protect you! Stay angry! Punish them! Never forget the wrong they did you!" We think that this protects us. But ill will hurts us, sometimes more than the other person did. Often, the person we resent doesn't even know about our hateful thoughts, and we are the only one who gets hurt. There's a saying in Alcoholics Anonymous that resentment is like swallowing rat poison and waiting for the rat to die. Similarly, the Buddhist tradition says that resentment is like

Forgiveness and compassion

throwing feces at someone; you *might* make them smell, but the only person guaranteed to stink is yourself. Bearing these similes in mind reminds us of the suffering that resentment causes, so we can recognize and let go of it.

Forgiveness is the opposite of resentment. It is a willingness to let go of ill will. Forgiveness offers protection from resentment's painful consequences and allows us to be at peace. Forgiving someone doesn't mean that you begin to trust them naively; they must earn our trust. If someone can't be trusted, simply remember that fact and keep your guard up. You can do that without hatred or resentment, and out of compassionate self-care instead. We don't need ill will to stay safe; we just need to remember. We can maintain safer boundaries through caring compassionately for our own well-being than we can from hating another person. A boundary based on hatred is one with spikes on the inside.

Resentments are often directed against those who have no desire to do us wrong. All that's going on is that they are, like everyone, imperfect human beings. They may even be people we love and who love us. But we're unable to accept their imperfect natures, and so we keep making ourselves angry about things they've done or neglected to do. The self-compassion practices I've outlined are ideal for helping us let go of resentment. When you find resentment arising, realize you're in pain, drop the story, drop your attention down into the body to notice your painful feelings, and offer them support. And then, with your empathy and compassion aroused, remind yourself that we're all flawed beings, struggling as we do this difficult thing of being human. Resentments keep arising because we don't know how to accept our own pain, while self-compassion brings acceptance, healing, and freedom from pain.

Exercise

Keep watching your mind and notice resentful thoughts. When you identify them, try applying the self-compassion steps I've laid out above.

20

Compassion versus utility

We can see with the eyes of compassion or with the eyes of utility. When we see with the eyes of utility, we gauge beings by their usefulness to us. When the checkout clerk works efficiently, we remain neutral, perhaps even friendly, but, if they have trouble finding the price for an item or need to ask for help, we can quickly become irritable. This person has become an enemy: an obstacle to the smooth functioning of our lives. They are now a target for our ill will. When the child is slow at getting ready for bed, sidetracked by seemingly endless distractions, we yell, because the child being awake is an impediment to our alone time. The lamb in the field is cute, but we like the taste of meat. The lamb is of more utility to us dead than it is alive.

With the eyes of compassion, we see that others' happiness and suffering are as real to them as our own are to us. We see that others desire happiness, but don't find it as often as they would like. We see that others want to be free from suffering, and yet keep suffering. We feel for the checkout clerk because we know they are stressed and frustrated, and not able to show it. And, for all we know, maybe they're just learning the job, they're undertrained, the systems have been changed, they're having to deal with someone else's errors, they've been working long hours, or they have personal problems that are making it hard to stay

The Heart's Awakening

focused. We don't know that any of these things is the case, but we are open to the possibilities.

When the child is distracted at bedtime, we recall that self-control is one of the first cognitive abilities to go when we're tired. So the child is literally unable at that point to control themselves. We see that getting angry will make things worse, and doesn't model self-control, which is what we want them to learn. We see that we need to take a breath, soothe ourselves, and offer kind, calming, but firm directions. And the lambs? I'd rather have tempeh or tofu. After many decades of enjoying a vegetarian diet, I can no longer think of farm animals as food, any more than I can think of pets or people as food. Seeing the world through the eyes of utility pits us against others, which is always painful, while seeing through the eyes of compassion, we see we're all in it together.

We often see ourselves with the eyes of utility. We might make a minor error, and give ourselves a hard time for not being perfect. We keep working until we're exhausted, seeing ourselves as "doing beings" rather than feeling beings. We blame the body for aging, as if that were a personality defect rather than a natural process. Seeing ourselves compassionately, we might smile at our errors, realizing that this is something we're all prone to. We notice we're getting tired and take a break, realizing that all organisms need rest. We notice the grief that accompanies aging, and support ourselves until it passes.

We can't switch from one way of seeing to another all at once. We bounce from one perspective to another, perhaps many times a day. Perhaps we'll only see through compassion's eyes for a short while, before we start to see the world in utilitarian terms once again. But it's a training. It's a practice. We get better at it. Just keep coming gently back to the thoughts: *this person suffers just as I suffer. This person, just like me, doesn't want to suffer.* As we keep gently reminding ourselves to see with the eyes of compassion, it more and more becomes part of who we are.

Exercise

Practice kind eyes as you go through life, also bearing in mind the phrase, "Feeling beings; suffering beings." The combination of these two things helps us to look with the eyes of compassion.

21

Compassionate news consumption

Since I'm teaching about compassion, you might assume I must follow the news closely to see what's happening in the world. In fact, I don't. The Swiss author Rolf Dobelli wrote the following:

> *News is toxic to your body. It constantly triggers the limbic system. Panicky stories spur the release of cascades of glucocorticoid (cortisol). This deregulates your immune system and inhibits the release of growth hormones. In other words, your body finds itself in a state of chronic stress. High glucocorticoid levels cause impaired digestion, lack of growth (cell, hair, bone), nervousness and susceptibility to infections. The other potential side-effects include fear, aggression, tunnel-vision and desensitization.*[60]

As it happens, I first read these words on the day of the Boston Marathon bombing, not far from where I live. At that time I didn't have a TV and saw none of the footage. But, as I went around my town that day, I could recognize those who had. As I wrote at the time, "They looked collapsed, shrunken, defeated. They looked haunted." One of my neighbors and I discussed how in the past we'd have learned about such disasters by word of mouth or through newspapers, perhaps days later, with no images at all. With the Boston bombing, television viewers saw explosions, blood, and wreckage – often repeatedly, because that's the only way news channels can provide twenty-four hours of content.

We didn't evolve to repeatedly witness violent events unfolding before us. Our minds don't respond well to being on the front line of disasters, day after day. Studies show that watching disasters on television is correlated with later depression, PTSD (post-traumatic stress disorder), and drug and alcohol use. I find it's enough to know that a tragedy has occurred. I don't need to see the blood.

I used to think that following the news would give me a sense of security. What if something awful happened and I didn't know about it? Then I'd come home from a vacation abroad, having been completely unplugged (this was pre-smartphone), and realize I hadn't missed anything. Newscasters recount the day's events with great urgency even if little has happened, and when major events do take place there is rarely anything I can do about it. We can't help others by watching the news. Usually we just get angry and sad, or numb and helpless.

Even if you quit the news entirely, which I've done for periods of time, you still know what's happening, because people talk about it, and you see news headlines in various places. If there's a humanitarian crisis you'll still know, and you'll still be able to respond. But usually you don't need to know the details. And how much do you retain, anyway? I'm guessing that you remember no more than someone who heard the news from another person. You don't miss out on anything but the stress.

The Heart's Awakening

I have a television now, but I still don't watch the news. It's too emotive a medium, so I stick to reading it. This allows me to pick and choose what and how much to read. Glancing at the headlines and reading a paragraph or two may tell me all I need to know. Sometimes, though, I'll read an article in its entirety, especially when it's educational. I used to listen to the news on my car radio. Then one day, as I was strapping my children into their car seats, a story came up about someone being stoned to death in Saudi Arabia. I decided toddlers didn't need to hear about that. I turned the radio off and never got into the habit of listening to it again.

Being mindful of what news we expose ourselves to can be a way of taking care of ourselves. It helps prevent us from being constantly outraged or exhausted, and from feeling helpless. It leaves our minds clearer so that we can thoughtfully reflect on what we can do to be of help to the world.

Exercise

As an experiment, try going a few days without consuming any news. Instead, spend your time on enriching activities, like reading books, having conversations, or meditating. Note any changes in the quality of your life.

22
Apology and compassion

Sean Thomas Dougherty wrote a poem called "Why bother?" that, in its entirety, says:

> *Because right now, there is someone*
> *out there with*
> *a wound   in the exact shape*
> *   of your words.*[61]

I'm good at apologizing. This is not exactly a boast; I've gotten good at apologizing because I've had plenty of opportunity to practice it. Although I try to be kind, when I'm under stress I can get irritable. Sometimes I get overly focused on myself and what I'm doing, and I forget to be empathetic to others.

When we act unskillfully, which is inevitable, it's important that we re-establish that this is not who we want to be. Apology does this by reorienting our being toward what is best within us. Refusing to apologize – for example when we try to justify our actions, rationalize, weasel our way out of admitting fault, or blame the other person – strengthens the unskillful within us. It ends up perpetuating our own and others' suffering. Apology reaffirms our commitment to living skillfully, and is itself an embodiment of honesty and empathy. Mainly, though, we apologize to help others. When we've hurt someone, a sincere apology can help them to feel better. It helps them to let go of their hurt. It reminds them that they matter. Often as part of an apology I'll say to the other person, "You don't deserve to be treated like that."

When you find yourself reluctant to apologize, remember that the other person is suffering and let that motivate you. Recognize as well that, in your stuck state, you're also suffering. It's best for everyone if you do it as soon as you can. Some find it hard to apologize because they assume that, if they apologize, they're putting themselves in an inferior position. I'll never forget a friend telling me that her husband can never bring himself to apologize to their children after yelling at them. His pride gets in the way. Instead, he'd be extra nice and take them out for treats. This isn't good for anyone involved. It doesn't engender trust, and the thing that needs to be heard – "You matter, and I'm sorry I hurt you" – goes unspoken. For a spiritual practitioner, apology should have nothing whatsoever to do with status. It's simply about being honest with yourself and others. You're realigning yourself with what's skillful, and helping others to move on from their hurt.

We might fear that the other person is going to use our apology as an excuse to air resentments. And this might happen, especially if we aren't in the habit of apologizing and they have a backlog of resentments. Given a rare opportunity to talk about unresolved hurt, they may sometimes distort the record and accuse us of things we didn't do. It's best if we just listen, compassionately, without trying to defend ourselves. Breathe. What they're saying may not be true, but their underlying hurt is real. A time when someone is hurt and angry is not a time to try to correct them. Let them vent.

Apology and compassion

Acknowledge their hurt. Let them know you want to do better in future. You can straighten out the facts later, if that even needs to be done. But also notice your own pain, and show it compassion. Support yourself with kind eyes, soothing internal speech and reassuring self-touch.

To be effective, an apology needs to be sincere. "I'm sorry you feel hurt" isn't an apology; you can't apologize for how someone else is feeling. "I'm sorry if you feel hurt" is even worse, because you're not even acknowledging how the other person feels. These are just apology-shaped sentences. "I'm sorry. I did something that hurt you. You don't deserve to be treated that way" is an apology.

It's not good if we keep offering the same apologies over and over but make little effort to change. For an apology to be sincere, it must be accompanied by a desire not to repeat the mistake we made. An apology is only one step in a larger journey toward living with more kindness and compassion. The larger part is working to bring about change in the way we act. We give our apologies value by living them.

It can be helpful if you share what the conditioned roots of your hurtful behavior are. For example, if I think I'm being ignored or unappreciated, I can feel hurt and irritable. It took me many years to realize that this was because of painful experiences in my early life. When I explain my conditioning as part of an apology, I remind us both that this isn't about me being bad – it's just me working with old and unhelpful "stuff." Apology can allow us to understand and love each other more deeply.

One last thing about apologizing: I think it's perfectly valid to apologize on behalf of others. I've heard people argue that apology can only be an expression of one's own personal regret. But, when someone has been hurt, they need a reminder that they matter. If I were to be rude to a restaurant worker, for example, it would be helpful if a friend who is with me were to apologize on my behalf. It soothes and reassures the person who is wounded, even if the friend is not the one who inflicted the wound. Similarly, if my ancestors dispossessed your ancestors and caused damage that persists even now, I think it's helpful for me to express my grief and regret for the actions of the people I'm descended from. In neither of these examples are we saying we are personally at fault because of others' actions; we're simply expressing our own pain, and letting those who have been hurt know that they matter, so that they may hopefully experience some healing. Perhaps I too can be healed by such apologies, since my knowledge of those harms creates a wound of grief within me.

Exercise

See if you can apologize quickly and straightforwardly. Notice any reservations or hesitance, and consider them as misguided attempts to protect yourself.

23

The mind imbued with compassion

The following description is found in dozens of places in the Buddhist scriptures:

> *An individual keeps pervading the first direction[62] – as well as the second direction, the third, and the fourth – with an awareness imbued with compassion. Thus they keep pervading above, below, and all around, everywhere and in every respect the all-encompassing cosmos with an awareness imbued with compassion: abundant, expansive, immeasurable, free from hostility, free from ill will.[63]*

Notice those words, "an awareness imbued with compassion." The final stage of compassion meditation involves permeating our awareness with empathy, so that any feeling, suffering being our attention touches is met with compassion.

Here is how this happens:

An expansive awareness

We let the eyes be soft. Our field of attention becomes open and expansive – like a lamp, radiating in all directions. It's as if the mind is filling the space around us. We let the eyes be kind, so that our field of awareness is filled with warmth, and so now the space around us, too, is filled with warmth. We remind ourselves, if necessary, that all beings suffer, although they don't want to, and that they need support. Our kind, open, expansive field of attention is now imbued with compassion, ready to encounter living beings.

Open to all beings

We're now aware, with kind, calm eyes, of the space in which we encounter living, feeling, suffering beings. So what do we perceive? We may hear beings moving around, driving vehicles, talking, or playing music. We might hear dogs barking or birds singing. We may just know that beings are there, even if we can't detect them. Our soft, calm, and kind field of attention meets them all with warmth and compassion. We know they suffer, and we wish them well. We can say, "May you be free from suffering. May you find peace. May you be compassionate to yourself and others."

Meeting beings in the mind

We don't encounter beings just in the world of the external senses. We also meet them in the space of the mind, in memory and imagination. We can call to mind those we remember or imagine who are sick, in pain, lonely, grieving, living through difficult times. But we can bear in mind that every being we encounter is a suffering being, and offer them support in the same way we ourselves would like to be supported. Meeting all beings with compassion, we wish: "May you be free from suffering. May you find peace. May you be compassionate to yourself and others."

You might remember or imagine beings in faraway places, to the north, south, east, and west, above you (birds, flying insects, people in planes), and below you (worms and other earth-dwelling creatures). Let this be an easy, gentle exploration, free from straining to achieve anything. Let your empathy effortlessly touch others, let compassion arise naturally. And so we have, in the Buddha's words, "an awareness imbued with compassion [...] abundant, expansive, immeasurable, free from hostility, free from ill will."

How far do you go?
The Buddha compared a meditator sending out compassion to a trumpeter heralding the four directions.[64] The sound of a trumpet travels far but not infinitely so. The important thing, I think, is just that your field of compassionate awareness be as expansive as you can allow it to be. It cannot touch the whole world, but it can touch your whole world. I recommend putting a gentle effort into reaching out with your mind, but not straining.

The expansive, open, non-self-focused awareness I've described is easily accessible. Just let the eyes be soft, imbue your awareness with empathy, and then every being you encounter will be met with compassion.

Exercise

In daily life, try pausing and letting the eyes be soft. Be aware of the space around you, and of the beings in that space. Bear in mind the thought, "May beings in every direction be free from suffering."

GUIDED MEDITATION: Karuna bhavana

24

Compassion for others as an antidote to our own suffering

One time a splinter flew off a falling rock and cut the Buddha's foot to the bone. In intense pain and confined to bed, he was unable to teach. A visitor arrived in the form of Mara, the Buddhist personification of doubt and spiritual defeat. Mara taunts the Buddha, saying that he's useless, lying there like someone "drunk on poetry." Mara's presence implies that the Buddha was not entirely immune to those inner voices that taunt us that we're not good enough. Those voices, however, are never able to fully take hold of his mind. He's always able to recognize them and send them packing, which is what happens here. The Buddha replies to Mara, "I lie down full of empathy for all living creatures," and the Evil One, defeated, vanishes.[65]

What is it about the Buddha's statement that makes it such a powerful defense against doubt? Falling into self-pity, we assume we've been singled out: "Why me?" We think we've been uniquely afflicted: "This is terrible! I can't bear it! It's so unfair!" And these thoughts, these second arrows, intensify our suffering. But when we consider others' sufferings – when we lie down full of empathy for all living creatures – we realize we're all in it together.

With empathy for all beings, we recognize that many other people are worse off than we are. You have a cold? Someone else has just been diagnosed with cancer. You have cancer? Someone else has just learned that their child has cancer. With empathy for all creatures, we put our own suffering in perspective and are less prone to overreact.

Recognizing the universality of suffering, and with empathy and compassion for others' pain, we let go of the story that we have been singled out, that our pain is unbearable, that our suffering is unfair. We no longer fire those second arrows, and our pain diminishes. The empathy and compassion we've developed for others helps us to support ourselves through our own difficulties.

Another way that the Buddha's statement reduces suffering is that it affirms that he is not useless. He reminds himself that he's still "on mission." Yes, he may temporarily be unable to teach, but he can still practice. He can still strengthen his empathy and compassion – qualities that will benefit others in the future. This is something we can bear in mind at times when we're ill, too. Even when we can't do much, we can make our lives useful.

Exercise

When you recognize that your own mind is causing you suffering, regard this as a trigger for recognizing Mara. Regard your thoughts, painful feelings, and reactive emotions as Mara. See if this helps you be more at peace.

25

The heart of tenderness

When the Buddha said he lay down with empathy for all beings, the word translated as "empathy" is *anukampa*, which literally means "resonating emotionally." Just as when a wineglass vibrates sympathetically when certain notes are played on a musical instrument, empathy is one person's heart resonating with another's. Anukampa is receptive; it's the feeling that stirs us to compassionate action, through karuna, which is active.

The Buddha told the first five followers he had guided to enlightenment to go forth out of anukampa for the world. He said that everything he taught, he taught out of anukampa. Many Buddhists have never heard the word "anukampa," and yet it was the entire basis of the Buddha's life and his mission to teach and help beings liberate themselves from suffering. Anukampa is a natural sense of solidarity with others, recognizing that we all suffer. In neuroscientific terms it results from "mirror neurons," which allow us to create internal models of the thoughts and feelings of others.

We feel empathy in the body, often around the heart. This seems to be to do with the vagus nerve, which runs into the body directly from the brain itself rather than through the spinal cord, carrying information to and from virtually every organ in the body. It's the vagus that creates or perceives feelings such as an open, tender heart, heartache, the warm

The heart of tenderness

glow of love and admiration, and so on. The more active our compassion, the more "tone" there is in the vagus.[66]

The Buddha made it clear that empathy is the basis of all ethical behavior:

> *"A person with evil wishes and dominated by evil wishes is displeasing and disagreeable to me. If I were to have evil wishes and be dominated by evil wishes, I would be displeasing to others." A practitioner who knows this should arouse their mind thus: "I shall not have evil wishes and be dominated by evil wishes."*[67]

Living ethically isn't about following rules or "being good." It's to do with maintaining a connection with our own hearts and feeling their resonance with others' hearts, so that we can treat them as feeling, suffering beings, rather than as things.

Exercise

Stay in touch with your tenderheartedness, and notice how the heart resonates with others' suffering. Observe how this feeling evokes the desire to be helpful.

26

The fall and rise of compassion

Compassion was of great importance in early Buddhism, but eventually the tradition became, with some exceptions, insular, scholastic, and dry. Later, a reform movement sprang up that re-emphasized compassion: the Great Vehicle, or Mahayana. Mahayana practitioners aimed to become bodhisattvas, meaning "those set upon enlightenment for the sake of all beings." In the eighth century, a Mahayana monk called Shantideva wrote a profound text called the *Guide to the Bodhisattva's Way of Life*. In a chapter on meditation, Shantideva outlined a practice of "exchanging self and other." He says:

> 90. [...] *earnestly meditate on the equality of oneself and others in this way: "All equally experience suffering and happiness, and I must protect them as I do myself."*[68]

He explores this theme in a series of verses, encouraging us to see seemingly separate human beings as if they were parts of one body.

> 91. *Just as the body, which has many parts owing to its division into arms and so forth, should be protected as a whole, so should this entire world, which is differentiated and yet has the nature of the same suffering and happiness.*

He points out that the way we cherish ourselves over others is something we learn, and that can be unlearned.

> *111. Due to habituation, there is a sense that "I" exists in the drops of blood and semen that belong to others, even though the being in question does not exist.*
>
> *112. Why do I not also consider another's body as myself in the same way, since the otherness of my own body is not difficult to determine?*

Shantideva means that, through reflection, we can recognize that everything constituting our own bodies has come from elsewhere, including from the semen and eggs ("drops of blood") of our parents, as well as the food we've ingested.[69] Since nothing in our bodies is truly ours, yet we care for them anyway, why should we not care for others, whose bodies are also not ours?

Shantideva says we should reflect both on the disadvantages of self-cherishing and on the advantages of caring about others.

Shantideva encourages us to imagine what it's like to *be* others – to have their unskillful thoughts and the suffering arising from them, as a practice of empathy. He suggests that we stop seeing things in terms of self and other. It doesn't matter in whose body or mind the suffering is found; our compassion can rise to meet it.

The Buddha articulated a similar perspective. Praising the way practitioners from another spiritual tradition practiced compassion, he said,

> *[T]hey don't think of themselves as an "ascetic" or "brahmin" [...] Nor do they think "I'm better" or "I'm equal" or "I'm worse." Rather, they simply practice out of kindness and sympathy for living creatures, having had insight into the truth of that.*[70]

The Buddha is saying that a truly compassionate person doesn't think of themselves as having any status at all, or any sense that they are "doing compassion." Compassion simply arises within them in response to suffering, wherever it might be found.

Shantideva's idea of exchanging self and other was developed into a meditation practice that the Tibetans call *tonglen* ("giving and taking"). In this practice, we take in an awareness of others' sufferings as we breathe in, and offer them compassion on the out-breath, exhaling relief and kindness upon them.[71]

Exercise

Reflect on the following verses from the *Guide to the Bodhisattva's Way of Life*, and let them be a guide as you go through life:

> *When happiness is equally dear to others and myself, then what is so special about me that I strive after happiness for myself alone? When fear and suffering are equally abhorrent to others and myself, then what is so special about me that I protect myself but not others?*[72]

27

Kindness, compassion, and communion

The Buddha said that an enlightened being doesn't see any separation into someone who does the experiencing and something that is experienced.

> *A Realized One sees what is to be seen, but does not conceive what is seen, does not conceive what is unseen, does not conceive what is to be seen, and does not conceive one who sees.*[73]

The word translated as "conceive" is *mannati*, which also means "imagine" or "posit" – that is, to imagine something as real that isn't real. The separation of self and other, the Buddha is saying, is something we misconstrue or imagine. Although this may sound mysterious, it's territory we've had a taste of anytime we've been in a state of "flow." In a flow state we're completely absorbed in some activity, with few if any of the self-referential thoughts that create a sense of separation between ourselves and what it is we're doing. For example, when we're with a friend and we're each completely paying attention to what the other is saying, resonating with each other, we're not obsessing about the distinction between "me" and "them." Your relationship isn't a competition. Instead, it's an easy flow in which you're both participating, each of you with a diminished sense of self.

To say that you and your friend are two separate entities – at any time, not just when you're in a flow state together – is to imagine or posit (*mannati*) something that's not the case. Your beings overlap. You're entangled with one another. Thoughts that arise in one mind end up in the other. Your emotions vibrate together. Yet to say that the two of you are "one" is also to imagine or posit something that's not the case. There's a separateness-yet-entanglement that defies description. When we experience this, perhaps the word "communion" comes closest.[74]

All things are entangled, neither two nor one. When we empathize and have compassion for one another, we recognize our interconnectedness. When you know me to be, like you, doing this difficult thing of being human, your empathy is the felt sense of our entanglement. At other times, we're busy imagining separate selves and others. We're busy "selfing" – caught up in states like anxiety, anger, and craving, where we obsess about ourselves in opposition to something or someone else. Selfing removes the possibility of communion.

Very practically, selfing can take the form of keeping score about whose turn it is to speak. Keeping score may be based on the conceit of equality. Anxious to demonstrate that we're just as important as the other person, we anxiously wait for them to finish so that we can have our turn. While they're speaking, we mentally rehearse what we're going to say, only half paying attention to them. When we insist on equality in this way, communion cannot emerge.

Kindness, compassion, and communion

Keeping score may sometimes be based on the conceits of superiority and inferiority; what you have to say is *surely* more important than anything they have to say. When someone shares their suffering, you compete by sharing something even more impressive. Competing prevents empathy and compassion from arising, making communion impossible. Superiority and inferiority also come in when we want to "fix" the person who is suffering. We can see ourselves as the superior dispenser of wisdom. Usually this alienates the other person. They do not feel understood. They crave connection but are offered correction.

Compassion dissolves the reactive emotions that drive selfing. With compassion, we become less self-obsessed. We no longer keep score. We don't compete. Rather than correct, we connect. We recognize that everyone is at the center of their own world. We still experience our own thoughts, feelings, and urges in a way that others never can, but we see that others' thoughts, feelings, and urges are just as real to them as ours are to us. We're not any more or less special than others. The world becomes a massively multicentric field of overlapping beings, often selfing, reacting, and competing, but in precious moments resonating, loving, and in communion with one another.

Although the Buddha's words above might seem abstruse, all he's saying is: *just be present with others. Notice your selfing and let go of it. There's just suffering, and compassion that responds to that suffering. Just let that happen, and when the communion of compassion happens, be present with that, too.*

Exercise

Notice when you yearn for your "turn" to come up in a conversation. Recognize this as the manifestation of conceit. See if you can let go of those preprepared thoughts and simply stay with what another person is saying. If this is at all painful, offer yourself some support as you continue listening.

Part III
JOYFUL APPRECIATION

The essentials of mudita

Mudita (Pali and Sanskrit) is the desire, based on empathy, that beings, ourselves included, experience long-term happiness and well-being as a result of their skillful actions. It recognizes and celebrates the good in the world, and encourages its growth and development. When we see good qualities in others that are more developed than our own, we desire to emulate them.

Other translations
Sympathetic joy, empathetic joy, gladness, appreciative joy, joy, rejoicing.

The stages of the meditation
We cultivate appreciation for:
- Ourselves.
- A person who experiences peace and joy as a result of their skillful actions.
- A relative stranger.
- A person we have difficulty with.
- All beings.

Suggested phrases
- May you appreciate goodness wherever you find it.
- May your good qualities continue and increase.
- May your skillful qualities bring joy to yourself and others.

One crucial thing to know
Mudita is not simply "being happy because others are happy." It involves recognizing the skillful wherever we find it, and encouraging its growth and development.

1

Cultivating joyful appreciation

Mudita is usually translated as "sympathetic or empathetic joy," and described as "feeling happy because others are happy." I profoundly disagree with this interpretation. *The Path of Freedom* describes how we cultivate mudita:

> *When we see or hear that some person's qualities are esteemed by others, and that they are at peace and are joyful, we think: "Wonderful! Wonderful! May they continue joyful for a long time!"*[75]

Our records of the Buddha's teachings don't define mudita, and the text above is the earliest I know of that gives us an indication of what mudita is and how it's to be cultivated. There are several things that are significant here.

1. Mudita begins with recognizing what's skillful. We're asked to recollect someone whose skillful qualities are developed to the point where others esteem them.
2. Mudita involves recognizing conditionality. We know that happiness and peace arise in dependence upon skillful qualities.
3. Mudita is about appreciation. We recognize skillful qualities and the peace and joy they bring as being good things.

Cultivating joyful appreciation

4. Mudita is a loving quality. The reason we support, rejoice in, and encourage someone's skillfulness is because we want them to have long-term happiness and well-being.
5. Mudita creates joy. In appreciating and admiring another person's skillfulness, we become uplifted.

This all goes far beyond "being happy because someone is happy." And that's good, because a lot of the happiness we see around us arises from unskillful actions, and we shouldn't be glad, for example, that someone is happy because they've just defrauded an old lady of her life savings. Just as we can define compassion as kindness meeting suffering, we can define mudita as kindness meeting the good. This meeting is a joyful experience, or at least can arouse joy. Because mudita is a state of appreciation that is joyful, I call it "joyful appreciation."[76]

With mudita defined in this way, we can see that the first three brahma viharas form a progression.

With kindness, we want what is best for others' long-term happiness and well-being. We want them to be happy. We think, speak, and act kindly, so that they feel supported and valued, and are put at ease.

With compassion, we want beings to be happy but are aware that they are suffering. To help them be happy we want to remove their suffering, or at least support them while their suffering persists.

With mudita, we want beings to be happy, but we see that happiness is based on skillful qualities and actions. And so we see, rejoice in, and encourage skillfulness, so that beings can attain happiness.

Joyful appreciation is something we can and should cultivate in daily life as well as in meditation. We can recognize skillful words and actions that we encounter, and we can also be generally appreciative – recognizing and being glad for anything whatsoever that brings benefits to ourselves or others.

We begin mudita meditation by cultivating appreciation of our own skillful qualities, or at least establish kindness toward ourselves. Although this stage is not found in the earliest description of the practice, it's a healthy place to begin, given that we often lack appreciation of our own skillful qualities. Or perhaps we need to start one step before that, by recognizing how happiness arises. That is the topic of the next chapter.

Exercise

Today, carry around an attitude of appreciation as best you can. As you encounter others, or even just think of them, be aware that they contain the seeds of goodness. When good things happen to you, however minor they seem, dwell on them appreciatively.

2

Where does happiness come from?

Here's a test for you. Imagine you've taken a photography course, and you're asked to choose your two best photographs. You love them both, but you're told that you can only keep one. Which of the following options would make you happier?

a. You choose one photograph now, and you're stuck with the choice you make. The photograph you do not choose will be sent away, forever.
b. You choose one photograph now, but you can change your mind at any time. The photograph you didn't keep will be held for you, just in case.

Most of us would choose option B, because we think being able to change our minds would make us happier. What psychologist Dan Gilbert found in a study that employed this scenario was that those who were stuck with their original choice were happier than the others. The downside of having the option to change your mind is that you start doubting your decision.[77] The fact that most people guess wrongly which scenario would make them happiest illustrates that we're not very good at anticipating what will make us happy or unhappy. As Gilbert says, divorce lawyers and tattoo removal parlors always have plenty of work.

The Heart's Awakening

The Buddha used the Pali word *vipallasa* (Sanskrit *viparyasa*) to describe our difficulty in identifying the causes of happiness. In modern parlance a vipallasa is a cognitive distortion – specifically, the cognitive distortion of mistakenly believing sources of suffering to be sources of happiness.[78] This works in reverse, too: we often assume things that would make us happy would make us miserable. Most people think, for example, that quitting social media would make them unhappy, while studies show it does the opposite.[79]

So what does make us happy? Beauty? Money? Power? Buddhism points to the quality of the mind as the primary factor. To what extent is the mind caught up in selfishness, hostility, and confusion? These are qualities that create conflict and unhappiness. To what extent is the mind empathetic, kind, and endowed with self-understanding? These are qualities that bring peace and joy.

To live more happily, we abandon the unskillful mental habits that cause suffering. Much of what we do falls into this category – clinging to things we desire, resisting experiences we don't like, anger, hatred, complaining, worrying, and doubting ourselves and others. Even wanting to be happy can make us unhappy if it's imbued with clinging. These are things to let go of, as best we can, whenever we recognize them. But to be happy we must also cultivate the skillful mental habits and behaviors that create happiness. These include kindness, compassion, appreciation, generosity, patience, curiosity, having close relationships, having a spiritual orientation in life, and having the capacity to become absorbed in enjoyable activities. Eliminating unskillfulness and cultivating skillful qualities makes us happier, but it helps us bring happiness to others, too, because we clash with them less and are more caring and empathetic.

External events, like winning the lottery or losing our job, certainly influence our levels of happiness. But the quality of the mind that experiences these things determines the degree to which they make us happy or unhappy. If you're a miserable person and you become rich, you'll now be rich and miserable, rather than simply miserable. Most of our happiness results from the skillful attitudes that exist within us, and the actions that flow from them. If you want to be happier, become more skillful.

Exercise

Watch your words, actions, and especially your thoughts. Notice whether these things are contributing joy and ease, or unhappiness and conflict, both for yourself and for others.

3

On gratitude and appreciation

Appreciation and gratitude involve recognizing and being glad for those things that are good and beneficial. I can have gratitude for the sunlight on my face, or for recovering from a cold, or for having access to the internet. That's not mudita, which is more specifically recognizing and being glad for the existence of skillful qualities in ourselves and other beings. But becoming more appreciative and grateful in general will support mudita's arising. If we can't appreciate and be grateful for life's ordinary blessings, it's unlikely we'll appreciate other people's skillful qualities.

For many years, to help me become a more appreciative person, I've kept a daily gratitude list. Every day, first thing in the morning, I write down at least five things that I'm grateful for. This helps train my mind to notice what's going right in life, rather than what isn't. Doing this often brings me great joy, and, in case you'd like to take up this practice as well, here are some practical suggestions:

- I suggest writing a minimum of five things. If your list is shorter, make sure you're choosing things that aren't obvious or that you haven't thought of before.
- Do this every day. You'll soon find that you start noticing things you appreciate, because you know you'll be writing them down.

On gratitude and appreciation

- Look for small things – things that bring pleasure or gratitude you take for granted because they're so routine, such as a moment of quiet or the sound of birdsong. If you only record major things, you'll think you don't have much to be grateful for. But, when you celebrate the little things, your day is full of blessings.
- Challenge yourself. If it feels hard to come up with the last one or two things, that's good. It means you're noticing things that are less obvious.
- Hold the things you're grateful for in your heart so you can feel their goodness. That is, bear them in mind and watch your heart until you notice a shift in your experience. Your practice is more effective when it is heart-based.
- But remember that it's okay if you don't feel anything when you first begin. This happens. Keep holding beneficial things in your heart, and in time you'll start to feel gratitude.
- Be specific. It's too easy to say, "I'm grateful for my spouse." Dig deeper, and recall specific qualities or traits your spouse has, or things they've done, that are worthy of appreciation.
- If you feel stuck, think of what life would be without the things you take for granted – being sheltered from the elements, having electricity and flowing water, being able to listen to music, having food in the fridge, coffee.
- Think about how things were in the past. Not long ago, an eight-mile journey might take a day,

dentistry was done without anesthetic, and infant deaths were common. Remembering this, it becomes easier to appreciate what you have.

- If you're able to read other people's expressions of gratitude, give yourself time to empathize. Hold the things they describe in your heart, and see what happens.

When I get to the end of my list, I often find myself grateful just for breathing and for existing. Every moment becomes precious. My meditation students and I share our daily expressions of gratitude on my meditation community website, and we find ourselves grateful to witness each other's appreciation and gain insight into each other's lives, which builds friendship.[80] Mudita, like compassion, can be a form of communion.

Exercise

I suggest that every day from now on, for as long as you find it helpful, you write down five things you're grateful for. If you can, share your gratitude with others.

4

The challenge of appreciating ourselves

Many years ago, when I was a community education worker in Scotland, a colleague and I took a youth group on a weekend retreat to help them resolve their conflicts with each other. My colleague sprang an exercise on us. We had to share one thing about ourselves that we liked. He asked me to go first, and reader, I froze! It wasn't that I couldn't think of anything, but that, as soon as anything did come to mind, I just couldn't say it. It seemed too risky, as if I were inviting contradiction or ridicule – which wouldn't have happened in that context. I'd have no difficulty with that exercise now, but a lot of people would. It's easier for us to share our self-criticisms with others, because usually someone will take pity, and point out our good qualities. This is a cultural ritual: we prompt others to say appreciative things about us because we can't do it for ourselves.

The Path of Freedom says that mudita practice begins with calling to mind someone we admire, but normally we start with ourselves. This makes sense: if we happen to be feeling a bit down, then, rather than being inspired and uplifted by a skillful person's good qualities, we might obsess about our perceived relative lack of them, cultivating self-doubt or envy rather than admiration.

So, as you're sitting in meditation, having connected with yourself empathetically as a feeling being, remind yourself that happiness arises from skillful qualities, and accept that skillful qualities exist within you. And then begin to say:

- May you appreciate goodness wherever you find it.
- May your good qualities continue and increase.
- May your skillful qualities bring joy to yourself and others.

Just drop these words into the heart and let their effects ripple through your being. If you like, you can replace the words "good qualities" and "skillful qualities" in the second and third phrases with specific qualities you have. You might say, "May your *kindness* continue and increase. May your *patience* bring joy to yourself and others," and so on. This makes the practice more personal.

We all possess any skillful quality you care to name. No one is without at least a little wisdom, kindness, courage, patience, and so on. You can know this, and name various skillful qualities, encouraging them to grow. The practice becomes more real, though, if we recognize, name, and encourage the growth of specific skillful qualities we're aware of having. These qualities don't have to be well-developed. Even if they're there in embryonic form, you can recognize and value them.

It can be as challenging, though, for us to name our good qualities to ourselves as it is to name them to others. The *yes-but* voice speaks up. We think, "Well, I can be kind." And then we hear a voice saying, "Yes, *but* you can be unkind too." When this happens, remember that the presence of an unskillful quality doesn't negate the existence of a skillful quality. *Of course* you're sometimes unkind. That's true for absolutely everyone. If you didn't have unskillful qualities, you wouldn't need spiritual practice. So it's irrelevant that you're not always skillful; you can still celebrate your skillful qualities. Recognize the *yes-but* voice when it appears, smile at it, and choose to ignore it. It's well-meaning, because it wants to stop you becoming inflated, but it's misguided, because it stops you becoming more skillful and confident about your own goodness.

You can experiment and find what works best for you at a given time. The phrases that I use are constantly changing and evolving. There is no set of words that is clearly "the best." In whatever way that's effective for you, remember there is goodness within you, that it is the basis of your present and future peace and joy, and that the world needs you to encourage its development.

Exercise

Set aside time to reflect on your skillful qualities, even those that are not well-developed. Remember that the presence of unskillful qualities doesn't negate the presence of the skillful ones. If it helps, think of times people have rejoiced in you. If you have a spiritual context for doing so, share these things.

GUIDED MEDITATION: Self-appreciation

5

Ethics isn't about being good

When the Buddha was speaking to ordinary people about ethics, he'd often use the words *punna* and *papa*, which respectively mean "merit" (or "good") and "bad" (or "evil"). He also used these words in poetry. But when he was talking technically to serious Dharma practitioners, usually he used the terms "skillful" and "unskillful," which are *kusala* and *akusala* in Pali.

I used to find these words puzzling. For a long time, I assumed that they were some kind of non-judgmental Buddhist "code" for good and bad. But eventually I realized that they're to be taken literally. Having skill means you're able to achieve what you set out to do, especially when it's challenging. If a skilled carpenter aims to make a beautiful coffee table, that's what appears. They have the skill to accomplish what they set out to do. They have that skill because of their practice.

What's the "coffee table" we're trying to make in our lives? What's our overall aim in life? If you look closely at everything you do, you'll find that the aim is to find freedom from suffering. Every action has behind it the intention to bring about well-being. When we're selfish, it's because we assume that "looking after number one" will bring happiness. When we're hateful, it's because we want to drive away things and people we don't like, so we can be at peace. When we embrace deluded ideas, it's because we assume on some level

Ethics isn't about being good

that they will help us in some way. The thing is, none of these things *works*. We aim to be free from suffering but end up creating pain and distress. Lacking ethical skill is when we try to make a coffee table and end up with a crooked object that gives us splinters.

When we're kind, or generous, or compassionate, we find that those things do "work." They do free us from suffering. They do make us happier. They are skilled actions because they help us achieve the peace and joy we want in life. They're the ethical equivalent of the carpenter's elegant coffee table.

The Buddha advised us to give up greed, hatred, and delusion because they get in the way of our deepest yearnings to be free from suffering, not because they are bad. He said:

If this abandoning of what is unskillful were conducive to harm and pain, I would not say to you, "Abandon what is unskillful." But because this abandoning of what is unskillful is conducive to benefit and pleasure, I say to you, "Abandon what is unskillful."[81]

This is a truly radical statement. The Buddha's saying that, if greed, hatred, and delusion led to happiness, he wouldn't tell us to give them up. We abandon them not because they're morally bad, but because *they don't work*. They don't take us where we want to go. This is what the Buddha meant by skillful and unskillful. Skillfulness is what frees us and others from suffering.

It just so happens that what's generally considered "bad" is also unskillful, and what's usually considered "good" is skillful – that is, it leads to happiness. But this isn't always the case, so the Buddha's teaching on skillfulness offers us a powerful tool for examining the moral conventions of our time and place. The unwritten moral conventions around us might say things like, "It's okay to 'pile on' to someone on social media when they've done something bad. It helps improve society." An understanding of the Buddha's ethics of skillfulness might bring us to the opposite conclusion – that sanctioned cruelty is not good for us, for its victims, or for our society.

We train, but we'll never be perfect. Buddhist practice is what I call "the fine art of making mistakes." Our mistakes – those times we make ourselves or others suffer – are how we learn. Through trial and error, guided by intelligence and what we learn from those who are wiser than us, we practice and refine our spiritual skills. We develop the skill of liberating ourselves and others from suffering. Mudita is an important part of that. In cultivating mudita we open our minds to recognizing skillful thoughts, words, and actions. We open our hearts so that we can respond to skillfulness with appreciation and admiration. And, seeing that skillful qualities lead to freedom from suffering, we encourage their continuance and development. Mudita is the skillful action of recognizing, rejoicing in, and encouraging further skillfulness.

Exercise

If the concept of ethics as being about training in the qualities that lead to freedom is new to you, reflect on this to see how it agrees with and contradicts your existing understandings.

6

There's more right with you than wrong with you

Jon Kabat-Zinn said, "As long as you are breathing, there is more right with you than there is wrong, no matter how ill or how hopeless you may feel."[82] We might resist acknowledging Kabat-Zinn's message because we're so used to focusing on what's going wrong. We have what's called a "negativity bias." Someone says an unkind word, and we repeatedly obsess about it, making ourselves miserable. Yet someone says something complimentary, and we might not even want to hear it. Most of us don't vividly recall compliments months after they were delivered, the way we would with insults.

One way negativity bias shows up is in the way that we generally don't like our bodies. We think there's a lot wrong with them. Even people who are regarded as having "perfect" bodies manage to find fault with how they look. And sometimes our bodies have aches and pains, and get sick and don't function as well as we'd like, and so we blame them, as if they're letting us down. But think of it this way: your body is always there for you. It shows up for you every day. Even if it's in pain, it does its best to serve you and get you through life. What kind of friend does that for us? When your body has aches and pains, those are the sensations of healing. The inflammation that causes pain is part of the body's healing response. We should be grateful to those sensations of pain: "Thank you, body, for trying to heal yourself for me!"

How unfair we are when we are critical of this good friend who shows up each day, in sickness and in health, and who faithfully tries to repair the damage done to it by life. Let's not do that! Instead, let's thank the body. Take time out to do a body scan, moving your focus – soft eyes, kind eyes! – gently around the body. Thank each part in turn – and by that I mean clearly articulate the words "thank you" in your mind. Thank your toes, your feet, and so on, right up to the top of your head (which protects your precious brain), and out to your fingertips. Thank your skin for keeping your insides inside and the outside outside. Thank all your inner organs for what they do for you. Thank your senses; even if they don't work as well as they used to, they are doing their best to connect you with the world. Thank that precious brain, and the consciousness that it supports. Thank your ability to be self-aware. Thank everything.

Notice how saying "thank you" over and over awakens your appreciation and creates joy. Perhaps you'll also notice that your body likes being regarded with a warm inner gaze, and being thanked. It shows appreciation in turn by softening and releasing pleasurable sensations. Being grateful for what's going right with our bodies is itself a practice of self-care. It's good for us both physically and mentally. The Buddha said that a kind person should have thoughts like this: "May these beings [...] look after themselves joyfully."[83] The phrase "look after themselves joyfully" implies not just that we should take care of ourselves, but that we should appreciate the miraculousness of the precious being we're taking care of. This isn't selfish, because we recognize that others too are precious miracles.

Let's make a conscious effort to recognize how much is going right in our lives. Let's take care of ourselves with appreciation and joy.

Exercise

Try the gratitude body scan I suggested above. You can also take your awareness into the world and say "thank you" to all the supportive conditions you find there.

7

Innate purity versus original sin

A Freudian analyst with a stereotypical Viennese accent asks a criminal about his childhood:

"Were you unhappy as a child?"

"Not really. I had a perfectly normal childhood."

"I see. You wanted to kill your father and sleep with your mother!"[84]

Freud believed that only a veneer of decency prevents us from being monsters, and, as this idea has percolated into our culture, many of us have come to assume that we are inherently bad, with our good qualities being nothing more than a facade. As a result, we have difficulty trusting ourselves. This reinforces the religious view, dating back to the second century, of original sin, where we inherit Adam's sin from eating the fruit of the tree of knowledge. Incredibly, St. Augustine believed that even babies are sinful, and that unbaptized infants are tortured in hell for eternity.

Some forms of Buddhism teach instead that we are inherently pure, and that greed, hatred, and delusion are superficial contaminants. That may not be strictly what the Buddha taught, but this view of innate purity makes practical sense. Take a jar of water, mixed with mud, that has just been shaken vigorously. You see a murky swirling mixture. But leave the jar undisturbed: the water stills, the mud settles out, and finally you're left with clear water. The mud was never

Innate purity versus original sin

inherently part of the water. The inherent clarity of the water is revealed by stillness. Likewise, sit still in meditation, attending to the breathing, and your emotions quiet themselves. Thoughts arise less often, becoming somehow lighter, and passing through the mind without disturbing it. You become happier, kinder, calmer, and clearer. Just by sitting, these qualities reveal themselves.

The muddy water illustration is an imperfect metaphor. Practice is not just about letting the unskillful fall away. It is also about bhavana: cultivating and maintaining the skillful. Although skillful qualities are inherent in the mind, they need to be nurtured. That is what the brahma vihara practices involve.

We've seen that empathy, kindness, and compassion are qualities inherent in the human mind. We don't create them – we simply set up the conditions whereby they reveal themselves. And, once that happens, we exercise and strengthen them, helping them to flourish. This development becomes much easier if we learn to trust ourselves, and to believe we are fundamentally pure rather than filled with original sin.

We can recognize that our greed, hatred, and delusion are not "evil," but are simply clumsy and ineffective ways of finding happiness. Deeper than any of our habits, whether skillful or unskillful, is a desire for peace and happiness that motivates every action. This desire is perfectly wholesome; it's whether it expresses itself skillfully or unskillfully that is important. So beneath even our most unskillful actions is something good. Our task is to recognize which habits and actions help us achieve the peace and joy we seek, and which do not. And this is the job of mudita – recognizing and encouraging the skillful, both in ourselves and in others, so that beings can find the peace and joy they have been stumbling toward their whole lives.

Exercise

When you sit to meditate, adopt an attitude of trusting the mind. Regard it with gratitude and admiration. Just sit, and observe how clarity and kindness sometimes reveal their presence, and how sometimes they are hidden by the swirling mud of unskillful thoughts.

8

To believe in the heroic makes heroes

The second stage of the mudita bhavana practice involves cultivating admiration for a person who is esteemed for their good qualities and who experiences peace and joy as a result. In other words, we're admiring our heroes, and we do this so that we can emulate them. As the nineteenth-century British prime minister Benjamin Disraeli wrote, "To believe in the heroic makes heroes."[85]

Upatissa, the author of *The Path to Freedom*, implies that we might only know our hero from reputation. But it's good to ask, who do you know personally who has admirable qualities, and who is generally joyful and at peace? I am fortunate to know several people like this, some of whom I regard as friends. They are joyful, dignified, and at peace. They are ethical, kind, and careful in how they talk about others. I'll find myself complaining about a third party, and a skillful friend will say something that makes that person's actions understandable and forgivable. My ethical friends are almost always quick to laugh and don't take themselves too seriously.

There are others I know mainly by reputation. I think of people like the Dalai Lama, Nelson Mandela, Eleanor Roosevelt, Paul Robeson, and Maya Angelou. These people are giants in their own ways, embodying highly admirable qualities. The Dalai Lama is most obviously joyful, while the others seem to exhibit more of a sense of dignity and peace. I feel uplifted simply by calling them to mind. Moral psychologist Jonathan Haidt coined the term "elevation" to describe this feeling. He wrote:

> *Powerful moments of elevation sometimes seem to push a mental "reset button," wiping out feelings of cynicism and replacing them with feelings of hope, love, and optimism, and a sense of moral inspiration.*[86]

Dacher Keltner, a professor of psychology at the University of California, Berkeley, aptly describes the bodily sensation of elevation as "a feeling of spreading, liquid warmth in the chest and a lump in the throat."[87]

So, in the second stage of the practice, call to mind someone you admire. You might just sit with a mental image of them, and let their good qualities touch your heart. You might name their good qualities. Upatissa recommends saying: "*Sadhu! Sadhu!* May they continue joyful for a long time!" (*Sadhu* is a word meaning "wonderful!") Since he mentions both peace and joy as the outcomes of a skillful life, we could end up with a set of phrases along the lines of:

- May your good qualities continue and increase.
- May your joy continue and increase.
- May you enjoy peace for a long time.

I find it doesn't matter if my heroes are no longer among the living. Wishing these things for them is still meaningful.

To believe in the heroic makes heroes

Fortunately, the heroes we reflect on do not have to be perfect, since nobody is. I can know that Nelson Mandela had an affair and hurt his family, and still admire him for his dignity and capacity for forgiveness. I can know that Maya Angelou once worked as a pimp, and still have respect for the wise, thoughtful person she evolved into.[88] With mudita, we're not judging people as "good." We're simply focusing on their skillful qualities. The flaws and mistakes of my heroes help me to have *more* respect for them, not less. Their humanness, as shown by their weaknesses, makes them easier to relate to. They are flawed beings who developed remarkable qualities. I too am a flawed being, and I can take inspiration from their path.

Exercise

Who do you admire, and what qualities or actions of theirs inspire this admiration?

GUIDED MEDITATION: Admiration

9

The near enemy of joyful appreciation

Buddhaghosa describes the near enemy of mudita as rejoicing in "Happiness based on the home life." He clarifies this with a reference to a scripture that discusses how happiness can arise from worldly pleasures.[89] Buddhaghosa is saying that celebrating worldly gains and the pleasure that comes from them is not mudita. Interestingly, this is precisely how many people do teach mudita. One of my students reflected this when they wrote, "I always thought of mudita as rejoicing in another person's good fortune – things like buying a first house, having a baby, celebrating a special occasion."

Yes, celebrate your friends' good fortune! But, if we focus purely on the material events, such as the buying of the house or the arrival of the baby, we're missing celebrating the skillful qualities involved in those achievements. Buying a house may involve perseverance, optimism, thrift, and so on. Having a baby involves enduring physical discomfort, overcoming challenges in relationships, the practice of self-care, conquering fears, and preparing for unconditionally loving a new being.

If we fail to draw our friends' attention to their own skillful qualities, the friend may overlook them too. It's great to say, "Congratulations on your new house!" but it's far more powerful to point out to someone the good qualities we saw in them as they made that happen. They feel seen, come to

The near enemy of joyful appreciation

appreciate themselves more, and, having been reminded of their own skillful qualities, they may well be inspired to develop them further. Being joyfully appreciative of skillful qualities and actions is a powerful practice compared to celebrating material success.

Celebrating people's material successes is still healthy (assuming they were achieved ethically) and to be encouraged. The near enemy of mudita is not something that destroys it; it's just a shallower form of appreciation that can, if that's *all* we do, distract us from appreciating the skillful. Celebrating worldly achievements is a good thing – but it's even better to go further. Celebrate often and widely, but especially remember to look for people's good qualities, and to celebrate and encourage them, since that's what mudita is.

Exercise

In your practice of appreciation, try to make sure that at least some of what you celebrate acknowledges your own and others' skillful qualities, words, or actions.

10

Accepting compliments as a spiritual practice

Many of us are uncomfortable receiving compliments. We squirm and offer up self-deprecating rebuttals – it wasn't such a big deal, someone else could have done it better, and so on. It can even be traumatizing to be praised: one woman wrote in a discussion forum, "I won some academic awards a few years back and got lots of positive attention [...] and my response was to fall into a depression – some part of me couldn't accept that I deserved any of the congratulations or compliments." This is "imposter syndrome," where we believe we're unworthy of the position or respect we've earned, and where praise can trigger crippling waves of self-doubt.

In the Triratna Buddhist Community in which I practice, we often formally rejoice in others' skillful qualities. Often at the end of a retreat – usually in a small study group, where people have got to know each other well – everyone takes a turn being celebrated by everyone else. If one person paying you a compliment makes you squirm, how would you feel about a room full of people doing it? This practice of "rejoicing in merits" trains us to accept compliments graciously, and to let go of our resistance to praise. We learn to accept compliments and to be grateful to the person who gave them.

In case you feel uncomfortable accepting compliments, here are some lessons drawn from the Triratna community:

Accepting compliments as a spiritual practice

- Let yourself be still. Don't squirm or deflect. Don't discount the praise. Stay present. If you feel discomfort, just allow it to be there. Breathe.
- Look at and listen mindfully to the other person. When someone is doing you a favor, it's appropriate to give them your attention wholeheartedly.
- If you feel like smiling, smile. If you don't, don't. Sometimes accepting a compliment is a serious business.
- Accept blushes. Blushing is a physiological phenomenon that's outside your control. It's not a sign of weakness.
- Give thanks. Acknowledging the other person's observations with a simple "thank you" is the best repayment that you can offer. Giving a compliment back discounts the praise you've been given.
- Complimenting the compliment is fine. If you say something like "Thank you. That was a lovely thing to say," you're acknowledging the compliment giver's skillfulness.
- Don't take credit where credit's not due. It's dishonest to accept praise you haven't earned. If you genuinely played no role in what you're being praised for, you can still thank the person for their kind intentions, but tell them who actually deserves credit.
- Be open to learning something new about yourself. The appreciation you've been offered might clash with your self-view, but let it in.

Having our skillful actions being pointed out to us can help us overcome self-doubt. We can't nurture skillful qualities we don't know we have, so we need to have them pointed out to us. When someone points out skillful qualities that we didn't know we had, we are more likely to exercise that quality in the future. This can also bring up self-doubts, but when that happens we have an opportunity to question and overcome them.

Exercise

I encourage you to accept compliments graciously when they're offered.

11

"For my long-term well-being and happiness"

I've said that our most fundamental drive is to seek happiness, peace, or well-being. Sometimes, though, we might doubt whether that's truly our deepest motivation. There are times we court misery by wallowing in self-pity, delaying necessary tasks, making decisions we know will have unpleasant consequences, and hurting others in ways that are guaranteed to come back to bite us. This is where it's helpful to remember that our unskillful actions are simply misguided strategies for finding happiness. Shantideva talks about this in his *Guide to the Bodhisattva's Way of Life*, when he says,

> *Those desiring to escape from suffering hasten right toward suffering. With the very desire for happiness, out of delusion they destroy their own happiness as if it were an enemy.*[90]

Delusion is the problem. Our brains are incredible, but they've evolved to assume that if something is pleasant then we should embrace it, and if something's unpleasant we should avoid it. And that's often wrong. To be happy in the long term, we often must do things that are unpleasant right now. Think of exercising, apologizing when we've made a mistake, or restraining our anger. None of these things is pleasant, but they lead to our long-term happiness. And often, as we all know, the things that give us pleasure in the short term are not good for us in the long term.

An important part of spiritual practice is to retrain our brains to be motivated by something more than immediate pleasures and pains. We need to look at the lasting effects of the choices we make. The Buddha talked about this when he said we should bear in mind questions like: "What kind of action will lead to my lasting harm and suffering? Or what kind of action will lead to my lasting welfare and happiness?"[91]

Only by taking a long-term view can we overcome our ethical shortsightedness. As the Buddha said in the *Dhammapada*, "Even evil-doers experience good things as long as their bad acts haven't come to fruition. But when those bad acts come to fruition, then evil-doers experience bad things."[92] It takes time and intelligent effort to learn what brings happiness and well-being in the long term. We often have to make mistakes, experience the pain of them, and learn from them. This is the Dharma as the fine art of making mistakes.

The Buddha suggested a shortcut, though, which is that we can learn from "the wise" – those who have already been through the painful process of learning. We need to identify who the wise are, however. This requires assessing how reliable their advice is, and looking carefully at how ethical they are. We can also learn from the mistakes of the unwise; the *Dhammapada* verse above is from an entire chapter filled with such lessons.

On a moment-by-moment level we can look at our emotional states and gauge whether they support our long-term happiness and well-being. If I find myself about to act out of anger, I often think, "Uh oh! Been there, done that!" and

"For my long-term well-being and happiness"

look for a more skillful response. In the midst of our complex lives, we can't consult "the wise" at every turn, but we can look carefully at our past experience and see what has been unhelpful and what's promoted our well-being.

Exercise

Think of examples of insights you've learned from others, and things you've learned through trial and error.

12

Joyful appreciation and reverence

A few weeks after I started attending the Glasgow Buddhist Centre in my native Scotland, I was invited to attend a regulars' evening. This was very different from the secular introductory classes I'd been going to. Before the meditation there was bowing and chanting. After the main event, which was a talk, there was a collective *puja* or act of worship, in which we recited verses and chanted mantras. Some people offered sticks of lighted incense to the Buddha.

I found all this perplexing. I wondered if it was all necessary. Wasn't it enough just to meditate?

Eventually I came to understand that ritual is a spiritual practice like any other. Chanting is a mindfulness practice. When we chant, we can be aware of the body, its breathing, and the movements that take place in the mouth and throat as we create sounds. If we're chanting with others, then we can be mindful of them too, so that we harmonize and synchronize with each other. In chanting sacred verses, we can be mindful of the meaning of the words we're saying and be moved and inspired by them. Bowing has nothing to do with obedience to authority – it's a normal form of greeting in many parts of the world. Often Dharma practitioners in the West bow to each other, finding it a gracious way to show mutual respect. In fact, I bow to you right now, dear reader.

Joyful appreciation and reverence

Bowing to a buddha statue is similar. The statue reminds us of the Buddha as a historical teacher. If we were to meet him, we'd want to show him respect. Bowing to him wouldn't be demeaning; we would simply be acknowledging that the Buddha had insights and qualities that we appreciate and aspire to emulate. Bowing is an embodiment of mudita: it's rejoicing in the good qualities of others. It's an expression of receptivity toward and respect for them. It's a sign we'd like to develop those skills too. When we bow to a statue of the Buddha, we also salute our own potential as enlightened beings.

Many people say that the first time they bowed to a representation of the Buddha, they felt that a bubble of egotism "popped." They realized in that moment that their resistance to physical demonstrations of gratitude toward the Buddha had been a form of clinging to self, or conceit. Bowing to the Buddha, we release any idea of our own superiority, equality, or inferiority. Bowing is what is skillful in us recognizing what is skillful in him.

Even at the peak of human development, with no one to look up to, the Buddha saw respect and reverence as so intrinsic to a life of well-being that he thought, "Why don't I honor and respect and rely on the same Dhamma to which I was awakened?"[93] Having reverence opens a kind of spiritual portal, allowing movement in two directions. On the one hand, our respect flows toward whoever or whatever it is that we respect. On the other hand, we also become more receptive to the positive influence of whoever or whatever it is that we respect.

The Buddha talked about this two-way flow when he said, "Respect and humility, contentment and gratitude, and timely listening to the teaching: this is the highest blessing."[94] *Respect* is the way we relate to those who have benefited us. *Humility* is letting go of our egotistic ideas of equality. *Contentment* is the sense of relief we have when we do this. *Gratitude* is what we feel as we acknowledge how we benefit from the teachings. And, because of our openness to the skillful, we *listen* to the teachings wholeheartedly, letting them influence us.

Exercise

I suggest that you find some symbol of skillful qualities that you respect, and experiment with bowing to it. It doesn't have to be a human figure; it could be an object or image that represents some spiritual quality. See how this makes you feel.

13

Looking deeper for the good

I often find that other people notice skillful qualities that I miss. I've mentioned that, on Wildmind's community website, people express gratitude for what's going on in their lives. We comment on each other's posts, and I'm frequently surprised and delighted to see people rejoice in qualities or actions I hadn't fully registered. I'm grateful I'm able to learn from others who are better at observing these things than I am. I notice, though, that I become more receptive to others' skillfulness if I slow down, read things repeatedly, imagine what it would be like to have the experience that someone has written about, and stay aware of my heart. In the third stage of the mudita bhavana meditation, we rejoice in the good qualities of a relative stranger, or "neutral person." This can involve a similar problem: not knowing what we're rejoicing in.

At the very least, you can call them to mind and recognize that, although you don't know this person, they're just like you. They're a feeling being, doing this difficult thing of being human, where happiness is often elusive, and suffering appears all too frequently. And they, just like you, embody skillful qualities that are the basis of any peace and joy they experience. Then begin to wish them well, specifically recognizing, celebrating, and encouraging the growth of what's best in them. You can say things like:

The Heart's Awakening

- May you appreciate goodness wherever you find it.
- May your good qualities continue and increase.
- May your skillful qualities bring joy to yourself and others.

You may assume that, because you don't know this person, you don't know about their skillful qualities. I suggest, however, that you may know more than you realize. Research shows that, within a tenth of a second of first meeting someone, we automatically make evaluations about their friendliness, approachability, trustworthiness, and so on. If you sit with your memories of this person, you may begin to appreciate qualities you haven't consciously noticed, realizing, for example, that they're honest, have a good sense of humor, are patient, or stay calm under pressure.

If you've identified some of the skillful qualities this person embodies, you can name those qualities:

- May your kindness continue and increase.
- May your good humor bring joy to yourself and others.
- May your patience bring you joy.

However, if you've no clue at all about what skillful qualities your relative stranger might embody, assume that they must have them, and use the more generic phrases. Whatever unknown good qualities this person has, wish that they grow, so that they will experience peace and joy.

Exercise

Practice noticing strangers' skillful qualities. Simply be attentive, and notice the way they speak, what they do, and their body language and facial expressions. What goodness do you see?

GUIDED MEDITATION: Appreciating a stranger

14

Mudita, spiritual friendship, and spiritual community

When the Buddha gave advice to a young householder, he described how we can recognize various types of good-hearted friends:

> *Recognize a good-hearted friend who's a counsellor on four grounds. They keep you from doing bad. They support you in doing good. They teach you what you do not know. They explain the path to heaven.*
>
> *Recognize a good-hearted friend who's empathetic on four grounds. They don't delight in your misfortune. They delight in your good fortune. They keep others from criticizing you. They encourage praise of you.*[95]

Good friends draw out the best in you. They show you what your weaknesses and strengths are, so that you can work on becoming more skillful. They support you when you feel like giving up. It's hard to imagine how we could make progress without that kind of feedback.

The Buddha had high praise for monks who had close and harmonious friendships. When he asked the monk Anuruddha how he was able to live harmoniously with his companions, Nandiya and Kimbila, Anuruddha replied,

Mudita, spiritual friendship, and spiritual community

I think, "I'm fortunate, so very fortunate, to live together with spiritual companions such as these." I consistently treat these venerable ones with kindness by way of body, speech, and mind, both in public and in private. I think, "Why don't I set aside my own ideas and just go along with these venerable ones' ideas." And that's what I do.[96]

Anuruddha opens with gratitude, relating how appreciative he is of his companions. That gratitude and appreciation lead to kindness.

The Buddha talked about how mutual appreciation creates communal harmony:

What is a harmonious assembly? An assembly where the mendicants live in harmony, appreciating each other, without quarrelling, blending like milk and water, and regarding each other with kindly eyes.[97]

When we focus on the skillful in each other – "appreciating each other, without quarrelling" – we're less likely to seek out things to grumble and argue about. I also love that reference to "kindly eyes," which has become central to my own practice.

The Buddha advised that we choose friends who have skillful qualities, and emulate them:

What is accomplishment in spiritual friendship? It's when someone resides in a town or village, and in that place there are householders or their children who may be young or old, but are mature in conduct, accomplished in faith, ethics, generosity, and wisdom. They associate with them, converse

215

and engage in discussion. And they emulate the same kind of accomplishment in faith, ethics, generosity, and wisdom. This is called accomplishment in spiritual friendship.[98]

Note how appreciation and emulation are the defining characteristics of "accomplishment in spiritual friendship."

I'm inspired by the skillful, appreciative communication I see daily in my own spiritual community. Virtually all the communication I witness is people supporting each other, rejoicing in each other, and building each other up. I learn from this. In a spiritual community, everyone is our teacher.

Exercise

What contexts do you have for practicing spiritual community and spiritual friendship? What can you do to create or deepen them?

15

There's a crack in everything

I'd like to share some recollections of a day, more than a decade ago, when I was leading a month-long course on mudita.

> *I've been noticing, in the weeks since I started to practice the mudita bhavana every day, that I'm becoming much more appreciative. Yesterday I was walking to my local cafe, and saw Larry sitting on a doorstep, smoking a cigarette. I was struck by the style of his baseball boots. Their color perfectly complemented the rest of his outfit. I commented on this, and we got into a conversation about them. He said that they're cheap shoes, but that he loves them. It seemed he was pleased to have permission to like his shoes rather than feel embarrassed about them being cheap.*
>
> *In the cafe, there was a new display of paintings by a local artist. They were all good, but three were outstanding. The way that the paintings had been displayed was beautiful, and I couldn't help but think that those artworks belonged in that space. I shared that with Michelle, the cafe's owner. She liked that. Michelle herself is a lovely person, and I noticed that there was a touching vulnerability about her, like she was perhaps feeling a bit down, but dealing with it in her usual patient way, remaining calm and graceful under pressure. Running a cafe isn't easy, and I admire her.*

The Heart's Awakening

This morning as I was walking to work, I became aware that I hadn't been letting in the world's beauty. It's early summer, and the trees, of which there are many on my route to work, are resplendent. Last night's rains have left the greens and purples of the leaves rich and saturated, and the world is alive and vibrant. Yet, although I had been physically seeing the world, I hadn't allowed myself to resonate emotionally with it. My mind's preoccupations were a filter that stripped out all the beauty. As I let my thinking drop away, the world's beauty came flooding in. It was deeply enriching and satisfying, appreciating all this beauty. Everything was beautiful. Everything.

When we have an appreciative mind, it can seem as if everything is beautiful. It's not just the obviously beautiful things (trees, flowers) that you can resonate with. Even cracks in concrete, a Coke can that a car's run over, a pair of cheap baseball boots, or a pile of dirty dishes can all be received with appreciation and so have their own beauty.

Even brokenness is beautiful if we look the right way. A few weeks ago, I dropped my iPad, and the screen cracked right across. I now like my iPad more, not less. It's unique. Mine is the only iPad that's cracked in that particular way. Interestingly, when other people see the crack, they're aghast. They seem shocked, as if I had broken a limb. But to me, it's beautiful.

The Japanese have an art called kintsugi. When some ceramic household object, like a favorite teapot, breaks, it is repaired with gold resin, so that the cracks are highlighted. Objects repaired in this way are considered more precious and beautiful than undamaged items. This makes me think *of Leonard Cohen's words, "There is a crack, a crack in everything / That's how the light gets in." Appreciation seems to have the ability to make things whole again, because the cracks in things are more beautiful than anything else. They're where the light shines strongest.*

I still remember and appreciate everything I wrote about that day. It's as if the writing opens a direct portal from my heart today to my heart then. This is another benefit of writing down things we're appreciative of. In the future, reading over them can be a simple yet powerful way of reconnecting with gratitude, appreciation, and admiration.

Exercise

Give yourself a day of mudita. Keep letting self-preoccupation drop away and let your heart be open. Note what you're grateful for, what you feel appreciative of, and what you admire. Write down your experiences and share them with others. At some point re-read them and have your heart opened again.

16

Appreciation and confession

To learn to be more skillful, we have to train ourselves to see the ways in which we're unskillful. This is why the Buddha talked to his son about the art of reflection:

> *"What do you think, Rahula? What is the purpose of a mirror?"*
> *"It's for checking your reflection, sir."*
> *"In the same way, deeds of body, speech, and mind should be done only after repeated checking."*[99]

Here's his guidance (slightly condensed) on how we should reflect on past unskillful actions:

> *After you have acted [with the body, in speech, or in thought], you should check on that act: "Does this act [...] that I have done lead to hurting myself, hurting others, or hurting both? Is it unskillful, with suffering as its outcome and result?" If, while checking in this way, you know: "This act [...] that I have done leads to hurting myself, hurting others, or hurting both. It's unskillful, with suffering as its outcome and result," then, Rahula, you should confess, reveal, and clarify such a deed to a teacher or a fellow practitioner. And having revealed it you should restrain yourself in future.*[100]

There's a lot there, but, in essence, we're checking on both the impact and the intent of our actions. Did we hurt anyone? What was our intention in acting? Did it embody ill will or craving? Did it come from confusion?

Knowing our intentions isn't always easy. We often want to see ourselves as good, and rationalize or refuse to acknowledge anything that contradicts that view. Intention isn't always *conscious* intention. When someone is hurt by your speech or actions, give serious thought to whether you could have been more skillful. Considering the impact of our actions can help us become aware of hidden intentions.

Having acknowledged we've done something unskillful, we "confess, reveal, and clarify" it to others. Often, it's only when we confess to others that our remorse becomes real to us. That's when we *feel* the ethical reality of our actions. That's when there is unexpected emotion, a lump in the throat, a catch in the voice, or tears. It may only be then that we begin to understand how someone we've hurt must feel. Now, remorse may be painful, but it's also skillful. Just as a ship at sea might groan and creak as it changes direction, our emotional being aches as it reorients itself toward the skillful. However, this pain is short-lived compared to the long-standing distress of a guilty conscience, or of unresolved conflicts with others. The pain of confessing is cathartic, and soon turns to relief.

The first person we should turn to is usually whoever we've hurt. Our apology may be a necessary part of their healing. If that's not possible or appropriate – and sometimes it isn't – then we turn to someone else. The Buddha suggests we confess to a teacher or fellow spiritual practitioner.[101]

Choose carefully: the person you confess to should be trustworthy and ethical. If you've offended someone, for example, and share this with someone who isn't ethical, it's not helpful when, rather than receive your words compassionately, they say, "That's nothing. Just listen to what I did!"

The prospect of confessing may terrify you. It did me, at first. We fear that others will reject us if they learn our faults. But people who hear your confessions will not think less of you. They will admire your honesty. They may also offer clarifying questions, point out things that sound evasive, or make suggestions about how to handle difficult situations in the future. A spiritual community can develop a culture of confession, so that we see how normal and healthy it is to discuss ethical struggles. We see others showing remorse, learning, and moving on, and we do the same ourselves. We realize that confession is simultaneously wonderful and no big deal. Confession builds spiritual community; allowing yourself to be vulnerable with spiritual friends builds deep bonds of trust and mutual respect. In confessing we model openness, vulnerability, and courage. This is a gift.

Confessing leaves us feeling happier and lighter. We don't confess just to feel better. We do it so that we can act more skillfully in future. As the Buddha said, "Having revealed [your unskillful act], you should restrain yourself in future." And so our confession can conclude with a resolution – a renewed determination to be true to what's best in us.

Appreciation and confession

Exercise

Try sharing with trusted friends, especially friends in the spiritual life, the more difficult stuff you're working with, like the old habits that cause you and others pain. You'll find that as you do this your courage grows.

17

Appreciation and toxic positivity

Praise is common in the early scriptures. The Buddha often praises others, and there's a whole collection of discourses where he highlights the good qualities and attainments of his followers. He pointed out, for example, that the monk with the most charming manner of speaking was Bhaddiya the Dwarf, that the nun who was foremost in wisdom was Khema, that the male householder who was best at inspiring potential followers was Hatthaka of Alavi, and that the female householder foremost in developing deep meditative absorption was Uttarananda's mother. This touching praise reaches our hearts across a gulf of 2,500 years.

The Buddha himself was praised, as you would expect, both during his life and in the centuries after. In the first or second century CE, Matrceta wrote a hymn in praise of the Buddha, which includes this rather telling verse:

Generally your speech was wholly sweet
but when necessary it would be otherwise.
But either way, every word was well spoken
because it always achieved its purpose.[102]

The first line might sound like criticism, but Matrceta is praising the Buddha precisely because he had a critical edge when it was needed. The Buddha was sometimes not "nice." He did not practice idiot compassion. If he thought someone was going to suffer because of the harmful actions and doctrines they'd embraced, he'd challenge them out of concern for their well-being and the well-being of those they might mislead.

The mudita equivalent of niceness and idiot compassion is "toxic positivity." Author Susan Cain describes this as a "cultural directive" that says, "Whatever you do, don't tell the truth of what it's like to be alive."[103] Although it's crucial to rejoice in the good we see in ourselves and in the world, and be grateful for life's blessings, we also need to be aware of the things about us that need work, and that there are problems in the world that need our attention.

We don't help ourselves when we deny the things that are difficult in our lives. We don't help other people when we try to convince them that their problems don't exist, or blandly reassure them that everything will work out fine. Telling people that "happiness is a choice" and that they should stop feeling their grief denies them the empathy they need. Saying that people are being "negative" for seeing actual or potential problems is just a form of avoidance. Remaining naively optimistic regarding the world's problems leads to apathy, and to problems going unaddressed.

One form of toxic positivity we sometimes see in Buddhism involves the statement, "All things are perfect as they are." It's true that in meditation we can have experiences of deep equanimity where nothing can upset us, and our experience is perfect as it is. But it's narcissistic for us to assume that, because we are at peace, other beings' sufferings aren't real. Some people falsely claim the Buddha said this, but had he thought everything was "perfect just as it is" he wouldn't have bothered teaching.

Zen teacher Shunryu Suzuki struck a beautiful balance by saying to his students, "You're all perfect exactly as you are, *and* you could use a little improvement."[104] Saying we're all perfect exactly as we are suggests that we can stop fretting about "not being good enough"; we all have what it takes to become enlightened. If we have faith in our innate goodness, we'll be happier and kinder. And I don't need to explain, "You all need a little improvement." Don't we just! Practicing appreciation and being clear about our faults – non-judgmentally – is what will bring about that improvement.

Exercise

Don't ignore you own, others', or the world's problems. Recognize them, recognize the work needed to tackle them, and then find the optimism that will inspire you to do that work.

18

The far enemy of joyful appreciation

We've all at some point been annoyed by someone else's happiness. They're in a good mood, and we're inwardly grumbling; "What are they so happy about!" That's what Buddhism calls *arati*. It's the far enemy of mudita, the enemy of joy. Arati is a Pali word that combines the negative prefix *a-* (not, un-, or dis-) with the word *rati*, which means "pleasure, liking for, fondness, delight." *Arati* means not simply lacking those qualities, but opposing them. Arati is "anti-appreciation." It's aversion, bitterness, grumpiness, cynicism, nitpicking, and resentment.

I remember in my twenties being at a party with my girlfriend and two roommates, where the main attraction was a chance to win a flight to Paris for the weekend, plus hotel accommodation. We'd all chipped in a certain amount of money, and names were to be drawn from a hat. My two roommates won the prize! One of them, a sweet girl called Susie, came dancing up to me with her eyes sparkling and a huge smile on her face. "I won a weekend in Paris!" she said. Sadly, I was so jealous and resentful I couldn't even smile back, and certainly couldn't celebrate with her.

The old saying, "No good deed goes unpunished" describes a form of arati. There's always someone willing to criticize or diminish good things that happen, often out of jealousy or from wanting to appear clever. Arati can also manifest as indifference. Others may be celebrating, but we're attached to being unhappy and our attitude is a weary sigh.

Arati isn't usually as strong an emotion as hatred, the far enemy of kindness, or cruelty, the far enemy of compassion. But it's an addictive emotional state. You see some elderly people with permanently sour faces who grumble about everything and everyone, and have got stuck that way because they've spent decades practicing being miserable. The more you complain about the world, the more it seems there is to complain about.

Arati is a state of suffering, and we can overcome it through self-compassion. Notice where the suffering is in the body, and send it thoughts of compassion, such as, "May you be well, may you be happy." This can help soften and dissolve the closed-off tight feeling that comes with arati, and open us up to feeling joy. Since having empathy for ourselves allows us to have empathy for others, a little self-kindness or self-compassion can open the way for us to be happy for others.

Expressing gratitude is a powerful way to overcome arati. This comes up a lot in my daily practice of writing five things I'm grateful for. When I first sit down, I often can't think of anything. The world feels dull and flat – that's arati. But when I look for things to be grateful for, there's always something. Soon I find my resistance dissipates, and I become genuinely grateful.

The gratitude practice I explained, where I mentally go through my body and thank each part of it for serving me, also dislodges arati. I go from being disgruntled with my body to being deeply appreciative of it. Say "Thank you" enough, and arati is replaced by appreciation and joy.

The far enemy of joyful appreciation

The fourth stage of the mudita bhavana meditation helps overcome arati as well. We call to mind someone we are in conflict with and are reluctant to celebrate. We open up to the fact that they contain skillful qualities, and we appreciate and rejoice in those qualities. We may have trouble acknowledging anything positive about this person at first, but it comes with practice.

Exercise

Watch your thoughts and your speech for grumbling, criticism, and so on. When you find those things happening, practice saying "Thank you" for everything, until joy arises, or practice self-compassion.

GUIDED MEDITATION: Appreciating someone we struggle with

19

Having gratitude for our enemies

The eighth-century Indian teacher Shantideva encourages us to appreciate even those who wish us harm:

Since my adversary assists me in my Bodhisattva way of life, I should long for him like a treasure discovered in the house and acquired without effort.

[...] patience arises only in dependence on that malicious intention, so he alone is a cause of my patience. I should respect him just like the sublime Dharma.[105]

In this creative and radical approach, we cultivate gratitude toward our enemies not because of any skillful qualities they may have, but for giving us the opportunity to practice patience. The bodhisattva way of life Shantideva is discussing is the path of living with compassion for all beings. It's very important within that context to swiftly eliminate all forms of ill will. There are always going to be people who hate us, dislike us, or make life difficult for us, and we can't force them to change. But we can change our attitude toward them so that we become less reactive. And this is what appreciating our enemies does.

This practice works. One time on social media, I attracted the attention of someone whose communication started off as brash and rapidly degenerated into graphic threats of violence. I felt a powerful urge to retaliate, but then I remembered Shantideva's advice, and felt gratitude toward this person for giving me an opportunity to be compassionate. My anger for him vanished, and I even felt affection for him. In the end I decided not to respond at all, preventing the conflict from escalating.

It can be hard to find something to appreciate in someone we feel antagonistic toward. They certainly have skillful qualities, but we find it hard to recognize them. Shantideva gets around this difficulty, because it's people's challenging behaviors themselves that we appreciate, because they test us, challenge us, and give us the opportunity to go deeper into our practice.

It's important to remember that, even if we managed to create a bubble of cozy pleasantness around us, our tendency toward anger would still be there, encoded in the substrate of our brains. We can only work with that anger if it has been triggered. And this is why, under normal circumstances, we resent our enemies: they show us who we are, and we don't like it. Shantideva's teaching turns this around, so we're saying, in effect, "Thank you for showing me who I am! I'd never have been able to work with my messy anger if you hadn't helped me make it visible." Our opponent becomes a collaborator in our spiritual practice.

It's difficult to remember all this in the heat of the moment. When we're provoked, our first instinct is often to retaliate. So it helps if we rehearse. We can practice cultivating this gratitude for our enemies when we're calmer. So right now, think of someone you get annoyed by. Vividly imagine them doing whatever it is that angers you. Feel the annoyance arise, or at least remember what it feels like when that happens. See if you can find appreciation toward this person helping you see what it is you need to work on.

Exercise

I've suggested a rehearsal in the final paragraph above. You can do it as a standalone exercise, or bring it into the fourth stage of the mudita meditation.

20

All people and all circumstances are my allies

I was struck by something I read in an interview with Lynn Jurich, the founder and CEO of the solar energy company Sunrun: "Every morning my meditation is: 'All people and all circumstances are my allies.' I repeat it every morning: 'All people and all circumstances are my allies.'"[106] Jurich's practice is broader than Shantideva's suggestion that we be grateful for our enemies. Shantideva had in mind people who actively wish us harm, while Jurich includes everyone. There is no distinction between those trying to help us, those who might accidentally cause us difficulties, and those who might actively try to harm us, such as, in Jurich's case, competitors who might want to take business away from her. They are all allies.

Jurich considers not just all people, but all circumstances to be allies as well. Challenging circumstances not only test our powers of patience and our ability to handle anxiety and frustration, but they force us to be creative. When things are going well, circumstances are her ally. When they're going against her, circumstances are her ally. We can appreciate everything and everyone.

She notes that other competing businesses in the solar power market share a concern for the climate. Ultimately they're on the same side: mitigating climate change.

Competitors also keep Jurich on her toes; a competitor coming out with an improved solar project or a great advertising campaign spurs Jurich's own company to do better. If she feels jealous of others for their successes, then there's something to learn there about the need to refocus emotions in a positive direction.

Jurich's mantra possibly goes back to one of Tibetan Buddhism's *lojong* slogans, which says, "Transform all mishaps into the path of awakening."[107] But I find Jurich's teaching more appealing, because it's not just about mishaps, and it encapsulates so much, so neatly. It's perfect for memorizing and for using as a meditation practice.

Here's a test: if you close your eyes right now, can you remember Jurich's mantra, word for word? Or do you just remember the general idea? The more vaguely you remember it, the less you'll be able to practice it. So try memorizing the words: "All people and all circumstances are my allies." Say it over several times. Then close your eyes and see if you have it word for word. Wait a few minutes and try again. Keep testing yourself to make sure that the phrase is locked away in your long-term memory.

Next, find five minutes for meditation. Just drop the phrase, "All people and all circumstances are my allies" into the mind. Breathe. Let the words just sink in. Then say them again. From time to time as you're doing this, call to mind people and circumstances that try your patience. Don't go into the whole background story. Just remind yourself of some challenging circumstance or person, and say, "All people and all circumstances are my allies." Call to mind people who aim to support you and appreciate them as allies as well. At least

All people and all circumstances are my allies

sometimes, you'll start to regard everyone and everything with gratitude and appreciation.

Even as I'm writing these words, I'm being interrupted repeatedly by my son asking me questions. And I remember that these interruptions are my ally. They give me an opportunity to maintain love rather than express irritation. They give me an opportunity to communicate more skillfully, and to learn from the mistakes I make. They give me an opportunity to be a better person. And they arouse confidence and courage, because the world appears as a less frustrating, threatening place. "All people and all circumstances are my allies."

Exercise

Try my suggestion for memorizing Jurich's mantra.

GUIDED MEDITATION: All people and all circumstances are my allies

21

Seeing goodness through others' eyes

The mind likes saving energy, and one way it does that is by reducing complexity to simple binaries. One of these is "good versus bad." If we dislike someone for whatever reason, then they must be bad. Once we've put someone in the "bad" category, we look for things to dislike about them so we can confirm their badness. We assume they can't have any goodness in them, and so we fail to appreciate any skillful qualities they have, even if they're right in front of us. If they're unkind to us but show kindness to others, they're hypocritical. If they help us, they're being manipulative. If they do something good, we find a reason not to give them credit. We get stuck in a state of arati, or anti-appreciation.

Once, when I was on a large retreat, there was one person I took an instant dislike to. I'll call him Ignatius, since I've never met anyone by that name.[108] I found everything about Ignatius – his voice, his mannerisms, his laugh – irritating. I really couldn't see anything likable about him at all. Now, as it happened, there was a practice on this retreat where the retreat leader would single out each person and talk about their good qualities in depth. This is one form of the practice of "rejoicing in merits" that I discussed earlier. The time approached for my bête noire to have his good qualities celebrated, and I simply could not imagine what our leader would find to say about him.

Yet he found plenty. He pointed out many of Ignatius's skillful qualities and did so with obvious warmth and admiration. And the weird thing was that, every time he pointed out something skillful Ignatius had done, or some good quality he had, I recognized, "You know, that's right! He does do that! He does have that good quality! He does have that talent!" Because I recognized the praise as accurate, I'd evidently seen Ignatius's good qualities, but hadn't allowed them to consciously register. They contradicted the view I'd built up about the person I'd turned into an enemy, and so I excluded them from awareness. This rejoicing in merit permanently changed my view of Ignatius. I now think of him with nothing but warmth. Even recalling the mannerisms that had annoyed me so profoundly, I feel only affection. I remember him now as creative and funny, and as a fascinating person. My ill will toward him has been completely eradicated.

This is another reminder of the importance of spiritual friendship and spiritual community. We often need to borrow the eyes of someone who can see the world more accurately and more appreciatively than we ourselves can. We become intoxicated by our own views. We see someone as annoying, and we can't imagine that there might be other perspectives. Being exposed to wiser and kinder views allows us to appreciate how limited and inadequate our own are. We need each other's help to see the world more as it is, with its abundance of goodness that's often right in front of us, unacknowledged.

Exercise

Notice when other people celebrate things that you might have overlooked. Try sharing with that person how they've opened your eyes.

22

Laughter, delight, and appreciation

There's no record of the Buddha ever laughing, and if the scriptures are to be believed it was unusual for him even to smile. One time Ananda, the Buddha's cousin, saw the Buddha smile and thought, "What is the cause, what is the reason why the Buddha smiled? Realized Ones do not smile for no reason."[109] The fact that Ananda regarded a smile by the Buddha as worthy of comment gives you the impression that the Buddha took life very seriously, but not so seriously that he didn't smile. He seems to have had a very poor opinion of laughter, however. The *Dhammapada* suggests that merriment is inappropriate in the face of the suffering we see around us: "When this world is ever ablaze, why this laughter, why this jubilation?"[110] In another discourse the Buddha puts laughter in the same category as sloth, deception, and fornication – things to be abandoned.[111]

I once wrote an article for *Tricycle* magazine about the Buddha and laughter, and discussed how psychologists have found that the funniest jokes are those that trigger a sense of superiority in the reader.[112] Here's an example:

Texan: "Where are you from?"
Harvard graduate: "I come from a place where we do not end our sentences with prepositions."

Texan: "Okay. Where are you from, jackass?"

See how it works? We're encouraged to look down on the Harvard graduate for being pretentious. Humor is often a form of arati, or anti-appreciation, reinforcing feelings of conceit. But not always. I had a dear friend in Glasgow, called Neil, who was fond of saying, "You have to laugh!" – often in response to some unkind or foolish thing he'd heard about. Instead of getting angry or bitter, Neil would laugh at the absurdity of life. He'd laugh at himself, too.

After I'd written the *Tricycle* article, I discovered there are references in the early scriptures to "the laughing wisdom" (*hasapanna*). It would have been nice to have discovered this before I'd written the article, of course. You have to laugh! As far as I know, the scriptures don't explain what this laughing wisdom is, but my assumption is that it's the burst of delight that accompanies a sudden insight. We see something for the first time, and it's new and fresh and amazing. And simultaneously we realize that we've been wrong all along about something. The conjunction of "Boy, I was so wrong!" and "Wow! Isn't the truth amazing!" makes us laugh.

Laughter as a response to insight is common in the Zen tradition. Here's one story:

When Venerable Shui-lao of Hung-chou came to see the Patriarch for the first time, he asked, "What is the meaning of [Bodhidharma's] coming from the West?"
The Patriarch said, "Bow down!"
As soon as Shui-lao went down to bow, the Patriarch kicked him. Shui-lao had a great Awakening. He rose

up clapping his hands and laughing heartily, and said, "Wonderful! Wonderful! The source of myriad samadhi and limitless subtle meanings can all be realized on the tip of a single hair." He then paid his respects to the Patriarch and withdrew.

Later he told the assembly, "Since the day I was kicked by Master Ma, I have not stopped laughing."[113]

Sometimes we laugh in delight when we see something done well. This can be another way of mudita showing itself: we are delighted in the way goodness appears unexpectedly. It's the opposite of looking down on people: it's looking up at people with admiration, delight, and joyful appreciation of their good qualities.

Exercise

Observe what makes you laugh. Is a sense of superiority involved? What skillful things give rise to sudden delight?

23

Impermanence and mudita

The Buddha encouraged us to reflect on five things. The first four are that (1) old age, (2) sickness, (3) death, and (4) separation from what we love are inevitable. The fifth reflection is that we're responsible for our own lives and our actions. He was saying, in essence, "Life is short and difficult; live it wisely." He also suggested that we reflect that all beings are in the same situation as ourselves, so that we recognize that the time we have together is precious.[114]

I opened my book *Living as a River* by reporting on a study where married couples were asked to reflect on the fact that one day they would be separated by death.[115] They were not, as you might assume, depressed by this. Instead, they were uplifted. They found that they were less interested in their partner's faults, and instead felt more appreciative of them. What do those socks on the bedroom floor matter, when we have so little time together?

The Buddha used the image of a violent, unpredictable flood to represent life's precariousness. Echoing this, Leonard Cohen, who was profoundly influenced by Buddhism, said:

What is the appropriate behavior for a man or a woman in the midst of this world, where each person is clinging to his piece of debris? What is the proper salutation between people as they pass each other in this flood?[116]

Impermanence and mudita

The unpredictability of our lives can suggest either "Every man for himself" or "We're all in it together." The former view is depressing, isolating, and ignoble. I prefer the latter way of seeing things. Through these five contemplations, we can dramatically overcome our sense of being in it alone. Instead, we can begin to see that we're all on the same journey together, and learn to inspire and support each other along the way, drawing out one another's goodness. Our lives are not separate, but intertwined. My practice is not separate from yours, nor yours from mine.

According to the Buddha, the benefit of applying these five reflections to your own life is that you "entirely give up bad conduct, or at least reduce it."[117] This is a worthy and noble goal: you'll become a better person through contemplating your own existential situation. But the benefit of reflecting that the same five things apply to others is much more profound: you "give up the fetters and eliminate the underlying tendencies [to unskillfulness]." In other words, you'll become enlightened. So let's reflect on those around us – those dear to us, those we're connected to with ties of blood or love, those who barely register, those we don't like. They're all going to die, just as we are. We don't have long with them, and, as we all fumble half-blind through life, we can help each other by recognizing one another's goodness. We can rejoice in it, bring it to each other's attention, and encourage its growth.

There's urgency in this. You may think you will have time later to seek the good in yourself and others. You might think you can rejoice tomorrow in others' skillful qualities. But there may be no later. Tomorrow may never come. Knowing this, let's act as if we don't have time to waste. Let's support ourselves and others, right here, right now.

In the final stage of the mudita bhavava practice, we can remind ourselves that our time here together is short, and that the best use of that time is to draw out what's best in one another. "May all beings appreciate each other's goodness. May our skillful qualities continue and increase. May our goodness bring joy to ourselves and to others."

Exercise

Spend some time reflecting that you are subject to old age, sickness, death, and being separated from what you love, and that you are responsible for your own life. Then apply the same reflections to others. Can you feel a sense of time being precious? Since the future is uncertain, let's set an intention that our next encounter with others will be a kind and appreciative one.

GUIDED MEDITATION: Mudita bhavana

24

When mudita hurts

Sometimes admiration can be so intense it's painful. I noticed this when I was asked to speak at my mother's funeral. She'd had a prolonged passing. Her body had been reacting badly to the dialysis she needed to keep her alive, and she had been so sick and in such pain that she'd asked for the dialysis to stop. This meant that she'd die within a week or two. The family supported my mum's wishes, but my nephew reminded her that I would want to fly over from the US to say goodbye. So she said she'd keep going with the dialysis until I could get over to Scotland.

I told this to those who'd gathered to say farewell to my mum. I said what an amazing thing it was that a mother would keep herself alive, in pain and discomfort, for the sake of her son. I knew the words I wanted to say, but I kept choking up, unable to speak. This wasn't sadness. The lump in my throat and the aching in my heart were those of "elevation" – the powerful sense of admiration we can have for the heroism of others. These feelings can be so strong that it's hard to bear them, especially in a public setting, which is where they often happen.

Something similar happened to me recently in a Buddhist group where we are exploring our racial conditioning. At this gathering, which I was facilitating, we started by watching a video of the song "Stand up," from the film *Harriet*.[118] Both the film and the video portray Harriet Tubman's escape from slavery and her involvement in the Underground Railroad, which helped people to escape the brutality of the slave system. Astonishingly, Tubman returned to the South thirteen times to rescue hundreds of others from slavery. The courage she displayed is astonishing. Every time she crossed into territory where it was legal for white people to regard black people as property, she risked her life as well as her hard-won freedom.

This song had moved me every time I'd heard it, but listening to it with others was especially powerful. I felt stirred by the sufferings of those who were enslaved. I empathized with their yearning for freedom and the fear of getting caught. I was shocked at the cruelty of those who treated people as possessions. I felt admiration for the compassion and courage of those who organized the rescues – especially Tubman herself. And the imagery in the song, about Tubman crossing a river and bringing her people to safety, resonated both with the bodhisattva ideal and with the need for white people opposed to racism to reach out to and change the minds of other white people who harbor feelings of racial superiority.

The feelings welled up so powerfully that I struggled to bear them. I had to just keep breathing with these overwhelming sensations, practicing self-compassion with them, accepting them as best I could, and reminding myself, "It's okay to feel this. Let me feel this." At the end of the song, when as leader it was my job to conduct the meeting, I had to accept that it was okay to be unable to speak for several minutes, and be seen with tears in my eyes. These are the things we sometimes need to do when admiration gives rise to feelings of elevation so strong they are uncomfortable.

Exercise

I suggest watching the video I discussed. Does it evoke admiration, inspiration, elevation – or other emotions? You may not respond the same way I did, but be prepared to offer yourself support if you need it.

25

An antidote to fear

The Path of Freedom says that joyful appreciation creates "non-fear." In more positive terms, it gives us courage. The connection between appreciation and courage, which might not be immediately obvious, is to do with what kind of world we think we live in. The news we consume can easily give us the impression that the world is full of wars, conflict, murder, theft, natural disasters, and all manner of troubling things. But we have to remember that news reporting highlights negative events precisely because they are not common, and does not give us an accurate picture of the world. Because of the negative bias of news reporting, many in the US believe crime is rising, even though it's been falling for decades. Similarly, many believe that violent conflict in the world is increasing, even though the number of wars and the number of people killed in them has been declining for many centuries. Once again, perhaps we should watch less news, or at least consume it more selectively, or focus more on thoughtful and nuanced analyses of current events. We can even access publications that focus more on good news.

Believing that we live in a dangerous world where people are mostly bad and everything is getting worse is another form of arati, or anti-appreciation. Cultivating appreciation helps us to recognize that, in most people, goodness predominates. Every day, billions of people say the words "I love you," and

An antidote to fear

there are hundreds of millions of hugs. In every minute of the day, someone comes to the aid of a stranger. Look around you and notice the things that are working, even if it's just that you have access to roads and sidewalks, that there are streetlights and sewers. Most people's *lived* world, as opposed to the one they see on the evening news, is peaceful and orderly.

The practice of mudita can restore balance to our view of the world. We can recognize that the world is mostly a safe and kind place, in which we don't need to be in constant fear. I'm not suggesting being reckless. There are dangers in the world, and sometimes fear is appropriate. Neither am I suggesting naiveté. The world faces many significant problems. Many of those would be reduced if we were more confident. Our fear of the effects of global warming, for example, can be so paralyzing that we feel hopeless and become unable to take action to combat it.

We often misjudge others, seeing them as more judgmental than they really are. Who among us has not discovered a stain or flaw on our clothing while in public, and been anxious that others are judging us? But do others really obsess about such things? These fears are based on our *assuming* that others are full of judgment and criticism. Isn't it unkind to think about them that way? Shouldn't we give them the benefit of the doubt and assume they are predominantly kind and respectful human beings? After all, most of the behavior we see in the world around us shows mutual respect and kindness. If we assume goodness in others, then we experience less fear. If we experience less fear, we'll be kinder to others. If we're kinder to others they'll tend to be kinder in return, and so we've changed the nature of the world around us.

Exercise

When you fear being judged by others, try cultivating kind thoughts toward them. Consider that both you and they are suffering, and offer compassion. Consider that all beings have the roots of goodness, and are simply trying to muddle through life.

26

The magic ratio of appreciation

I remember a time I made a critical comment to my ex-wife. Upset, she complained that I criticized her a lot, which surprised me, because I didn't think I did. So I asked – I think curiously, not as a challenge: when was the last time that I'd said something critical? She couldn't remember. I asked if it was within the last two weeks. No, it was longer ago than that. The last month? She was pretty sure it was longer ago even than that. This was a sobering reminder of how careful I need to be with my speech. Criticisms stick in the mind.

According to psychologist John Gottman, for a relationship to be stable in the long term there must be at least five affirming interactions for every critical or challenging one. Probably many of us are not even close to that ratio. Interacting affirmingly can involve giving compliments, affectionate touch, smiling, laughing, making friendly eye contact, showing non-verbally that you're listening to a conversation, responding to a bid for attention, sharing jokes, and so on. Negative interactions include sarcasm and criticism, but some of the most damaging are signs of contempt, such as eye-rolling. Gottman has found that signs of contempt are the single most accurate predictor of divorce.

If there are more critical than supportive interactions in a relationship, both parties can feel that they don't matter and that they're under constant attack. And, when that happens, even completely neutral interactions can be interpreted as criticisms. Both our tendency to be critical and our sensitivity to criticism can result from a lack of appreciation and overabundance of criticism in early life. We may have lived in a childhood world where the ratio was inverted, with more critical than affirming interactions. We go around still expecting to be attacked, and become overly sensitive to perceived criticisms. To counterbalance this ingrained negativity bias, we need first to learn to see the good in each other, and then to reflect it back to the bearer.

Galway Kinnell wrote a poem whose opening lines read:

The bud
stands for all things,
even for those things that don't flower,
for everything flowers, from within, of self-blessing
though sometimes it is necessary
to reteach a thing its loveliness,
to put a hand on its brow
of the flower
and retell it in words and in touch
it is lovely
until it flowers again from within, of self-blessing.[119]

One thing I decided to do as I wrote this book was to jot down qualities I admire in my partner. It was fun and easy to do, and within the first two or three minutes I already had a list of more than twenty things – and that was just scratching the surface. Then my task was to express these things to her: to keep reminding her of her own worth and goodness.

The magic ratio of appreciation

When I was doing my master's degree I took some classes in the business school, one of which told us how to deliver critical feedback. This method sandwiches criticism between two pieces of praise: "Here's something that's good about your performance. You suck at doing this other thing. But here's something else good about your work." Many managers love this method; the rest of the world calls it "a shit sandwich." Since the praise is only being offered to soften the criticism, it comes over as being insincere. Because the ratio of praise to criticism is only two to one, it comes over as an attack. And it's clearly manipulative, so you'll distrust the praise anyway. So don't use praise to manipulate. Don't use it as a "technique" to improve your relationship. Let your appreciation be an act of genuine love. The person you love feels. They suffer. They have skillful qualities that they probably don't fully recognize. So be their mirror, or, in Kinnell's words, let them know in words and touch that they are lovely, until they can flower from within, of self-blessing.

Exercise

What's the balance of appreciative and critical thoughts in your mind, whether directed at yourself or others? I think probably many of us need to cultivate appreciative thoughts to balance up our critical tendencies. Making a list can help with that.

27

Gratitude for the teachers and teachings

I'm grateful you're here. I'm always grateful to anyone who shows up when I'm teaching or reads what I write. If you weren't interested in the Dharma then I'd have no opportunity to talk about practice, except to myself, and that wouldn't be as much fun. I benefit so much from teaching.

I learned meditation from many people, the first of whom was a man called Susiddhi, a fellow Scot who taught at the Glasgow Buddhist Centre in Scotland. I am grateful for what he taught me, and I'm grateful to the many other teachers I learned from. Some traditions talk about "lineages," but the process of teachings being passed on isn't linear. Teachers learn from each other. Students learn from each other. Students teach their teachers. So I'm going to say "Thank you" to all the teachers who have been my students and the students who have been my teachers.

Most of the people I learned meditation from were taught to meditate by Sangharakshita, an Englishman who went to India and became a Buddhist monk. I'm grateful to him for having explored Buddhism in India, and for finding teachers there, of whom one was Indian, several were Tibetans who had recently fled their homeland, and one was a Chinese Ch'an (Zen) teacher. Thank you, Dhardo Rinpoche, Yogi Chen, and all the other teachers who helped Sangharakshita along the way.

Gratitude for the teachers and teachings

How many teachers were there between the Buddha and those who taught me to meditate? The non-linear route back to the Buddha is like an entwined braid of crisscrossing streams. The number of teachers between us and the Buddha is literally uncountable. In essence it amounts to all practitioners there have been.

I'm grateful to the Buddha himself. One of the things that I'm most thankful for is that he refused to settle. He said that, until the moment of his enlightenment, he felt an "arrow in the heart."[120] He was never prepared to accept this. He had a comfortable early life, even if he wasn't the prince that legend makes him out to have been. Refusing to settle with that, he went off wandering. He attained deep states of meditation with Alara Kalama and Uddaka Ramaputta, and could have settled for these spiritual accomplishments, or for becoming a leader of either man's spiritual community, but he didn't. Gotama explored extreme asceticism, and refused to settle with that. And then he rediscovered the *jhanas* – deep states of meditative absorption – and he recognized that this was the path that would lead to awakening. He didn't settle for the jhanas as blissful states, however, but used them to question the very way he perceived himself and the world. He didn't settle until he'd found that arrow and plucked it out.

Here again, he could have settled, enjoying the enlightened experience in solitude, but instead he spent forty-five years wandering and teaching. Even on his deathbed, his eighty-year-old body broken and racked with pain, he continued teaching, exhorting, and inspiring others to practice. I'm deeply grateful for his heroism, and, even though he's long dead, I say "Thank you" and bow deeply. Gratitude turns naturally into puja, or devotion.

Every moment in our lives is an opportunity to be grateful. Gratitude makes us happier. Gratitude leads to emulation, and in emulating our heroes we become better people. But, if we're going to emulate the Buddha, then perhaps we need to let ourselves be influenced by his most outstanding quality, which was his refusal to settle for anything short of enlightenment. Being a happier, more skillful person isn't enough. We need to go all the way along the path, until we too can pull out that arrow.

Exercise

Spend time reflecting on people you've learned important life lessons from. Those may be formal teachers, fellow practitioners, or something else entirely. Remember what you learned and how it's benefited you. Hold those moments in your heart until you feel the goodness of them.

Part IV

OVERCOMING OBSTACLES TO LOVE

The essentials of upekkha

Upekkha (Sanskrit *upeksha*) is the desire, based on empathy, that beings, ourselves included, attain the insight that eradicates craving, aversion, and ignorance, which are obstacles to love.

Other translations
Equanimity, even-mindedness.

The stages of the meditation
Cultivating a wish that the following attain insight:
- Ourselves.
- A relative stranger.
- A friend.
- A person we have difficulty with.
- All beings.

Suggested phrases
- May all beings accept the arising and passing of things.
- May all beings abide in equanimity, free from attachment or aversion.
- May all beings know the deep peace of awakening.

Two crucial things to know
If we want beings to be truly happy, then we should wish for them the deepest possible level of happiness, which is spiritual awakening. We don't merely wish for insight to arise in ourselves, but instead actively seek it. Nor do we merely wish for it to arise in others, but instead actively encourage it within them.

The practice of upekkha as a brahma vihara is very rich and multifaceted. It might at first seem confusing. Just remember that it's about overcoming grasping, aversion, and delusion, which are obstacles to love. It's about deepening our capacity for love. Ultimately it's a practice that leads us to awakening, which is the fulfillment of love and compassion.

1

The culmination of the brahma viharas

In all the brahma viharas, we want to help beings attain well-being and happiness. With kindness, we want beings to be at ease, well, and happy. With compassion, we want to relieve them of suffering so that they can be well and happy. With appreciation, we want them to have the skillful qualities that are the cause of well-being and happiness. Where do we go from there? A major turning point in my understanding of the brahma viharas was realizing that mudita was not "being happy because others are happy." If mudita is a deeper practice than metta and karuna, encouraging the development of skillful qualities in them, I wondered how upekkha could continue this progression. The only way to go deeper seemed to be supporting all beings, ourselves included, to move toward awakening. Enlightenment, after all, is the most profound experience of peace and joy that can be attained.

Upekkha is usually seen as a "cool" quality rather than a loving one. Buddhaghosa says, for example, that in upekkha there is "no further concern, such as 'May beings be happy' or 'May they be released from pain.'"[121] In this understanding, upekkha is devoid of love and compassion. I find this unsatisfactory. Seeing upekkha as a loving practice where we desire the spiritual growth of beings, not just in terms of cultivating skillful behaviors but also in terms of developing

The culmination of the brahma viharas

insight, seems a more appropriate culmination of the brahma viharas.

We can see traditional descriptions of upekkha in terms of it being the work we do to perfect our love by becoming awakened. *The Path of Freedom* names three goals or characteristics of upekkha practice:

1. Developing non-attachment.
2. Ridding ourselves of our likes and dislikes toward beings.
3. Regarding all beings as equal.[122]

These all relate to the process of developing insight. "Non-attachment" here means overcoming our attachment to self. When we're attached to self, we see the world in terms of what we think threatens or benefits our own well-being. This leads to likes and dislikes. We like others when we think they'll benefit us, and dislike them when we see them as threats to our well-being. Because of this, we do not regard or love beings equally. Complete non-attachment to self, ridding ourselves entirely of likes and dislikes toward beings, seeing all beings with the wisdom of equality, and having unconditional love and compassion for them are all marks of enlightenment.

Metta, karuna, and mudita are not enough. They help us to be loving, but they can't entirely rid us of craving and aversion, liking and disliking, and so they don't allow us to be entirely loving. Until we're enlightened, we can never be totally loving because of ignorance, craving, and ill will, which are obstacles to love. Upekkha removes these obstacles.

Although *upekkha* is usually translated as "equanimity"

or "even-mindedness," etymologically it is related to insight. It comes from a prefix, *upa-*, which denotes closeness, and a verb root, *ikkha*, which means "to see." *Upa-ikkha* – upekkha – is "seeing closely," or "looking deeply."[123] This is not that different from another word that describes cultivating insight – *vipassana*, which means "truly seeing." With upekkha, we look closely at the obstacles that inhibit our ability to love, so that we can overcome them.

Although the Theravada tradition came to see upekkha as a retreat from love, for Mahayana Buddhists upekkha was always a loving quality that was related to helping beings become enlightened. There are many different expressions of upekkha in the various Mahayana schools, but they are typically along the lines of, "May all beings abide in equanimity, free from liking and disliking." This was not just the wish that beings learn to be mindful amongst the ups and downs of life. The equanimity that is "free from liking and disliking" is enlightenment. What *upekkha* is about, in the Mahayana traditions, is the wish that oneself and others become enlightened. This is the perspective I embrace here.

To practice upekkha is to move ourselves and all beings toward living as the Buddha lived, with unconditional love. It's to practice the bodhisattva ideal. Upatissa talked about unconditional love when he wrote:

The Bodhisatta and the Mahasatta develop loving-kindness for all beings. For the sake of benefitting all beings, they regard friends, indifferent ones and enemies, equally, without hatred and without attachment. Thus they fulfil the perfection of equanimity [upekkha-paramita].[124]

Notice how we begin with metta, cultivate the perspective that all beings are equally deserving of love, and eradicate hatred and attachment. That this eradication is complete, and not just a temporary state of non-judgment, is marked by the fact that it fulfills upekkha as a *paramita* or perfection – which indicates a virtue of enlightened beings. For Upatissa, upekkha was a bodhisattva practice.[125] The bodhisattva loves unconditionally, free of the biases of selfish craving and ill will, and wishes to guide all beings to awakening. This form of love also came to be known as *maha karuna* or awakened compassion.

This is the approach to upekkha that we'll be exploring, not just in meditation, but in daily life as well. If you've learned about upekkha as a brahma vihara before, my approach is probably different from what you were taught. I'm not saying I'm right – we don't know exactly what the Buddha taught – but many of my meditation students have found this perspective helpful. I suggest exploring it and seeing if it benefits you.

Exercise

I invite you to look, in your daily life, at all the ways your mind reacts to others with non-love: defensiveness, hostility, passive-aggressiveness, indifference, and so on. Notice that, when these things happen, there is always a sense that you are defending something. Next, ask yourself: *what, exactly, is it that I am defending?*

2

Wisdom in the service of love

Bhikkhu Bodhi explains that upekkha is not the cool indifference that it's often thought to be:

> *True [upekkha] is the pinnacle of the four social attitudes that the Buddhist texts call the "divine abodes": boundless loving-kindness, compassion, altruistic joy, and equanimity. The last does not override and negate the preceding three, but perfects and consummates them.*[126]

That, too, is how I see upekkha – not as a retreat into a personal state of peace, but as love's perfection and consummation. Upatissa, in *The Path of Freedom*, acknowledges this when he says, "Equanimity is the purification of loving-kindness, compassion, and appreciative joy, because through it hatred and lust are destroyed."[127] To achieve this, we cultivate wisdom. But what is wisdom?

In Buddhist terms, wisdom (Pali *panna*; Sanskrit *prajna*) is insight into the nature of reality. Specifically, we cultivate insight into three things:

1. We see that everything that has a beginning has an end. Everything is impermanent.

2. We see that nothing that is impermanent could possibly give us lasting peace and joy. Everything impermanent is unsatisfactory, or dukkha.
3. We see that nothing that is impermanent or unsatisfactory can be taken to be a self. So we stop trying to define ourselves, or cling to anything as being our self.[128]

There is a direct connection between wisdom and love. We experience clinging and ill will because we believe we exist as separate selves, inhabiting a world of other separate selves, which our own self naturally comes into conflict with. Clinging and ill will are obstacles to love. To undermine these obstacles to love, we have to see that everything is impermanent, that clinging to impermanent things is unsatisfactory or painful, and that there is no self at the center of this clinging anyway. Losing our belief in a self, and seeing clinging as fruitless, we no longer come into conflict with others. We are free instead to love them and have compassion for them.

Kindness, compassion, and appreciation help us to "unself" by widening the circle of our concern, so that we live in a less self-centered world, and also by lessening the craving and ill will that reinforce our sense of existing as separate selves.

In Buddhism, wisdom and love are not separate, but complementary. Love helps us have wisdom, and wisdom helps us love more fully. Traditionally, the love that emerges from insight is talked of as compassion, because, as we lose our sense of existing as an atomized self, bouncing around in a world full of other selves, we realize that the self-conceit we are abandoning is a source of suffering. And we recognize that, although we are becoming free of the burden of self, others are still trapped with the suffering it causes. We want them to be free, too. This is compassion. In fact it is maha karuna, the compassion of the enlightened.

This is what upekkha does. It helps us perfect and consummate the previous brahma viharas. It helps us to be more perfectly and unconditionally loving. This may sound very advanced, but in practice it's often simple. Consider, for example, what happened when we considered that all beings are impermanent. Typically, our self-centered resentments begin to drop away. We become more loving and appreciative. This is wisdom perfecting our capacity to love. Consider, too, what happens as we notice that our feelings are impermanent. Knowing that a feeling will naturally pass away, we are more likely to be patient with it, less likely to react with craving or ill will, and are able to be kind and compassionate instead. This too is wisdom perfecting our capacity to love. There are many ways in which wisdom can perfect our kindness, compassion, and appreciation. We will explore many such practices as we come to understand the practice of upekkha.

Upekkha is a practice of ever-deepening insight, accompanied by ever-deepening love. Its working ground is anything that holds us back from being loving. When we encounter obstacles to love – imperfections and failures in our kindness, compassion, and appreciation – we look deeper. We overcome those obstacles until eventually we root out craving, hatred, and delusion. Enlightenment happens, at which point there are no longer any barriers to love and we are able to love unconditionally, as bodhisattvas.

Exercise

In your daily life, catch yourself when you're not being loving, and observe what's going on. What inner barriers to love do you notice? What do you cling to that obstructs love? What aversions do you have that make it hard to be loving?

3

Will the real upekkha please stand up?

The word "upekkha" has several meanings in the early teachings, and this can cause confusion. Let's look at three types of upekkha, and see how they relate to each other.[129] All three can be understood in terms of "looking closely" – the etymological meaning of "upekkha." I've provided a diagram (on page 270) to help you understand how I see the relationship between the three.

1. When we explored the practice of self-compassion, we saw that we could observe our feelings, mindfully, and return from reactivity to calmness. Although I didn't mention the word "upekkha" at that time, that's what we were exploring. This form of upekkha is not the brahma vihara, although it may play a role in its practice. I'm going to call this "ordinary upekkha." It's the non-reactive calm that comes from mindfully observing pleasant, unpleasant, and neutral feelings.[130]
2. There is upekkha as a brahma vihara – Bhikkhu Bodhi's "perfection and consummation" of kindness, compassion, and appreciation. Despite our attempts to be loving, we inevitably find ourselves reacting to others and being unloving. To overcome this, we bring in wise perspectives to help us let go of our reactivity

Will the real upekkha please stand up?

and bias. For example, we might be profoundly irritated by someone, but in looking more closely – that is, practicing upekkha – we might consider that this person is only on this earth a short time, as are we. We lose interest in having aversion, and abandon it. The insight practice of seeing impermanence can liberate us from our ill will and allow us to arouse compassion.[131]

3. "Upekkha" is also a synonym for "enlightenment." It refers to the deep peace that is characteristic of the awakened mind. Awakening comes about when we have trained ourselves to closely observe the arising and passing of things, so that we see the nature of reality as thoroughly impermanent. Once we realize that nothing has any substantial reality, but is instead changing in every moment, we recognize that there is nothing to grasp onto or to have aversion for. We don't even see any self that can grasp or have aversion. We become disenchanted with grasping and aversion, seeing both as pointless, and in time the mind becomes completely free from greed, hate, and delusion. This is an unshakable level of peace. Enlightenment is a state of permanent love and compassion. It is not the brahma vihara of upekkha; it is the goal to which the brahma viharas lead.[132]

These three forms of upekkha are related. Ordinary upekkha helps us to still our reactivity so that we can cultivate kindness, compassion, and appreciation. Its aim is usually just to find calmness, but, if we practice it with the motivation to be more loving, it becomes part of upekkha as a brahma vihara.

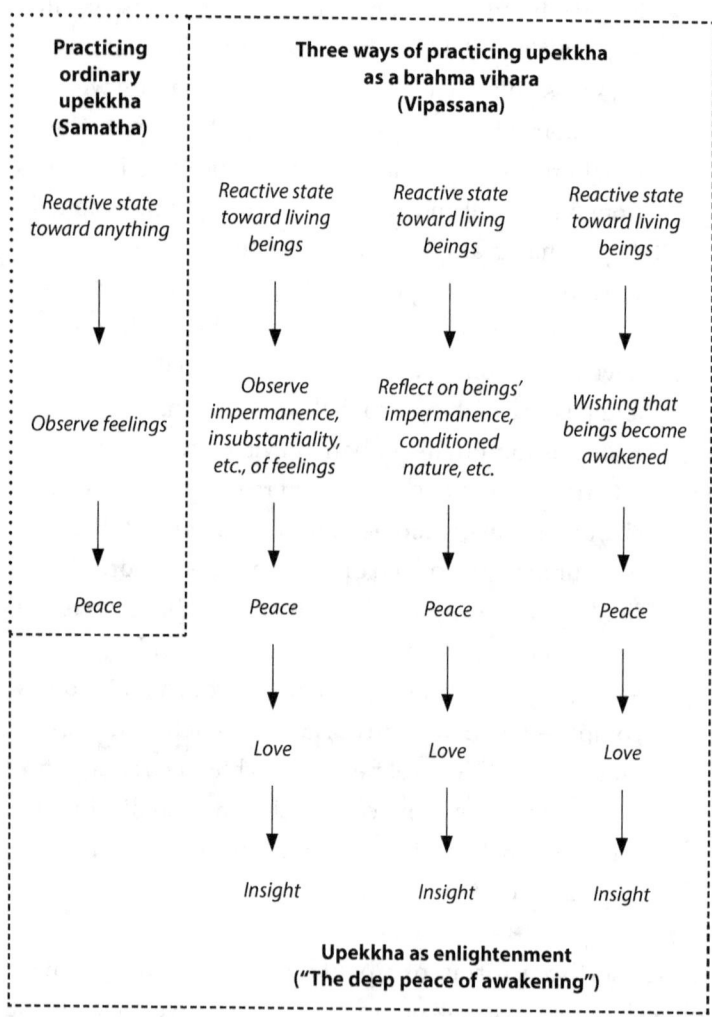

Types of upekkha

Upekkha as a brahma vihara involves cultivating insight, and enlightenment is the fullness of insight. So the practice of upekkha as a brahma vihara leads to the experience of upekkha as awakening. Enlightenment is also the perfection and consummation of love, compassion, and appreciation, so upekkha as a brahma vihara helps us move toward buddhahood in that way, too.

It's important to see how these forms of upekkha are different from each other. The ancient scholar-monks tended to lump them all in together. Since ordinary upekkha is a state of calm detachment from feelings, they assumed that the brahma vihara of upekkha was a state of calm detachment from beings, and they sometimes saw this as a state devoid of love. But the brahma vihara of upekkha is the deepest kind of love there is. It's what leads to the awakened love and compassion that the bodhisattvas and buddhas feel for all beings. That awakened love and compassion wants to lead others from delusion to awakening, from conflict to love. This is the culmination of the brahma viharas.

Exercise

In your daily life, and especially when you're thinking about or directly relating to others, keep noticing your feelings, and let this awareness bring you back to calm, and then to love.

4

Beginning in humility

Voltaire wrote, "We are all formed of frailty and error; let us reciprocally pardon each other's folly." This is a powerful teaching on forgiveness, and one that we should remember to turn upon ourselves as well as others. Our frailties and errors don't separate us from others; they show how we are just the same as them, and how we are connected to them.[133]

The Path of Freedom says that we begin the upekkha bhavana by recalling love's "severe trials."[134] This means that we should recall that it's hard to be loving, because our kindness, compassion, and appreciation often fail us, and we sometimes fall prey to their far or near enemies. So we begin the upekkha bhavana in a state of humility, recognizing our limitations and reactivity, knowing ourselves to be fallible, as all beings are. As best we can, we acknowledge these things with kindness and self-compassion, so that we don't become self-critical.

As we begin the first stage of the practice, I suggest the following:

Start with self-empathy and kindness

- Remind yourself that you are a feeling, suffering being. Recall that your feelings of peace, joy, and suffering are important to you.
- Remember you're doing a difficult thing in being human, and remind yourself that you want to be kind and compassionate.
- Share that kind and compassionate impulse with yourself. Regard yourself with kind eyes. Say things like, "I care about you, and I want you to be happy. I'm here for you."

Remember how love fails

- Now, call to mind a specific example of how you become reactive to others. This could be in the context of an intimate relationship, or the reactive feelings you have for a political figure. Recall this as vividly as possible.
- Notice any feelings that arise. Observe them. What shape do they have? Are they changing? Accept them as if they were any other sensation.
- Note any blaming, aversive, or angry thoughts that arise, and let go of them, coming back to being aware of your body and the feelings it contains.

Practice self-upekkha

- Offer yourself reassurance as you stay with your discomfort, by saying things like, "It's okay to feel this. We can do this. This is simply a moment of suffering. Let me be present with it. You're okay. It's just a sensation."
- As best you can, meet these uncomfortable feelings with kind eyes. Talk to them, saying, "May you be well. May you be at peace. I know this is painful, but I'm here for you. I love you and I want you to be happy."
- Remind yourself that you didn't choose to have reactive tendencies. This is just part of your conditioning.
- If you feel calmer and less reactive now, try bringing in the following upekkha phrases:
    - May I understand my own heart.
    - May I overcome attachment and aversion.
    - May I know the deep peace of awakening.
- Continue in this way for the remainder of your meditation session.

There are many ways to begin the first stage of the upekkha bhavana practice, and this is just one suggestion. It brings together ordinary upekkha as observing and accepting feelings. It includes upekkha as the desire to overcome obstacles to love. And it includes the aspiration to move toward the upekkha that is the deep peace of awakening.

Exercise

Set an intention to notice when your mind strays into unloving (cold, blaming, or hostile) ways of being. Whenever you find this happening, meet any painful feelings and reactive thoughts with kindness and understanding. Let this be your path back to love.

GUIDED MEDITATION: Self-upekkha

5

Give your feelings space

I'm driving into town, and for some reason I'm feeling down. Gloomy thoughts gather in my mind, like vultures with sharp talons, ready to tear into me. I realize that I need to take care not to slip into depression, so I become curious first of all about the feeling itself. It's like a weight pulling painfully on my heart. I notice its size, shape, and texture. Then I become curious about everything that is not that feeling – the space outside it. This space is filled by the sensations of the body, and of the world, in the form of colors, shapes, and sounds. It is open and expansive – vast compared to the feeling that was troubling me moments before. The feeling, which at first dominated my attention, is just one small part of a wider space. It's small, and no longer troubles me. Now, I'm at peace.

The Buddha said, "When you meditate like space, pleasant and unpleasant contacts will not occupy your mind."[135] Shunryu Suzuki expressed the same thing when he said, "To give your sheep or cow a large, spacious meadow is how to control him."[136] If you try to box in a wild animal, it will panic and try to escape. Give it space and it'll just stand around contentedly. It's like that with feelings, too. When our attention is like a small, restrictive cage, the mind becomes reactive. When our attention is more spacious, the mind calms down.

Letting the eyes be soft helps create this sense of space. As we've seen, we usually go through the world with our eyes tight and our attention like a spotlight. We pay attention to what's directly at the focal point of our visual field, ignoring everything else. And this tight, narrow way of paying attention is carried over into the way we observe things internally. With a narrow inner field of attention, we focus on one part of our experience at a time. A feeling, when we observe it with a narrow beam of attention, is akin to a stage actor picked out by a spotlight – it's intense and dramatic, and we have a heightened emotional response to it.

Imagine turning up the lights on the stage, revealing that the central actor is surrounded by other people, things, and action. The central actor is still there, but they have less impact so the drama is reduced. We do something similar internally by letting the eyes be soft and relaxed. This triggers a corresponding softness and openness in the way we pay attention inwardly. With soft eyes we can be aware of the whole body. Now just one part of a larger landscape, our feelings no longer dominate our attention, and we're less likely to react to them. We can accept whatever we're feeling. No longer reacting, the mind is calmer. This is ordinary equanimity.

In this state of equanimity, we experience pleasant and unpleasant feelings without, as the Buddha says, their occupying the mind. They still occupy space in your attention, but they no longer direct your thoughts and emotions. You can have a feeling of dislike for someone, and, instead of the mind going into overdrive, with thoughts about how awful this person is and how you'd like bad things to happen to them, you simply hold the unpleasant feeling that's at the core of the experience, allowing it space. The mind is freed from its normal reactivity. You're already kinder, simply because you are no longer having unkind thoughts and urges, as you normally would. You also have more freedom to awaken skillful – kind, compassionate, appreciative – thoughts and volitions. You can recognize that the feeling of dislike is painful, and surround it with kindness and empathy. You can extend that kindness and empathy to the person who has aroused your feelings of dislike. You have moved from reactivity to spaciousness, to equanimity, to love. This is the cultivation of upekkha as a brahma vihara – as a practice of love.

When obstacles to love arise within you, in the form of strong aversion or attraction, soften the eyes. Let your inner field of attention become open and expansive, so that you can observe your feelings as just part of a wider landscape. Let your feelings have space. Don't try to do anything with them. Just let them settle on their own. Then you'll find that your mind is calmer, and ready once more for love.

Exercise

In your meditations, sit with soft eyes and notice how this brings a sense of spaciousness into your experience. Call to mind situations in which you fail to be loving, and re-experience the painful feelings involved in them. See if experiencing the space around the feeling makes it easier to sit with, in a non-reactive state of equanimity.

6
No feeling is final

I remember times when I've felt miserable and have dreaded that I was going to remain stuck that way forever. This is something many people have been through. An unpleasant experience is bad enough, but the prospect of having one going on endlessly is hellish. Fortunately, any painful feeling you or I have ever had has ended. Despite knowing on a rational level that this always happens, our minds have a strange tendency to believe in the permanence of these transient experiences. This is another form of what the Buddha called a *vipallasa* (cognitive distortion), a word we've encountered before.[137] Specifically, this is the distortion of taking what's impermanent to be permanent, while the reality is that, in Rilke's words, "No feeling is final."[138]

I often practice recollecting the impermanence of feelings when I'm on social media. It sometimes happens that in these places I encounter material that's emotionally provocative, and even people who are rude and critical. Restraining the urge to retaliate is the best thing to do, but it can itself be painfully frustrating. What to do with that frustration? My wiser instincts remind me that the discomfort, if left alone, will pass in its own time. It's impermanent, and, once it's gone, the desire to retaliate will have gone, too, and I'll be at peace. I just have to ride it out.

But this isn't easy. I breathe with the discomfort. I keep reminding myself that retaliation will just create more suffering. I keep telling myself, "This will pass. No, really, it *will* pass." I notice the feeling and its accompanying urge coming and going, in waves. But, eventually, everything settles down. The next day, the feeling, if it is there at all, is a pale shadow. In time, I forget all about the provocation.

What I've described gets easier with repetition. Sometimes, as soon as you're provoked, you see the unpleasant feeling as impermanent, and no longer take it seriously. This takes away the feeling's power, and it quickly passes. Freed from the feeling, you're also freed from the need to react aggressively or defensively. You're calm, and you can shift more easily into an empathetic and kind way of relating to the other person. Other times it's more like a wrestling match with your reactive side.

Whether online or in other areas of your life, when you find that reactivity is creating a rift between you and others, remind yourself that your feelings and reactions are impermanent. Surf the urge to retaliate, and ride out your painful feelings until you find yourself once again at peace. Since the brahma viharas are loving practices, remind yourself that, just as you had suffered because of forgetting that feelings are impermanent, so are other people suffering, including those you have difficulty with. Extend your love to them. Wish them well: "May all beings accept the arising and passing of things."

No feeling is final

Exercise

Try reflecting on past strong feelings. Remind yourself that they are gone, like melted snow. It's especially helpful to do this when you're experiencing another round of similar feelings. Also notice in daily life how feelings come and go. Let that remind you that there is no compulsion to react to them.

7

Be creatively reductive

The Buddha used the word *samskara* (*sankhara* in Pali) to mean something like "a habitual pattern of thought, emotion, and action." It's formed from a prefix, *sam-*, meaning "together," and a verb root *kr*, meaning "make," "do," or "create."[139] Our samskaric pathways are triggered by feelings. For example, faced with uncertainty we might have a feeling of anxiety, then the mind starts worrying – gaming out all the things that could go wrong and trying to come up with potential solutions. All this second-arrow catastrophizing we do makes us feel worse. Attempting to ease the distress of all this, we might take out our frustrations on someone else. By repeatedly following that pathway – uncertainty-anxiety-worry-attack – we cement these components together, forming an established habit. The stronger these habits become, the less freedom we have to prevent them.

Many different feelings can trigger samskaras, including anxiety, shame, joy, boredom, sadness, disgust, loneliness, hurt, warmth, open-heartedness, frustration, grief, indignation, a heavy heart, heartbreak, heartache, anticipation, disappointment, butterflies in the tummy, feeling "gutted," and embarrassment, to mention just some that we have names for. And the number of emotional and behavioral pathways we create is almost infinite. You might think we'd therefore need an enormous array of techniques to address these feelings and the many kinds of reactive habits that spring from them, but the Buddha's teachings offer a way to radically simplify things. Whatever the unpleasant feeling is that's present, and whatever samskaric pattern springs from it, we simply acknowledge that the feeling is unpleasant.

"But I'm so worried, because this might happen or that might happen, and what will I do if..."

Observe: an unpleasant feeling is present.

"But I made a mistake and I'm embarrassed and ashamed, and all these people are judging me and..."

Just look: an unpleasant feeling is present.

"I'm so frustrated because I keep trying and trying to make this thing happen in my life and it seems like..."

Just notice: an unpleasant feeling is present.

This simple observation disrupts the samskaric flow. Our mind's energy and attention are now drawn away from the usual patterns of thought and action that would normally follow on from a particular feeling. Noticing – as a simple fact, not as a sign something is wrong – "an unpleasant feeling is present" disrupts our storytelling. It takes us out of imagined futures, and back into the present moment, where we address the obvious yet usually ignored fact that we're in pain. And what does pain need? It needs acceptance and compassion.

As, in the first stage of the upekkha bhavana, you recall the difficulties of being kind, compassionate, and appreciative, as you recall the "severe trials" and challenges of being loving, notice, "An unpleasant feeling is present." Whatever it is, simply experience it. Let it be present. Offer compassion to the part of you that is suffering, because that's how we respond skillfully to suffering. And the situation that provoked the unpleasant feeling response in the first place? Well, you are free to deal with that as a practical problem – if it even needs to be dealt with at all – with clarity and wisdom, because those qualities become available when you've become mindful and compassionate.

The Buddha's approach to feelings is reductive in that it simplifies complex situations: our feelings are pleasant, unpleasant, or neutral. It's a helpful simplification. But it's *creatively* reductive. We've chosen not to take a feeling as a sign that we must react toward others in a particular way, or at all. And so we can feel the feeling, whatever it may be, be free from reactive habits, and give ourselves permission to be loving.

Exercise

Keep observing feelings, and simply notice them as pleasant, unpleasant, or neutral. Although I talked about unpleasant feelings above, pleasant and neutral feelings can also trigger reactive patterns. Notice how labelling their "hedonic tone" begins to free you from reactivity.

8

Seeing feelings as non-self

The Buddha said that we become emotionally reactive because we are "yoked" (*sannutta*) to our feelings.[140] When we react to other people with anger, hatred, or contempt, we don't experience separation between ourselves and the feelings we experience. We are so identified with our feelings that, when they go one way, so do we. Seeing feelings as *not being part of us* can allow us to move from conflict to peace, and thence to love.

Imagine a blue sky. In it appears a single, white cloud. Watching the cloud carefully, you see that it's constantly changing. Even if the shape stays roughly the same, it is dissolving in some places and materializing in others. After a time, the cloud dissolves completely, and we are left once more with a clear blue expanse. Now, let's ask the question, "Was the cloud intrinsically part of the sky?"

Of course it wasn't. The sky was there before the cloud appeared, and remained after the cloud had gone. The cloud was just passing through. It's just the same with our feelings. They appear when conditions are right. They change moment by moment while they exist. Eventually, they pass away. Yet *your being* remains. The feeling was never intrinsically a part of you. It was just a temporary phenomenon that you experienced as it went from one state of non-existence to another.

Feelings are not consciously created. They come from ancient parts of the mind that are inaccessible to conscious awareness. We don't make them; we receive them. You can observe this for yourself: you feel feelings in the same way as you hear sounds: they are delivered to you. You can't will them out of existence. You can't simply dispel depression or anxiety by saying, "Begone, unwanted feeling!" How can something that you simply receive, and can't control, be "you"? As the Buddha said:

> *Feeling is not-self. For if feeling were self, it wouldn't lead to affliction. And you could compel feeling: "May my feeling be like this! May it not be like that!" But because feeling is not-self, it leads to affliction. And you can't compel feeling: "May my feeling be like this! May it not be like that!"*[141]

Feelings being as insubstantial as clouds, there is nothing there for us to hold on to. We can call them *our* feelings, but we can never possess them. How can something we can never hold on to be us or ours? Nothing that's that ephemeral could be the basis of a separate self.

Talking or reading about all this is one thing. Maybe it's puzzling. Maybe it's frustrating. Maybe it gives rise to feelings of resistance. The thing to remember is that I'm talking about a practice, not an intellectual exercise. The point is to observe, not to think about it. Notice feelings coming-into-being and going-out-of-being. Notice how you do not choose them; they just arrive. Notice how you can step into the role of not simply feeling your feelings, but also observing them. The act of observation that stands between observer and observed is the space separating your feelings from your sense of self. To notice this gap is to unyoke yourself. It's to become emotionally freed.

Unyoked from feelings, notice how you do not have to go in

Seeing feelings as non-self

the direction they are trying to take you. An unpleasant feeling need not trigger aversion, nor a pleasant feeling craving or grasping. You can let your feelings be your feelings – and be free. And as you observe feelings you can remind yourself, as the Buddha advised many times, "This is not mine, I am not this, this is not my self."[142]

As we keep observing, we start to recognize our feelings as not ours, not us, not who we are, and we're a step closer to awakening, a step closer to dismantling this burden that is our belief in a separate and unchanging self. We can disentangle ourselves from the anger, hatred, resentment, and contempt that cause our love to fail. We can return to loving, and, as we do so, we can realize that others, caught up in delusion, are yoked to their own feelings, and we can desire that they also become free.

Exercise

What did you read here that resonates with you? What intrigues you? What puzzles you? What annoys you?

9

Feelings are physiological

There is no term in Pali for "hangry" – a portmanteau word combining "hungry" and "angry" – and yet no discussion of feelings would be complete without mention of this important topic. In my twenties I was prone to being hangry. My girlfriend and I would often head out to a market area in Glasgow called the Barras and browse the stalls. It wasn't a place noted for its healthy food, and usually we'd have coffee and a donut to sustain us. The combination of exercise, caffeine, and sugar wreaked havoc on my system. Everything began to annoy me. We'd bicker with each other. Strangers became infuriating, walking too slowly and always getting in my way.

Low blood sugar heightens unpleasant feelings – makes them arise when they otherwise wouldn't – and this makes us reactive. Other physiological events have their own emotional effects. Exhaustion can make us irritable, despondent, or depressed. Overwhelm can cause irritability, anxiety, or despair. It's helpful to recognize the signs of these physiological imbalances. Not only can this prompt us to take care of our body's needs, but it can also help us to drop our reactivity. As I've often noted to myself, "Ah! It's not that the world's become an awful place, full of terrible people. It's just that I'm hungry." Even before we've had a chance to eat or rest, simply understanding what's really going on can help us come back to a calmer state, and to be more empathetic, kinder, and more compassionate toward others.

Feelings are conditioned by our physiological states, but are also themselves physiological. They are sensations that take place in the body, through the action of sensory receptors. These signals are picked up by the vagus nerve, which has been described as the body's "information superhighway," running from every major organ directly into the brain. When your physiology is out of balance, the vagus relays unpleasant feelings to the brain. The brain treats these signals as a sign that something is wrong, activating its emotional defense mechanisms.

Feelings are physiological in that any sensation is the result of thousands of nerve endings repeatedly firing and resting. If, in a relaxed and mindful state, you bring awareness to a feeling, it no longer seems to be a solid object within the body. Instead, it is revealed as a pattern of sensation, translucent and twinkling, suspended in the three-dimensional matrix of the body. If we look closely enough at painful feelings, we see tingling, pressure, heat, cold, weight, movement, pulsing, and so on. Sometimes we see there is no pain there. There's nothing to react to – just a play of appearances, an ever-changing, insubstantial constellation of pinpoints of energy, suspended in space, rapidly winking in and out of existence.

Bringing in an altruistic perspective, we can remember that others, too, are physiological beings. When we see them getting irritable or despondent, we can recognize that this isn't something that they're doing to annoy us, personally. It's that their own physiological systems are out of balance, and so their emotions are too. When we can see this, we're less likely to react to them with our own irritability or defensiveness, and can instead offer them compassion.

Exercise

Which physiological changes have the biggest effect on your feelings? Try recognizing what's going on, and see if this helps to free you from reactivity.

10
To see equality in all beings

Both *The Path of Freedom* and *The Path of Purification* agree that the brahma vihara of upekkha involves seeing that all beings are equal.[143] Both emphasize having an attitude of neutrality toward all. To understand this, we need to bear in mind that being neutral is not the same as not caring. Neutrality means not taking sides. A neutral arbiter in a dispute, for example, needs to care about the well-being of the parties they're working with. In the context of the brahma viharas, equality means not being swayed by liking and disliking, so we can be kind and compassionate without bias. Neutrality, seeing beings as equal, and unconditional love are three different ways of saying the same thing.

Liking and disliking distort our ability to recognize that all beings are equally worthy of love and compassion. These biases start with the feelings we've been discussing so extensively. When we have pleasant feelings toward someone, we assume they are more deserving of kindness. We want to reward them for making us feel good. This, of course, isn't love at all. The reverse is also the case: my meditation students often say things like, "Why does a person who's done bad things deserve my kindness and compassion?" or "I find self-metta hard, so I just skip that stage." Those biases are rooted in our having unpleasant feelings toward certain beings. We assume that how we feel about someone determines their worth as a human being. We punish those who evoke unpleasant feelings by withholding love – even though our feelings are *our* creation.

Now, we might well be biased against a so-called "neutral person." We might find them boring and think them unworthy of our consideration. But at least when we try to wish them well we're not fighting against the bias caused by strong likes and dislikes. This is why, in the upekkha bhavana practice, we take the "neutral person" as our starting point for considering other beings.

The most fundamental thing that we all have in common is our potential for awakening. Shortly after his enlightenment, the Buddha looked around the world with the eyes of compassion and saw all beings as like lotus flowers growing in a pond: some were almost fully open; some were closed, but above the water; others were still submerged in the mud. All were at different stages, but all were capable of fully blooming.[144] This is what they had in common. This is how they are equal. We too can learn to see that all beings have the same potential for enlightenment.

C.S. Lewis wrote,

It is a serious thing to live in a society of possible gods and goddesses, to remember that the dullest and most uninteresting person you talk to may one day be a creature which, if you saw it now, you would be strongly tempted to worship.[145]

Cultivating upekkha for a relative stranger, seeing their potential buddhahood, might then mean something akin to reverence. Can we see our relative stranger as a buddha-to-be?

To see equality in all beings

Can we let our attention be like the sunlight falling on lotus flowers, encouraging them to open? Can we feel a desire to nurture beings' unfolding?

Whoever we've called to mind in this stage of the practice, as well as having the potential for buddhahood, also shares the same obstacles to enlightenment as any other being. And so we can wish:

- May you accept the arising and passing of things.
- May you abide in equanimity, free from attachment or aversion.
- May you know the deep peace of awakening.

These wishes are all expressions of upekkha. Accepting the arising and passing of things without reacting is upekkha. Being free from attachment and aversion is upekkha. The deep peace of awakening is upekkha. Wishing these things for ourselves and others is to cultivate upekkha as a loving, even reverential, quality. We are looking beneath the superficial differences between beings, looking past the feelings we have toward them, and are instead focusing on what's most essential to them: their capacity for awakening.

We might go a step further: a common trope in Buddhist teachings is the saint who appears as an ordinary person, and even as a miserable beggar. They may act in ways that seem very un-buddha-like. And yet this is a teaching: part of their skillful means. When you call to mind a relative stranger, try adopting the perspective that they have already attained buddhahood. Regard them with reverence.

Exercise

As you go through life and encounter others, try bearing in mind a phrase such as, "I recognize the potential buddhahood in you. May you swiftly find awakening!"

GUIDED MEDITATION: Upekkha for a stranger

11

Take the first step in faith

Many years ago, when I was visiting an old friend in Colorado, he and his wife took me rock climbing. Early in the morning we bundled our gear into their brown Isuzu Trooper and headed to the hills. At the cliff face, Clive and Julie stood below, yelling encouragement and advice as I inched higher. Being a novice, and not good with heights, I was terrified. "Don't look down," they said. Coincidentally, that was the last place I wanted to look. Even keeping my eyes fixed on the rock in front of and above me, my breathing was tight, my mouth was dry, and my heart was racing.

And then I got stuck. I couldn't see any way to continue. The rock above me was smooth, devoid of handholds. The longer I stayed there, my trembling toes improbably gripping tiny nubbins of stone, my aching fingers clinging to a barely discernible ripple in the rock, the shakier my legs became. Staying still wasn't an option, but I couldn't climb any higher. I began to panic. Then I realized that, although I couldn't go up, I could go sideways, just a few inches. It seemed utterly pointless, but it was my only option, so I did it. And, although my position barely changed, from this new perspective everything looked different. I could now see a handhold above me. It was small, but it was there. I reached for it and was able to move one step higher. And from there, I could move higher still. Paradoxically, my anxiety made me keen to get to the top of the cliff as quickly as possible, just so that I could put the experience behind me. Clive said afterward that I shot up the rest of the way "like a rat up a drainpipe."

Upekkha bhavana involves taking a step toward the unknown. It means aiming to move toward enlightenment. But enlightenment is something we haven't experienced for ourselves. We might struggle to understand what it is, doubt it exists, or even have serious reservations about whether it's desirable. We might not be sure how to get there, or whether we're equipped to do so.

I remember having fears that enlightenment meant "giving up attachments," and that sounded miserable, because it meant giving up pleasure. But you don't have to give up pleasure to be enlightened. You can still enjoy chocolate, for example. In fact, you'd enjoy it even more than you do now. Imagine really savoring every crumb of chocolate, each one like the first time you'd ever tasted it, fully alive to every atom of sensation. And imagine being so satisfied with that experience that you didn't then gobble down the entire bar and feel gross afterward. The only thing you're giving up is what stops you living joyfully.

I don't know exactly what enlightenment is, but I know what it's like to suffer, and I know what it's like to regret making others suffer because of my unskillfulness. I'm tired of being stuck with reactive tendencies I don't remember asking to have. If enlightenment is freedom from those things, then it's something I desire, even if I don't exactly understand it. Similarly, I care for others. I know that they're just like me, and that they too suffer and cause others to suffer, and for the most part they don't want those things to happen. So that means that I want them to be enlightened too.

Take the first step in faith

Martin Luther King, Jr. said: "Take the first step in faith. You don't have to see the whole staircase, just take the first step."[146] Even though we don't know where we're going, we keep moving toward it, step by step. We encounter obstacles to love, and look closely until we find a way around them. We learn to see feelings as sensations like any other, or even as empty clouds of energy, and we stop reacting to them. We look for the self that reacts and clings, and find it's not there. Step by step, we get closer to life where we have compassion for all.

Exercise

I suggest reflecting on what goal you have for spiritual practice. Is it enlightenment? Is it something else? Are you not clear?

12

Not caring: The near enemy of upekkha

Do you remember how shocking it was, in 2019, to hear that Notre-Dame cathedral was on fire? I'm sure you do. But what do you remember of the fire that devastated the National Museum of Rio de Janeiro just the year before? Do you remember anything? If so, what emotional impact did it have? The museum – the largest on the entire continent – was 200 years old, and its collection of 200 million items was almost entirely destroyed. This fire was a major cultural catastrophe, not identical to but at least in the same league as the Paris conflagration. Yet it didn't strike most of us as deeply as the tragedy in Paris. (Your perspective will of course be different if you're Brazilian or have strong connections with Brazil. We care more about things that are familiar to us, which is the theme of this chapter.)

Sometimes we feel nothing. We don't care, even when we should. So this is what upekkha's near enemy is. Our love fails, not because we're full of anger, hatred, resentment, or contempt, but because our empathy is turned off. What makes this a near enemy of upekkha is that we can think of not caring as being a spiritual state of "non-attachment." This ersatz upekkha allows us to bypass the messy business of caring. It absolves us of having to do anything. It allows us to rest comfortably in complacency – and to consider ourselves more

Not caring: The near enemy of upekkha

spiritually advanced than those poor deluded people who are touched by the joys and sorrows of others.

Of all the ways we can live our lives, the Buddha said, practicing for the benefit of both ourselves and others is the "foremost, best, chief, highest, and finest."[147] This is the ideal life. He wasn't attached – in the sense, for example, that he helped others without expectation of reward – but he also wasn't *detached*. He cared. He had compassion. He spent his entire life working for the benefit of others.

Selective not caring is part of the human condition. Empathy did not evolve so that we could love all beings. It evolved so that we would care about the well-being of those we were relatively close to. We lived in tribal groups, and everyone we knew was "Paris" – that is, related to us and known to us. Everyone else was "Rio de Janeiro," their sufferings far less important, and perhaps not important at all.

Dr. Helen Riess of Harvard Medical School wrote,

Individuals tend to have the most empathy for others who look or act like them, for others who have suffered in a similar way, or for those who share a common goal. We see these biases play out repeatedly in communities, schools, sports teams, and religious communities.[148]

We see those same biases in our own minds. If we hear that someone who lives on our street has been a victim of a crime, we'll have a strong emotional reaction. If they're in the next town over, our response will be more muted. Perhaps counterintuitively, the greater the number of people suffering, the less we care. Charities tell us about one hungry child rather than a thousand, because they know that one child's suffering moves us, while many children suffering is merely unwelcome information – a cold statistic.

Biases like these are inherent in the human mind. They are part of the tribal empathy we inherit, that says, "People are more worthy the more they are like you." Part of the function of upekkha is to override this biased empathy with a more intelligent yet still compassionate form of caring. When we have intelligent empathy, we are still touched more directly by the single child, but, hearing about many hungry children, we want to help because we know it's the right thing to do. We may not have the same gut reaction as to the single child, but we know it's important to give. This is a less sentimental and more considered form of empathy. It's still an emotional response, but it's a more intelligent one.

Part of our upekkha practice can be to learn to care about not caring, so that we work to overcome the biases that inhibit our compassion. We depend less on gut responses, which are invariably biased, and use our intelligence to stir the heart to action, knowing that many suffering children requires even more of a response than the one.

These are things to bear in mind as we cultivate upekkha for a neutral person. To dispel any tendency to not care, remember that this person, like you and everyone else, wants to be happy and well, and has the potential to become awakened, yet their mind is afflicted by greed, hatred, and delusion. Can we reverently recognize their potential, and wish them well in overcoming obstacles to peace, joy, and unconditional love of enlightenment?

Not caring: The near enemy of upekkha

Exercise

Notice, when you're reading, listening, or watching the news, when you start to disengage emotionally. Notice what is given more attention in the news, and what they barely mention.

13

Biased empathy

On Mastodon, the only social media site I use, I follow the Auschwitz Memorial project, which educates the public about the horrors of the infamous Nazi concentration and extermination camp in occupied Poland. It's a touching read. More than 1.1 million men, women, and children lost their lives in Auschwitz, but the memorial project focuses less on incomprehensible statistics and more on the individual human beings who stand behind them. Sometimes these people were murdered or died of sickness and starvation, and sometimes the cause of death is not known. A very small number survived or escaped.

Here are four typical entries, including the camp victims' photographs and the brief comments the project shared. I ask you to read them carefully, to look at the photographs, and to note your responses.

Feliks

20 May 1885 | A Polish man, Feliks Guliński, was born in Gostyn Wielkopolski. A soldier. In Auschwitz from 14 May 1942. No. 35434. He perished in the camp on 24 July 1942.

Chana

3 June 1864 | Polish Jewish woman, Chana Klos, was born in Pultusk. She emigrated to Belgium and lived in Antwerp. She was deported to Auschwitz from [Kazerne Dossin] in Mechelen on 10 October 1942. She was murdered in a gas chamber after arrival selection.

The Heart's Awakening

Henri

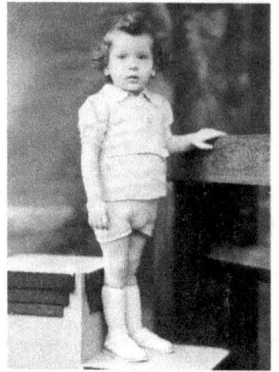

14 May 1940 | A French Jewish boy, Henri Latowicz, was born in Paris. He arrived at Auschwitz on 11 February 1943 in a transport of 1,000 Jews deported from Drancy. He was among 832 of them murdered in gas chambers after the selection.

Sura

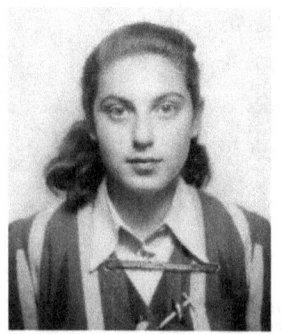

15 June 1925 | Polish Jewish girl, Sura (Sarah) Brombart, was born in Blaszki. She was deported to Auschwitz from Kazerne Dossin in Mechelen on 11 August 1942. She did not survive.

Biased empathy

* * *

As you read these stories, did any of the deaths affect you more than others? If so, can you say why?

Perhaps the fact that Henri was just a toddler was particularly moving. Maybe Sura being eighteen, and beautiful, and being deprived of the chance to lead her adult life just as it was beginning, was especially poignant. Maybe there's some other connection: you know Paris or Antwerp, or have Polish ancestry. Maybe you know someone with a similar name, or they remind you of someone.

The young children particularly get me, which is a common response. Our species is biologically programmed to be more protective of the young. As I read the accounts of children and babies who were killed in the camp, I think, "How could anyone do that to a child!" Then I remind myself, "How could anyone do that to *any* human being?"

My heart responds more strongly to young women, like Sura, on the verge of adulthood. This is another common emotional bias. Without wanting to ignore the realities of misogyny, sexual violence, and enforced (and stultifying) gender roles, our species is, on the whole, protective of young females. From an evolutionary perspective, females who have reached the age where they are capable of bearing young are hard to replace, and hence precious.

Attractiveness is another well-documented cause of bias. Good-looking people are more likely to get job interviews and promotions, and tend to be paid more. Fundraising campaigns often feature attractive people because we respond more.

Race matters. A young woman who has vanished is more likely to get extensive press coverage if she is white and blonde. One study in Canada found that missing white women got *twenty-seven times* the news coverage of missing Indigenous women, and that, while the reporting on missing Indigenous women was cooly factual, that on white women was more emotive. We're told by the media almost daily who matters and who doesn't, who we should care about, and who we should feel little or nothing for.

To be human is to have biases. We don't need to beat ourselves up over having them. But, if we're to practice upekkha, we need to become more aware of those biases and try to counteract them. We need to remind ourselves that every individual matters. Recognizing and overcoming our evolutionarily and culturally conditioned biases is not traditionally part of the teaching of upekkha, but I think it's a valuable area for us to explore. I suggest taking that into account while calling to mind a neutral person, and stretching your attention to include those who might normally be excluded by your mind's biases.

Exercise

In daily life, when meeting people, reading about them, seeing them on TV, and so on, ask yourself whether you might care more or less if this person had a different appearance, age, sex, race, and so on. Judging yourself is unhelpful. But see if you can look deeper, to find the underlying humanity of each person.

14

False equanimity

Sometimes people misuse the teaching that we are responsible for our own actions to avoid taking ethical responsibility. I've encountered Dharma practitioners who seem to take a quiet satisfaction in hurting people's feelings. They might, for example, make sweeping generalizations and judgments, and when people get upset they say, a little smugly, "Well, I'm just telling the truth. It's up to you whether you get upset or not." And they do this repeatedly. Their viewpoint seems to be, "If I didn't intend to hurt you, then getting hurt is your fault." The scriptures describe an occasion when the Buddha accused Ananda, his attendant, of false equanimity (*ajjhupekkhati*) when he failed to come to the defense of a senior disciple who was being verbally abused. Perhaps Ananda's perspective was, "If you get hurt, that's up to you."[149]

As we've seen, the Buddha explained to his son, Rahula, that we need to look not just at our intentions, but also at the results of our actions. We should ask whether our actions have resulted in ourselves or others being hurt, or allowed them to get hurt, and, if so, consider that we might have acted unskillfully. We need to do this because we aren't always clear about our intentions. Just because we tell ourselves that we are pure doesn't mean that we are.

There are many times I've hurt people's feelings, and only became aware of it because they told me. Sometimes I don't like this being pointed out, but increasingly I'm grateful that they've pointed out some kind of insensitivity on my part. I didn't have the conscious intention to cause hurt, but my words might have been careless and insensitive. Without the help of others, we would have great difficulty in uncovering our unacknowledged unskillful intentions. When we cause offense, especially if it happens repeatedly, we should examine our intentions. *Am I enjoying doing this? Is it giving me a sense of superiority? Can I learn from the feedback I'm getting and communicate more skillfully in future?* This is not the same as asking, "Am I a bad person?" It's a normal part of our conditioning that we want to see ourselves as good, and that we avoid seeing anything that contradicts that view.

Another way to practice false equanimity in order to avoid the challenge of responding compassionately is to misuse the teaching of karma. Karma is about how the way we act determines whether we'll create more suffering for ourselves, or whether we'll free ourselves from suffering. The Buddha never taught that everything that happens to us is the result of our own actions. In fact, he specifically said that was not the case.[150] Yet some Buddhists will look at people suffering and mistakenly think that they are absolved of any responsibility to act. They sometimes even say that they'd be interfering in someone else's karma if they relieved suffering.

People do similar things with teachings like emptiness and non-self: "Suffering is just an illusion... the self doesn't exist, so there's no one there to suffer." The mind can be remarkably creative when it comes to avoiding taking responsibility. A large part of the practice of upekkha is turning that creativity to good use – removing obstacles to love rather than constructing them.

False equanimity

Exercise

Notice when someone needs support. Sometimes we see people being attacked on social media and say nothing. We may hear someone being disparaged by others, and stay silent. Don't practice false equanimity. Don't walk by. Say something supportive.

15

Contempt: The far enemy of upekkha

A friend told me about a workshop that took place about a month after the UK's referendum on whether to leave or remain in the European Union. This was a Buddhist event, and, due to the emotional turmoil many were feeling, the workshop was packed. The ground rules included not debating each other, listening with empathy, and imaginatively identifying with others whose views and experience were different from their own. The participants, as an act of empathy, were asked to speak from the viewpoint of someone such as an EU citizen resident in Britain, a Remain journalist, or a working-class Leave voter. Some people who did this exercise couldn't stop themselves from mocking and parodying Leave voters, and others couldn't stop laughing at their performances. This was not what the workshop organizers had intended. Similarly, a Buddhist writer commenting on an article Stephen Batchelor[151] wrote, in which he articulated his deep grief at waking up in a country he no longer recognized, seemed to mock Batchelor's feelings of hurt and disorientation. I would describe the attitudes behind those actions as "contempt," which is an attitude of disgust and superiority. Contempt is *patigha*, which the Pali dictionary translates as "repulsion" or "repugnance."

Contempt often arises when others act in conflict with our most sacred values. If, for example, we consider fairness and

Contempt: The far enemy of upekkha

compassion as the central values in a truly human life, we won't perceive people we believe to violate those values as truly human. We will therefore not treat them with respect. If we see patriotism and self-determination as sacred values that give life meaning and dignity, we'll despise those who appear to ignore them. Contempt, as an attitude of superiority, is the opposite of seeing the equality of all beings, and it's one of the most damaging forms of ill will.

With apologies to Baudelaire, the greatest trick Mara ever pulled was convincing us that those we have contempt for *deserve* to be despised. Contempt fools us into not recognizing it as hatred. It's such a strong emotion that it throws us off balance and shuts down our mindfulness. This isn't helped by our tendency to isolate ourselves from opposing views by immersing ourselves in "information bubbles" where we're surrounded by others with similar views to ours. Within our bubbles, we congratulate each other on how good we are, while collectively denigrating the opposing side. Everyone agrees they are awful, and so our contempt goes unrecognized. (On the other side, in their own information bubbles, "they" are saying the same things about us.)

One way to overcome contempt is to see that all beings are equal in that they are all conditioned. When considering this, I like to bear in mind a quote by Eckhart Tolle: "If her past were your past, her pain your pain, her level of consciousness your level of consciousness, you would think and act exactly as she does."[152] Imagine growing up surrounded by views that are the opposite of those you have now. Imagine having constant reinforcement that those views are right and normal, and that the opposite views (those like the ones you hold, reader) are harmful and laughable. Imagine growing up with those you currently hate as your heroes, and those you currently admire as your enemy. You would, all other things being equal, be just like those you currently look down on as evil or stupid.

Often, when I ask people to do this empathetic exercise, they can't quite bring themselves to do it. They imagine themselves not as *being* the other person, but as *being inside* the other person. They wear the enemy as a costume, with their current self inside, its values and ways of thinking intact. And so they imagine themselves making different choices. But that's not the exercise. If you had the other person's genes, environment, and inner resources, you would be just like them.

I'm not arguing that our lives are entirely predetermined by our conditioning. But in some cases it's not far off that. Often the catalyst for change in our lives is not our innate capacity for breaking out of the views we've been conditioned to hold, but a chance encounter with someone we can learn from, because not only do they have different and more liberating views, but they have the empathy to listen without judgment, and the communication skills to offer us a different way of seeing.[153]

Reflecting this way – that is, practicing upekkha in the sense of looking deeply – can help us to let go of our contempt so that we can have a more balanced, equanimous state of mind. And from there we can cultivate greater kindness, compassion, and appreciation.

* * *

Contempt: The far enemy of upekkha

When we're cultivating upekkha for someone we clash with, it helps to remember that they are conditioned beings. To a large extent they are not free, but simply rehashing old scripts they have learned. Remember that they believe they are free, just as you believe you are free, and that you too are mainly working from old scripts you've learned.

Bearing them in mind, we can wish:

- May you accept the arising and passing of things.
- May you abide in equanimity, free from attachment or aversion.
- May you know the deep peace of awakening.

We can practice self-upekkha as we notice the arising of painful feelings that might normally lead to anger or resentment. We can accept these feelings, seeing them as impermanent, insubstantial, and non-self. And this makes it easier for us to be loving to this person we struggle to love.

Exercise

Try putting yourself in the shoes of a person you have contempt for. If necessary, find out more about them. Imagine having their limitations and their conditioning. Imagine seeing things the way they do. Make sure you're not imagining being yourself, hidden inside them. Does this change how you feel about them?

GUIDED MEDITATION: Upekkha for a difficult relationship

16

Accepting our limits

We can feel a sense of helplessness and despair when we compare the magnitude of the world's problems with our meager individual capabilities. Right now, for example, I'm very concerned about the micro- and nano-plastics that are building up in the soil, in the oceans, and in our bodies. I try to recycle as much plastic as possible, but I've no control over where it goes, and much of it is likely to end up contaminating the environment. I've got rid of all my plastic containers and reduced the amount of plastic I buy, but so many things are packaged in it that it seems like I'm set up to fail. Besides, others' use of plastic is growing, not diminishing, and what I can achieve on my own is insignificant.

When I start to feel despair about the state of the world and my inability to change it, I keep reminding myself that I can only do what I can do. I also remind myself not to become angry and frustrated with people who haven't yet recognized a problem I only became aware of myself five minutes ago. There is no room for feelings of superiority in the bodhisattva way of life.

Connected with this, traditional teachings on upekkha encourage us to reflect that others are the owners of their own actions. This is not an invitation to abandon being helpful, but an invitation to let go of clinging both to outcomes and to blame. Buddhaghosa talks about this when he says, "Through equanimity [great beings] expect no reward."[154] Others have their own lives and make their own decisions, and, although we can want what is best for them, we can't control them or choose their outcomes. We do what we can, and then let go of expectations.

In some cases there is nothing whatsoever we can do except let go. One woman told me she felt trapped in a double bind when she cultivated compassion for wild creatures. To wish a spider well means hoping that it will catch flies. To wish flies well means hoping they won't be eaten by spiders. Sometimes we cling to the desire to fix everything and to prevent all suffering, which is clearly impossible. Wild creatures cannot go without killing or being killed, and our compassion for bugs can be better expressed by not harming them. We can catch them when they come into our houses and set them free outside, but the moment we release the creepy-crawly we release ourselves from being responsible for them.

If you're caught up in wanting to fix everything, I advise that you say something to yourself like, "Dear Universe: with immediate effect I hereby tender my resignation as World Savior." I suggest you refocus your mind instead on the task of doing whatever you can do, however imperfectly you do it. When it comes to relieving suffering, bring kindness and compassion into your small part of the world. Agonizing over not being able to do the impossible is just another manifestation of the second arrow. It's a failure of love and compassion. It's a waste of energy. It's not a good way to spend this precious human birth.

At the same time, consider that you might be underestimating what's possible. Swedish activist Kata Nylén gives the following advice regarding climate action: "Act together.

Whatever you choose [...] do it together with others. It is the only way to create rapid change."[155] Joining or supporting existing organizations will help you feel better. Trying to move a large rock alone, you feel impotent. Putting your shoulder to the wheel with others, you feel you're making a contribution to an important task. Mostly, though, our principal work will likely remain close to home, with our immediate family, our friends, and our spiritual and secular communities.

There are some who have the vision and skills to found organizations that create large-scale change. If you can do that, great! But even those who have those talents – those who bring drinking water to thousands, or vaccinate millions against infectious diseases – must live knowing that the work they're doing only tackles a small part of the problems the world faces. Even the heroes of global good works need to practice equanimity, recognizing that they can only do what they can do. "I can only do so much" can be either a self-flagellating complaint or a declaration of wisdom, depending on how it's used.

Exercise

If you feel that it's your job description to be World Savior, ask who gave you that job description. What would be involved in resigning this post, and finding a way to balance compassion with self-compassion? If, reading this, you thought that perhaps your life errs too much on the side of complacency, how might you stretch yourself more?

17

Upekkha's other far enemy

According to Buddhaghosa there are two far enemies of upekkha. The first, which we've already looked at, is contempt. The second is greed, or *raga*, which is a spectrum of grasping attitudes ranging from attachment to outright raw desire. At the subtler end, we've seen that our biologically conditioned emotional empathy is biased, so that we care more about some people than others. We're so used to these biases that they seem natural to us: "Of course it's more tragic when a young woman on the verge of adult life dies than when an older woman dies!" we think. We don't question our perception that some lives are less valuable than others. But, if we want to be more loving, that's what we should do.

At the more extreme end, raw desire, I return to our attitude to animals. People don't eat just any animals. There is a division between animals whose welfare is of concern (pets, horses, rare species) and animals whose welfare doesn't matter much, if at all (mainly animals raised for slaughter, and those animals we dislike or fear). I've seen otherwise compassionate people drop live lobsters into boiling water, because those go in the category of "not mattering," and this happens because of raw craving. The fact that someone likes the taste of lobster suppresses their compassionate instincts.

One of my meditation students put it succinctly when she said that a common attitude is: "Your life is less important than my desire to eat you." Craving distorts our ability to think clearly, creating rationalizations such as, "Lobsters don't feel pain." We don't wonder how any creature could have survived for hundreds of millions of years without the ability to recognize things that are injurious to it. This same justification crops up with fish. If you tried to hunt rabbits or birds using baited hooks, you'd be arrested, because obviously that would be cruel. But baited hooks happen to be a good way to catch fish, and so we grow up with the myth that fish don't have nerve endings in their mouths. A fish's lips are its main way of touching things, so it makes no sense that they would have no sensation there, but, as I said, craving distorts our ability to think clearly. Craving creates justifications such as, "But these animals were raised to be eaten" and "What would happen to all the farm animals if we stopped eating them?" – and even, "Vegetables are alive too!" Craving persuades us that these statements make sense, even though a moment's thought shows them to be meaningless.

Even animal welfare organizations buy into the notion that some animal suffering matters and some doesn't. The UK's Royal Society for the Prevention of Cruelty to Animals would prosecute you if you kept a dozen dogs confined in one room for weeks, with injuries going untreated. But they'll ignore farms that do worse things. They've even issued their "RSPCA Assured" award to farms that have grossly abused animals.[156] Such is the reality-distorting effect of craving that an organization with the express purpose of preventing animal abuse says that animal abuse is acceptable.

Upekkha is about using wisdom to remove obstacles to love, and it involves questioning the way our minds operate.

Upekkha's other far enemy

We are challenged to see through craving's reality-distortion field and its irrational justifications. We are challenged to open our hearts and to allow empathy to arise for those we've previously considered as not mattering. We need to face the possibility that changing our habits is necessary. This involves equanimously confronting our fears and courageously facing our resistance to change. It's hard work, but only then can we stop craving from limiting our capacity to love.

I know from personal experience that none of this is easy. I was caught up in the reality-distortion field for many years. It was only when I first visited a slaughterhouse that I realized, against great resistance, that my desire to eat something I enjoy is not more valuable than another being's desire to live. I've been a vegetarian for more than forty years now, and a vegan for much of that time. I can no longer see a lamb or calf as potential food – any more than a kitten or a puppy. I hope one day all humans will feel that way.

Exercise

I know these issues are challenging. I even suspect that some people will have skipped reading this chapter rather than be confronted with the challenge of considering (again) whether farm animals are worthy of compassion. But I do encourage you to recall any affection you may have for companion animals, and then to include in awareness a farm animal as well, and consider that the latter's feelings are as real to it as the former's are to them.

18

The phenomenon of "othering"

Until 500 years ago, an English-speaking person would not have distinguished orange as a separate color from red, because the word "orange" didn't exist. What we call "orange" was just "red," or at best was seen as a blend of two colors: "yellow-red." Once the word "orange" was imported, however, the concept of red split, and now we have two distinct colors.[157] One day, English speakers might, like Russian speakers, regard light blue (*goluboy*) and dark blue (*siniy*) as fundamentally different colors. For now, though, they're just different shades of "blue." These are examples of how our minds divide things into different categories, and then perceive the world in terms of those categories.

The Buddha talked about how consciousness (*viññana*) is a condition for the arising of "name-and-form" (*namarupa*). I believe he was referring to the process I've described above. The mind takes undifferentiated perception, slices and dices it into different parts, and then names them.[158] Once we've given a name (*nama*) to the appearance (*rupa*) "orange," our minds forever see it as being separate from red. In using the term "consciousness," the Buddha was referring to the mind's tendency to see dualistic separation, rather than to "being aware" as such.[159] The *vi-* prefix in *viññana* means "separating," while *ñana* means "knowing." So *viññana* is dualistic knowing,

The phenomenon of "othering"

or *consciousness that separates* rather than the general faculty of perceiving.

The Buddha said that consciousness conditions name-and-form, but that name-and-form also conditions consciousness.[160] They are mutually conditioning. They prop each other up, like two bundles of reeds learning against each other.[161] The conceptual divisions we create become the apparent realities in which we live ("Of course *siniy* and *goluboy* are separate colors!"). As the Buddha said, "When a person sees, they see name and form, and having seen, they will know just these things"[162] – that is, all we can know is the categorizations we've created for ourselves.

Early in life, we separate self from other. We spend the rest of our lives taking that division to be real. We create many further divisions in our lives. We identify our parents or caregivers, distinguishing them from others. And then we create further distinctions, until every person we see is categorized in terms of gender, class, race, religion, nationality, sexual orientation, height, social power, and so on.

Cognitive scientists call these categorizations "knowledge schemas." They are not in themselves a problem: it's helpful to be able to recognize differences. But, having created these categories, we believe they are absolutely real. This can create problems. For example, there's a lot of hostility right now toward people who don't fit neatly into the male/female binary. People believe in their categories so passionately that they get angry when the world doesn't neatly correspond to them. Our minds may insist that everything exists in binaries, but the world is more complicated than that.

Schemas become toxic when cultural forces encourage us to see the categories we assign humans to as creating hierarchies of value. Some groups are seen as normal and better, and others as alien and inferior. Some are more worthy of respect and care, and others less. And so our knowledge schemas become overlaid with prejudice. The "other" becomes "othered" – that is, it becomes an other that is lesser, wrong, and not normal.

Since consciousness-that-separates and the nama-world of differences and hierarchies are mutually conditioning, you might despair about being able to escape this cycle. The important place to look, the Buddha says, is once again our feelings. ("All things converge on feelings," he said.)[163] It's our feeling responses that begin the process of othering. Conditioned responses leave us with unpleasant feelings regarding some, and pleasant feelings regarding others. Taking those feelings as a cue, we engage in patterns of reactive thought and emotion – judgments – that create hierarchies of value. When we choose not to be swayed by our feelings, we can experience our socially conditioned discomfort toward the "othered," but be kind and compassionate anyway. We work at dropping our judgments, which are unkind and uncompassionate. And, over time, the judgments that infiltrate our knowledge schemas begin to weaken and fade.

Blogger Lynn Kelly points out that we all have contempt, even though we don't want to acknowledge it:

Whom or what do we hold in contempt? Governments? Fat people? People with bad grammar? People who don't dress well? People who don't share our political views? People who don't speak our language? People without teeth? It may

The phenomenon of "othering"

not be a list we care to admit to – but it is probably there, possibly just below the level of consciousness.[164]

Reflect on what categories of people you feel contempt or disgust for. In your meditation, bring someone who fits that schema, and observe any feelings of discomfort that arise. Sit with those feelings, acknowledging them mindfully, while letting go of any judgmental thoughts that arise. See if you can find love for this person, recognizing their essential equality to yourself, and their potential buddhahood.

Exercise

We want to think we're fair, unbiased, and immune to our cultural conditioning. We need to look closer, and courageously, to see how we value some beings less than others. Look at your own responses to various groups to see how your conditioning has shaped those judgments.

19

All beings have been your mother

One traditional way of using wisdom to remove obstacles to love is to reflect that, as you've been reborn again and again over the unimaginable immensity of time, all beings have been related to you in every conceivable way. Anyone you find hard to love has been your mother, father, brother, sister, spouse, child, and so on. You have loved and cherished them, and they you. These recollections are intended to cut through our ill will as we imagine those former loving connections.

Having no personal evidence that rebirth exists, I find this exercise unconvincing, but I've found ways of adapting it to make it helpful. My test case was a politician for whom I had contempt. My dislike of him was so strong that I could barely stand to see his face or hear his voice. I found the policies he supported cruel and divisive. I'd not just disliked him, but had harbored ill will for him, taken pleasure in his discomfort, and had, to my shame, wished him harm.

I did not imagine that this person had been my child or mother in a past life. Instead, what I did was to imagine him as my wayward older brother *in this life*. I think most families have a black sheep – someone who is prone to exploiting others, or who lies, cheats, or steals. Perhaps they're an outright criminal. My own family had someone like that, in the form of an uncle who was almost certainly a sociopath.

Although this uncle was in many ways a terrible person, the fact that I was related to him softened my judgments of him.

Even if I believe this politician deserves to go to prison, my feelings are mixed. It becomes something I regrettably see as necessary for the good of society, rather than something I feel gleeful about. I can imagine visiting my wayward older brother in prison, not to gloat but to see if he's doing okay, and to be a support. I imagine hearing him protesting about being framed, and I feel compassion for him in his denial and delusion.

This approach helped me feel much softer around this politician. My heart's more open. Encountering him on the news is less disturbing. I suffer less. I still think that morally speaking he's a terrible individual, just as my uncle was. I do not like him, and probably never will, but I now care about him as a human being and want what's best for him (which is certainly not what he wants). I no longer harbor ill will for him. Perhaps this approach will help you, too.

We cling to our hatred because we think that to oppose our enemies we have to hate them. But that's not the case. We can set aside hatred and still tell right from wrong, still want to see our wayward elder brother prevented from causing further harm, and still believe it's right that they face the legal and moral consequences of their actions.

As the *Dhammapada* says:

For never is hatred
laid to rest by hate,
it's laid to rest by love:
this is an ancient teaching.[165]

We don't need hate. In fact we're much better off without it.

Exercise

Try imagining that someone you find especially difficult is a close family member. How does that change your feelings for them?

20

"All beings are, from the very beginning, buddhas"

I used to teach meditation and Buddhism to prison inmates. Most of the men I worked with were intelligent, thoughtful, and showed genuine compassion toward others. In their very challenging living situation, they were committed to their practice in a way that would put many Buddhists in the outside world to shame. Having ample time for reflection, they were often deeply regretful of the hurt they'd caused. I found much to admire about them and even considered them friends. Yet many of those men, I eventually came to discover, were murderers or sex offenders.

I was faced with the question: how should I relate to these people? At first I found myself torn between two perspectives. I could accept them at face value, as a collection of inspiring men. Or I could judge each by the worst thing he had ever done in his life. The former approach seemed naive; the latter uncompassionate. We are all arrows in flight. A human life is a trajectory, not a fixed point in space, and adopting a fixed view of another person limits both them and me. The only compassionate way to relate to these inmates was by recognizing their potential.

Sometimes I was privileged to see their potential unfolding. I used to meet up regularly with one of these men after his release. He'd done terrible things in his youth, and having done a lot of soul-searching he fully understood how he'd been acting, blindly, out of an inability to deal with his own pain. He deeply regretted his actions, and his victims had forgiven him. Entering old age in prison, he was a wise and kind man, who spent much time with inmates who were dying. Out of prison, in his final years, he struck anyone who spent time with him as a lovely individual. The arc of a life is long, and sometimes it tends toward buddhahood.

Sometimes, when I'm involved in a discussion about someone's spiritual progress, I find myself relying on impressions I formed years before. And I have to remind myself: people change. Our assessments of people are static snapshots, while they themselves are dynamic and ever-changing. Our internal images of people are simplifications, while they themselves are unimaginably complex. If we're to love others, it's important to remember that *they are change*. Even now, they are changing. Even as we see someone now, we're not seeing who they are: we're seeing this moment they're passing through on the way to being someone else. Being mindful of this is another way to practice upekkha.

I often bear in mind a line from a poem by Hakuin: "All beings are from the very beginning Buddhas."[166] I use this as a kind of mantra – a tool for changing the way my mind works. It reminds me to relate to others on the basis of who they can become, rather than what they've done or how they seem to be in the present. When we relate to another person as an ever-changing, evolving being containing the seeds of wisdom and compassion, we give them permission to develop those qualities. We help them to grow into their potential. And, because relating to them in this way involves acting with

"All beings are, from the very beginning, buddhas"

wisdom and compassion, it helps me grow into my potential as well.

Seeing others in this way doesn't mean ignoring what you see in front of you – the personality manifesting itself in the present moment – nor does it mean ignoring people's histories, even when those involve grossly unskillful acts. But we can see those things as moments in the flight of the arrow aimed at awakening. We are not defined by our mistakes. Those are just earlier points on the arrow's arc. And we're not fixed as we are right now. Now is just another point in time that the arrow is traversing on its way elsewhere. That "elsewhere" is buddhahood. We're all potential buddhas.

* * *

The fourth stage of the upekkha bhavana practice involves cultivating wisdom and love in relation to a friend. We can remind ourselves that they, like all of us, are afflicted with greed, hatred, and delusion. We are all capable, under the right circumstances, of doing very bad things. We can remember that they, like all of us, have the potential for enlightenment. We are all capable of great things. May we all find conditions that help us move toward awakening.

And so we can wish:

- May you accept the arising and passing of things.
- May you abide in equanimity, free from attachment or aversion.
- May you know the deep peace of awakening.

Exercise

When you see or think of others, remember, "This being is on the way to buddhahood," or, in Hakuin's words, "All beings are from the very beginning Buddhas." Remember that this applies to you, too. As you keep that perspective in mind, see how it changes the way you relate to yourself and others.

GUIDED MEDITATION: Upekkha for a friend

21
With reverence for all beings

One time when I was teaching in prison, Bobby, one of the inmates, shared an interaction he'd had in the prison yard. It had been raining heavily, and another inmate, seeing him pick his way slowly and carefully along the worm-covered paths, asked him incredulously why he was so bothered about killing worms. Bobby looked at him and said, "Well, can *you* make a worm?"

I find this a beautiful example not just of compassion, but also of upekkha. This is not upekkha in the cool uncaring sense that Buddhaghosa imagined it to be. It's a warm, nurturing quality. Bobby recognized something about worms that is easily overlooked. It's not just that worms suffer, but that they are miraculous. We humans take pride in our cleverness and our technology, but we've never made anything as complex as a worm.

But there's another form of upekkha at work here as well. Bobby *communicated* his sense of wonder and compassion. This implies that he recognized that his fellow inmate might be capable of wonder and compassion, too. He assumed the best in another human being, treating him as a friend, and, although I don't know if that person changed in any significant way, I imagine a seed was planted.

Empress Kōmyō was an important patron of Buddhism in eighth-century Japan. She saw taking care of the poor and the sick to be a religious duty, and there are paintings of her bathing a leper – his rags and foul appearance contrasting with her beauty and fine apparel. Many in Japan were scandalized that a high class woman would demean herself in such a way. Legend says that this leper revealed himself to be a buddha in disguise.

In a similar tale from India, the teacher Asanga had lived in a cave for twelve years, fruitlessly trying to visualize Bodhisattva Maitreya. Giving up in despair, he left his cave, only to encounter an injured dog by the side of the road. A festering wound on the animal's hindquarters was crawling with maggots, and Asanga wanted to help the dog by removing them. Realizing that picking out the maggots with his fingers would crush them, he decided to remove them, one by one, with the tip of his tongue. At this point the dog revealed itself as Bodhisattva Maitreya in disguise. At last Asanga's twelve years of practice had paid off!

In an important Mahayana text, the *Vimalakirti Nirdesha*, the bodhisattva householder Vimalakirti reveals that all the Maras in the world are secretly bodhisattvas, merely "playing the devil" in order to help ordinary beings become enlightened. He also says that most beggars are also bodhisattvas, who beg from other bodhisattvas (that is, us) in order to test them and help them on their spiritual path.[167]

Buddhas appeared to both Kōmyō and Asanga in order to teach them how to overcome disgust, which is an obstacle to love. Disgust (and contempt, which is a form of disgust) prevents us from seeing others' essential humanity. We have to overcome contempt and disgust in order to be fully compassionate.

Another implication of these stories is that we should regard all beings as potential buddhas, and treat them with respect and compassion. What would it be like for us to relate to everyone in this way? What would it be like to look at someone we struggle to like with enough love and imagination that we could see them as a potential buddha, or as a buddha in disguise? Perhaps we could try reminding ourselves not just that those we encounter are feeling beings and suffering beings, but that they are buddhas in the making. Every encounter we have with them is a teaching. Every obstacle is an opportunity for us to learn, and to move closer to our own buddhahood.

Exercise

Prepare yourself right now, and imagine that the next person you meet is a buddha in disguise. Now keep that thought in mind until you meet them, and see what difference it makes. You also might want to adopt the view that the next beggar you encounter is a bodhisattva, come to help you on your path.

22

Upekkha everywhere

Ordinary upekkha – being at peace with pleasant and unpleasant feelings – is an important part of all the brahma vihara practices. For example, when we consider the middle three stages of the metta bhavana meditation – friend, neutral person, enemy – we find that each evokes a distinct feeling tone. Thinking of a friend usually gives rise to pleasant feelings, a neutral person to neutral feelings (that is, we don't feel much), and a difficult person to unpleasant feelings. In each stage, the challenge is to maintain kindness without being swayed by our feelings. We allow them to be present, accepting them rather than reacting to them. We create a "gap" between feeling and emotion, and on the other side of that gap we maintain a skillful stance of kindness. If we lacked the ability to decouple our emotions from our feelings, we would be wholly on automatic pilot, reacting our way through life. Ordinary upekkha gives us freedom.

Upekkha as a brahma vihara – using wisdom to overcome obstacles to love – also finds its way into the other brahma viharas. For example, there are times we're cultivating kindness and we recognize the equality of others, seeing for example that our enemies are, just like us, struggling beings. Recognizing that someone we struggle with is going to die one day helps us to let go of our resentments and be more compassionate. Realizing that someone we care for is impermanent helps us to appreciate them more. Lynn Jurich's mantra – "All people and all circumstances are my allies" – is a powerful reflection on the equality of all beings. Both our friends and our enemies help us on our spiritual path. Upekkha is everywhere, which is to say that we can helpfully bring elements of wisdom into every meditation practice we do, using it to overcome obstacles to love.

Upekkha as a brahma vihara is not just a meditation practice. We can be aware of impermanence, non-self, conditionality, and other aspects of wisdom in our daily lives. In fact, because we spend most of our time in activities other than meditating, it's likely that most of our upekkha practice will take place in the world.

When I find myself frustrated with my children, I often remind myself of the fact that they were once helpless babies – the memory of which evokes love – and that they are on the way to being independent and accomplished adults. The challenges they bring into my life are virtually all to do with the bumpy transition from dependence to independence. Seeing them as arrows in flight, I find it easier to be understanding of their teenage moodiness or their reluctance to share my sense of priorities. When I find myself reacting to my partner, I remind myself that we are both working with our own conditioning. We each have forms of trauma from our childhoods, and, understanding that we are both conditioned beings, we find it easier to be patient and forgiving toward each other.

When someone drives aggressively close to my car and I become angry, I remind myself that the feeling of fear, and the reactive anger arising from it, are both impermanent, and that fairly soon I'll have forgotten about the incident altogether.

Reminding myself that I inherit the consequences of my actions, I consider that, if I allow myself to act unskillfully, I'll experience far more suffering than I otherwise would.

Seeing people acting badly in the world around me, I remind myself that all beings are blinded by delusion, that all have the potential to become awakened – and that big changes take a long time. Change is hard, and, however much we want it to take place, we need to find patience. Reacting to unskillfulness with ill will or despair is simply unhelpful. What this messed-up world needs is people who can work through their reactions, create calmness, and find their way back to love.

Exercise

In your daily life, look for opportunities to use wisdom to overcome obstacles to love. Practice upekkha everywhere.

23

There's no one to have compassion for, but have compassion for them anyway

One of my meditation students, as we were exploring upekkha practice together, said, "I'm noticing how something in me tightens or shuts down when confronted by another's different perspective. I'm silently defending my position as *right*. Guarding my self. But who or what is that?" Asking ourselves questions like "Who is defensive?" or "Where is the self that is resisting?" is an important practice of upekkha. Craving, aversion, and delusion are attempts to protect the self. But what is the self? Where is it? Maybe it doesn't exist? And, if so, what's the point of craving, aversion, and delusion?

We take it for granted that we have something called "a self." It's our essence, it defines who we are, it's unchanging (or relatively unchanging), and it's separate from the world (which is everything that is "non-self"). It's what receives inputs from the world, has thoughts and feelings about them, and then acts. This is how we think of it. Buddhism says that no such thing can exist.[168] So does science. So have many philosophers, such as the Scottish Enlightenment thinker David Hume, who wrote:

> *For my part, when I enter most intimately into what I call myself, I always stumble on some particular perception or*

other, of heat or cold, light or shade, love or hatred, pain or pleasure. I never can catch myself at any time without a perception, and never can observe any thing but the perception.[169]

In other words, when we're aware of ourselves, we're only ever aware of thoughts, sensations, feelings, and so on. And the things we're aware of come and go all the time. We are never aware of any "self" that has or creates them. The self we believe we have is a story. It doesn't correspond to anything that we can experience.

Our belief in a self is so ingrained and so central to the way we live our lives that it can be disturbing to consider that it might not exist. We think things like, "If I don't have a self, then who's here right now?" In other words, the idea of the self is equated with existing. We think things like, "If there were no self, how could I act?" – assuming that, if there were no self, then action could not take place. When you believe in a self, then you just can't imagine not doing so. It's like talking with people who believe in a certain idea of God. "If there's no God, then who created the universe?" they say. "If there's no God, then how can your life have meaning?" They can't imagine not having that belief.

Trying to *think* our way out of believing in a fixed or essential self is almost impossible. We need instead to *observe*. And, if we do, we'll eventually realize *it's just not there*. When people look for the self, they will still sometimes assume they've found it – "Aha! There it is!" – but all they're doing is labeling some perception or idea as "self." Here's Hume again:

There's no one to have compassion for ...

> *If any impression gives rise to the idea of self, that impression must continue invariably the same, through the whole course of our lives; since self is supposed to exist after that manner. But there is no impression constant and invariable. Pain and pleasure, grief and joy, passions and sensations succeed each other, and never all exist at the same time. It cannot, therefore, be from any of these impressions, or from any other, that the idea of self is derived; and consequently there is no such idea.*[170]

Hume probably had contact with Buddhist ideas, which might explain why his argument is so similar to the Buddha's.[171]

It's hard to see through the illusion of self, but it can be done, and when it happens it's a liberating and spiritually significant step, called stream entry. It's liberating, because our belief in a self inevitably causes suffering. As soon as we come up with the idea that we have a self, which happens at an early age, we wonder what kind of self we have. Seeing that we suffer in various ways, we inevitably come to the conclusion that the self we have is faulty. So we go through life believing that there is something fundamentally wrong with us, and often fear that others will discover "the real us" and stop loving us. Stream entry is spiritually significant because it's irreversible. Once it's happened, you've begun a new phase of spiritual progress that can only result in enlightenment.

Significant as it is, stream entry is only the first step on that new path. We find that we no longer believe we have a self, but we're forced to see that we still have an ego, in the form of craving, aversion, and delusion, which continue as habits, trying to defend a self we now know doesn't exist. The brahma viharas, and especially upekkha, play a role in uprooting these samskaras.

Buddhaghosa, in *The Path of Purification*, says that, at an advanced stage of development, the meditator's mind "has become skilled in apprehending what is non-existent in the ultimate sense, (that is to say, living beings, which are a concept)."[172] Recognizing that beings are trapped in a delusion that causes them suffering – imagining that they have selves – deepens our compassion and makes it easier for us to drop our aversions to them.

To quote Hume again:

> *I may venture to affirm of the rest of mankind, that they are nothing but a bundle or collection of different perceptions, which succeed each other with inconceivable rapidity, and are in a perpetual flux and movement.*[173]

When we see others as having selves, we inevitably categorize those selves as "good or bad," "worthy or unworthy," just as we had previously done with our own, and think that these qualities are inherent to who they are. Recognizing that people are bundles of ever-changing thoughts and emotions means that there is no permanent goodness or badness, worthiness or unworthiness, to be found in them. There are no selves there to have a bias toward or against, and so we can begin to love all equally.

Nevertheless, although there is no self that experiences suffering, suffering is real. So we compassionately wish that beings be free from suffering, while also recognizing that there are no beings to free from suffering.

There's no one to have compassion for ...

* * *

The final stage of the upekkha bhavana practice involves cultivating wisdom and love for all beings. At the same time, we can remember that beings do not have the kinds of selves they think they have. The selves they believe they have are a source of suffering. You can wish that, as they observe the arising and passing of things, they come to see their true nature, which is change.

And so we can wish:

- May you accept the arising and passing of things.
- May you abide in equanimity, free from attachment or aversion.
- May you know the deep peace of awakening.

Exercise

Yes, this can seem confusing! Don't try to force yourself to understand. Instead, look. Ask: where is this self that is confused? Don't take a concept (a verbal response) as an answer. Look for the actual thing: the self. Where is it? What is it like? Can you find it? Does it exist?

GUIDED MEDITATION: Upekkha bhavana

24

Living upekkha fully

The brahma vihara of upekkha can seem complicated. It can involve reflections on karma, impermanence, conditionality, and non-self. It addresses craving, aversion, and delusion. It can involve observing your own feelings or reflecting on others'. In essence, though, it's just *the use of wisdom to remove obstacles to love*. When anything that is non-love arises in our lives, we can change our perspectives and return to being loving. Because upekkha involves removing barriers to love, it also means cultivating a desire to be enlightened, since that's the only way we can remove *all* barriers to love. And, since we want others to be as free from suffering as they can possibly be, we want them to be enlightened too, and do what we can to help them move in that direction.

This might still sound complicated and abstract, but living upekkhafully is often very simple and practical. For example, a few months ago my partner and I adopted a puppy called Pippa. She became part of our household so quickly and easily that, after just an hour or two, our other dogs had fully accepted her. Several months later, though, Pippa was still not fully potty-trained. She was smart, but she just didn't get that we wanted her to do her business outside. This could be frustrating, and sometimes I got annoyed with her. But I knew that getting mad backfired. It stressed and confused her, making it harder for her to learn. So I needed to muster

Living upekkha fully

whatever patience I could. And, to do this, I practiced ordinary upekkha: on a good day, at least, I noticed my feelings of frustration and accepted them. Recognizing that I didn't have to react to them, I became calm again. And that calm state is always loving, because I already love her.

I reminded myself that her behaviors were conditioned. The foster family she'd been with had potty-trained her with disposable pee-pads. When she arrived here, she was already conditioned to see rectangular objects on the floor – such as rugs – as places to pee. She didn't choose to have this conditioning. It wasn't her fault. Remembering this, it was easier to be forgiving and loving. There was no point getting mad with her foster family either; with rescued animals constantly passing through their home, they just didn't have time to potty-train them. I reminded myself of the impermanence of this peeing habit, which I could know to be a passing phase. I reflected on non-self: the habit of peeing and pooping indoors was not a fixed part of who Pippa was, but just a transient part of her lovable being.

The reflections above helped me to return to calmness, and thence to love. This removed the suffering of getting angry as well as any that would come from regretting my anger. There are many times anger and frustration didn't arise at all – a sign that the upekkha practice was working. But, when I slipped up and did get frustrated, I reflected on how my own conditioning makes that inevitable. Given the punishment-oriented culture I grew up in, my first instinct when someone misbehaves is to get angry. I didn't choose to have that conditioning. I accept that it's going to take a while to undo it, and I accept that the tools I have for working on myself are imperfect. I forgive myself.

Eventually something clicked with Pippa. I realized one day that she had gone a week with no accidents. Then it was two weeks. Then she started making it clear when she needed to go out. Way to go, Pippa!

The chances are you don't have a puppy who pees and poops in your house, but I wanted to illustrate how the Dharma's wisdom teachings can be used to alleviate suffering in everyday situations that might otherwise cause frustration, anger, and self-blame. If you have a colleague who's difficult to work with, or a family member who does things you dislike, or an annoying neighbor, or you see politicians you can't stand on TV, you can adapt these practices to help bring more love, patience, and peace into your life and into the world. All experiences of non-love are invitations to look more deeply.

Exercise

Look for opportunities, even in the most mundane of frustrating daily activities, to apply wisdom teachings.

25

Upekkha and criticism

Once the Buddha was talking with a horse trainer called Kesi, who explained that sometimes he trained a horse through encouragement and rewards, sometimes through punishment, and sometimes through a mixture of the two. If none of those options worked, then he would have the horse killed so that it wouldn't damage his professional reputation. The Buddha said that he too sometimes trained people gently, through pointing out the benefits of living ethically. He'd train some people harshly, by telling them about the painful consequences of their unskillful actions. Some people required both approaches. And, when followers were unresponsive to training, he said – to Kesi's initial shock – he killed them. What he meant by this was that he stopped wasting his time giving guidance to those who refused to practice it.[174]

The Buddha taught out of love, to help beings move toward enlightenment. And sometimes, as we saw when he talked to Prince Abhaya, he had to say things that were critical. Being critical is something I often hesitate to do, because I used to be too critical, and I'm wary of it. Nevertheless, I want to offer a few suggestions for being critical in a loving way, so that you can model the kindness you want to encourage in others.

1. Refrain from speaking until you're calm. With heightened emotion, your words are likely to be hurtful.
2. Reconnect with love as much as you can. Speak out of care and concern for the other person.
3. Don't use the word "unskillful" as a polite Buddhist way of saying they're bad or wrong. They'll know what you mean.
4. Remember that it's the behavior that's the problem, not the person. You're not attacking them or saying they're bad or wrong.
5. Discuss the effects of actions. Let the other person know who you think is being hurt and in what way. If no one, not even them, will be hurt, is there really a problem to address?
6. Encourage skillful alternatives, and talk about the impact of those actions too. Say who you think will benefit, and in what way.
7. When it seems you're not going to make progress, let it go, or wait for a better time.
8. See this lack of progress in practical rather than in personal terms. It's not that the other person is stupid or bad, or that you're at fault. It's just that conditions aren't right for change to happen.

The initiative is now with the other person. They are responsible for their own actions, and they may change when they're ready. In the meantime, you've done what you can, so be at peace.

Again, living with upekkha is not necessarily easy to do, but upekkha is practical and it does help us to be more loving and to help others. It's a loving quality. It uses wisdom to overcome obstacles to love. And with that love we do what we can to steer ourselves and others in the direction of awakening.

Exercise

When you think it's helpful to offer criticism, bear in mind the points made above. Intelligently observe if any of these suggestions don't work for you. Keep experimenting until you find what does.

26

Mara and upekkha

Mara is a mythological figure from the Buddhist tradition. His name comes from a root meaning "death" and is related to English words like "mortal" and "murder." He represents the forces of fear, craving, hatred, and above all doubt, which derail our practice. He is what kills our spiritual practice.

In the early scriptures, Mara tries to sow doubt and distraction for spiritual practitioners. He appeared to the nun Soma, for example, trying to make her doubt that she, as a woman, could attain enlightenment. Recognizing Mara, Soma pointed out that her sex was irrelevant:

> *What difference does womanhood make*
> *when the mind is serene,*
> *and knowledge is present*
> *as you rightly discern the Dhamma.*[175]

Mara seems to have appeared very often to nuns. Perhaps that's because women practicing alone in the forest were more vulnerable, or because living in a male-dominated society left them more prone to doubt about their spiritual capacity.

Interestingly, the Buddha himself is the person in the early scriptures to whom Mara most often speaks. Mara sometimes challenges him in strangely mundane ways, like telling him that material prosperity is the way to happiness.

Mara and upekkha

Other times he's more subtle; Mara tried to persuade the Buddha that he shouldn't teach because this would get him caught up in the whole realm of popularity and unpopularity. This might be a believable doubt even for an advanced practitioner to have. The traditional view of the Buddha, however, is that he has transcended doubt, so it's odd that he hears the voice of Mara at all. The only way I can make sense of this is to assume that the Buddha did sometimes have doubting thoughts, but that he was *always* – unlike ourselves – able to recognize them for what they were. He saw through them. He recognized Mara, and the Evil One, as he's known, vanished.

Recognizing Mara is an important part of my own practice. When troubling thoughts and emotions arise, such as anger, despondency, or anxiety, I recognize them as Mara. Once I've done this, I no longer believe my thoughts and feelings in the way I did a moment before. I don't always manage to spot him; I imagine only the Buddha is aware enough to always recognize Mara. But it happens enough that it makes a significant difference to the quality of my life.

After recognizing Mara, I take a further step by congratulating him on having done such a good job of getting me worked up. He'd made it seem as if anger and anxiety were inevitable responses to life. The thoughts he'd created were completely believable, and the feelings utterly compelling. I think of them as being like the effects in a Hollywood movie. So I congratulate Mara: "Well done! You really had me fooled! Those special effects were amazing!" This makes the practice of recognizing Mara even more effective. It brings more appreciation, and hence joy, into my experience. It also helps to eradicate self-blame. After all, Mara is clever! No wonder he fools me!

So this is another tool for removing obstacles to love. When any pattern of thought, feeling, and emotion arises that prevents you from being kind, compassionate, and appreciative, recognize it as Mara, and congratulate him wholeheartedly. With those obstacles removed, you'll find you're able to return once again to a loving state.

Exercise

Try recognizing Mara and congratulating him.

27

Through love, to buddhahood

We've been on a long journey together, and it seems appropriate, for this final piece on the brahma viharas, to look back and see where we've been.

Kindness

We began with metta, or kindness. Kindness, however, rests on a foundation of empathy, so that's our true starting point. To be kind to others, we need to learn to empathize with ourselves, relating to ourselves as feeling beings whose happiness and suffering matter. Only then we can empathize with others, recognizing that their happiness and suffering are as real to them as our own are to us. Then we naturally want to act toward them with kindness. We think kindly about them, talk kindly to them, and act in kind ways toward them.

This isn't easy to sustain. We have deeply ingrained habits of ill will, and to live kindly requires constant training, both on and off the cushion. We make mistakes all the time, and learning to forgive ourselves becomes part of our training in kindness.

Compassion

Wanting beings to be well means wanting them to be free from suffering. Compassion is not a mere feeling, but rather a desire to relieve suffering or to support beings while they go through it. Compassion is active. Having compassion can involve simply being present, one feeling being to another, relieving them of the burden of being alone with their problems. Sometimes it means offering practical help.

Compassion doesn't mean taking on others' sufferings. We don't see someone drowning and think, "Oh, I should drown too, so that I can empathize with them." If we try to feel what they feel, we may well render ourselves useless. It's enough to know they're suffering. We learn to stand firmly on the bank, using our strength and stability to help them out of the water.

Joyful appreciation

Joyful appreciation goes deeper still. We recognize that, although we want beings to be well, happy, and at ease, those things arise from their skillful thoughts, words, and actions. So we recognize and appreciate the skillful in ourselves and others. We encourage the skillful to arise, so that beings can be happier and the world can become a better place. Mudita is a wisdom practice, insofar as seeing the workings of conditionality involves wisdom.

Removing obstacles to love

No matter how much progress we make in being kind, compassionate, and appreciative, as long as we're not enlightened, craving, aversion, and delusion – known as the three roots of unskillfulness – will act as obstacles to love.[176] Eradicating unskillfulness by cultivating the first three brahma viharas is like cutting a plant back to the earth: as long as the roots remain, it will keep growing back. To remove all obstacles to love, we must uproot unskillfulness entirely, and to do that we need to develop insight. Upekkha bhavana, on and off the cushion, is the process of using insight to overcome obstacles to love.

Enlightenment, which is what removes the last traces of the roots of unskillfulness, is what we aim for in practicing upekkha. But we aim for enlightenment for all beings, rather than for ourselves alone. This is because we want all beings to reach the deepest level of joy and peace possible, which is enlightenment. To practice upekkha bhavana is to practice the bodhisattva path.

Upekkha is the culmination of the brahma viharas. It perfects our ability to be kind, compassionate, and appreciative. It takes us to buddhahood, where compassion flows effortlessly and unobstructedly. The Buddha spent his entire life teaching, mentoring, and guiding others to attain the same state of compassionate peace that he had attained. He lived the four brahma viharas – which are the best ways of living life, and are also states of divine abiding – in order to benefit others.

I've mentioned that the Buddha refused to settle for anything short of complete freedom from the three roots of unskillfulness. He didn't settle for a position in government, or for being the leader of a meditation community. He didn't settle for being a renowned ascetic. He kept pushing on, until he'd uprooted every trace of craving, aversion, and delusion from his mind. This is the example he set. The brahma viharas are powerful tools that he offered so that we could emulate him. Together, let's follow that example. So long as life remains, may we commit ourselves to living with love, and to removing obstacles to love.

Exercise

Take a breath. We've come a long way! What shifts have you noticed in your life as you've followed this 108-step path through love and all its permutations?

Conclusion

In *Gravity and Grace*, Simone Weil writes, "Attention, taken to its highest degree, is the same thing as prayer."[177] Let us attend, prayerfully, meditatively.

Let your eyes be soft and kind. Notice your inner field of attention soften too, becoming ready to receive. Notice how sensations from all over the body present themselves to you, effortlessly. There's no need to seek them out; just let them come to you. Notice the soft tenderness of this breathing, animal body, softening further as it's held in kindness. Notice your living, tender heart, meeting whatever feelings you find there – whether they're pleasant, unpleasant, or neutral – with warmth.

If there's any pain or discomfort present, meet that too with kindness. Sit, knowing that it's a skillful thing to be aware, to look kindly, to accept whatever you find, without judgment. Know that there is, besides these things, abundant goodness within you. Feel the pulsating, tingling energy and brightness of skillful qualities that are waiting for action, hovering at the soft boundary between known and unknown.

Recognize your own being as a mystery, indefinable, and not capable of being pinned down by some crude label such as "self" or "non-self." Whatever-this-is is changing in every moment, capable of evolving beyond all apparent limitations into a state of unconditional love and wisdom. Sense the

The Heart's Awakening

potential buddha that you are, and let yourself resonate to the quiet song of your own future awakeness.

Let your eyes and your field of attention soften and open further, into the space, sound, light embracing you. Who is around you in this world, seen or unseen, heard or unheard, human or animal? Let your kind eyes smile upon them. When the warmth of your attention touches suffering, see it transform into compassion. May all beings be free from suffering. When the warmth of your mind joyfully touches goodness, let appreciation, admiration, and emulation arise. May the good qualities in yourself nurture the good in you, and may the good in them call forth your own goodness.

Even more than goodness, though, our world needs awakening; it needs the unconditional compassion – maha karuna – that recognizes and encourages the potential buddhahood in all beings. May all beings move swiftly toward that awakening. May all beings know the deep peace of the awakened mind, free from craving and aversion, and may they dwell in love's fullness, acting as guides to the world.

On this long journey together we have not gone anywhere. The whole time we've been right here, right now. And, although we may talk of it this way sometimes, enlightenment is not a destination. It's not place you go to. It's not far away. It's simply a different way of seeing, a change in perception. Feel the closeness of awakening. Sense that it's right here, surrounding and penetrating you, in this miraculous present moment, just waiting to be found, just waiting for that shift of perspective to take place.

May you and all beings know the deep peace of awakening.

Notes

Introduction

1 I still refer to "lovingkindness meditation" rather than "kindness meditation" so that people will know what I'm talking about.
2 For example, it's found in compounds like *brahma-deyya*, the best of gifts, *brahma-danda*, the worst punishment, *brahma-vada*, best speech, *brahma-yana*, best path or best vehicle.
3 We have compounds like *eka-vihara*, living alone, *jangha-vihara*, wandering on foot, *diva-vihara*, spending the time of day.
4 Buddhaghosa, *The Path of Purification*, trans. Nyanamoli Thera, 4th ed., Buddhist Publication Society, Kandy 2010.
5 Upatissa, *The Path of Freedom (Vimuttimagga)*, trans. Rev. N.R.M. Ehara, Soma Thera, and Kheminda Thera, Dr. D. Roland D. Weerasuria, Colombo 1961.

Part I, chapter 1

6 We Buddhists often talk about "sentient beings." Generally we think of "sentient" as meaning "being conscious," but its full meaning is "being able to perceive or *feel* things." Sentient beings are feeling beings.
7 See Bodhipaksa, *This Difficult Thing of Being Human*, Parallax Press, Berkeley, CA 2019.
8 *Families (Kulasutta)*, SN 20.3, translated by Bodhipaksa. Bhikkhu Sujato's translation is available at https://suttacentral.net/sn20.3/en/sujato, accessed on November 6, 2024.

Part I, chapter 2

9 *Dhammapada*, verse 130, translated from the Pali by Bodhipaksa.

Notes

10 *The People of Bamboo Gate* (*Veludvareyyasutta*), SN 55.7, translated from the Pali by Bhikkhu Sujato, available at https://suttacentral.net/sn55.7/en/sujato, accessed on November 6, 2024.

Part I, chapter 4

11 "Loving eyes," in Jan Chozen Bays, *How to Train a Wild Elephant, and Other Adventures in Mindfulness*, Shambhala, Boston, MA 2011, ch.14.

Part I, chapter 5

12 *The Shorter Analysis of Deeds* (*Culakammavibhangasutta*), MN 135, translated from the Pali by Bhikkhu Sujato, available at https://suttacentral.net/mn135/en/sujato, accessed on November 6, 2024.

Part I, chapter 7

13 This isn't a phrase I use much these days, even in its second-person form. But perhaps you do, and it may have conditioned how you think about the practice.

Part I, chapter 11

14 Tony Schwartz, "Relax! You'll be more productive," *New York Times*, February 9, 2013, available at https://www.nytimes.com/2013/02/10/opinion/sunday/relax-youll-be-more-productive.html, accessed on November 6, 2024.

Part I, chapter 12

15 John O'Donohue, *Anam Cara: A Book of Celtic Wisdom*, Cliff Street Books, New York 1997, p.13.

16 *Half the Holy Life* (*Upaddhasutta*), SN 45.2, translated from the Pali by Bhikkhu Bodhi, adapted by Bodhipaksa, original available at https://suttacentral.net/sn45.2/en/bodhi, accessed on November 6, 2024.

Notes

Part I, chapter 15

17 *The Discourse on Loving-Kindness* (*Mettasutta*), Snp 1.8, translated from the Pali by Piyadassi Thera, available at https://suttacentral.net/snp1.8/en/piyadassi, accessed on November 6, 2024. (Wording altered to be gender-neutral.)

Part I, chapter 17

18 "L'attention est la forme la plus rare et la plus pure de la générosité." From an April 13, 1942 letter to poet Joë Bousquet, published in *Correspondance*, L'Âge d'Homme, Lausanne 1982, p.18.

19 Sometimes we'll not want to approach someone because we sense in some way that they are a threat. Trust your gut on this.

Part I, chapter 22

20 See, for example, *Analysis* (*Vibhangasutta*), SN 12.2, translated from the Pali by Bhikkhu Sujato, available at https://suttacentral.net/sn12.2/en/sujato, accessed on November 6, 2024.

Part I, chapter 23

21 *With Anuruddha* (*Anuruddhasutta*), MN 127, translated from the Pali by Bhikkhu Sujato, available at https://suttacentral.net/mn127/en/sujato, accessed on November 6, 2024.

Part I, chapter 24

22 Jamil Zaki, "Kindness contagion," *Scientific American*, July 26, 2016, available at https://www.scientificamerican.com/article/kindness-contagion/, accessed on November 6, 2024.

23 "Partisan conflict and congressional outreach," *Pew Research Center*, February 23, 2017, available at https://www.pewresearch.org/politics/2017/02/23/partisan-conflict-and-congressional-outreach, accessed on November 6, 2024.

Part I, chapter 25

24 *The People of Bamboo Gate* (*Veludvareyyasutta*), SN 55.7.

25 *To Cunda the Silversmith* (*Cundasutta*), AN 10.176, translated from the Pali by Thanissaro Bhikkhu, https://suttacentral.net/an10.176/en/thanissaro, accessed on November 6, 2024.

26 *About Araka* (*Arakasutta*), AN 7.74, translated from the Pali by Bhikkhu Sujato, available at https://suttacentral.net/an7.74/en/sujato, accessed on November 6, 2024.

27 *With Jivaka* (*Jivakasutta*), MN 55, translated from the Pali by Bhikkhu Sujato, https://suttacentral.net/mn55/en/sujato, accessed on November 6, 2024.

Part I, chapter 26

28 *The Meditation on Love* (*Mettabhavanasutta*), Iti 27, translated from the Pali by Bhikkhu Sujato, available at https://suttacentral.net/iti27/en/sujato, accessed on November 6, 2024.

Part I, chapter 27

29 Adapted from Bodhipaksa, *Wildmind: A Step-by-Step Guide to Meditation*, 2nd ed., Windhorse Publications, Birmingham 2010, p.329.

Part II, The essentials of karuna

30 Following the pattern in *The Path of Freedom*, there is no "friend stage" here. The metta bhavana includes a friend because that's a natural place to start connecting with our innate kindness for others. The karuna bhavana includes a suffering person in this stage because that's a natural place for connecting with our innate compassion toward others.

Part II, chapter 1

31 *The Path of Freedom*, p.190 (wording modernized).

Part II, chapter 4

32 *The Longer Discourse on Mindfulness Meditation* (*Mahasatipatthanasutta*), DN 22, translated from the Pali by Bhikkhu Sujato, available at https://suttacentral.net/dn22/en/sujato, accessed on November 8, 2024.

Notes

Part II, chapter 5

33 I'm an introvert with a very low need for social contact, but even I need to get out and see people sometimes.

Part II, chapter 6

34 *A Question about Suffering* (*Dukkhapanhasutta*), SN 38.14, translated from the Pali by Bhikkhu Sujato, available at https://suttacentral.net/sn38.14/en/sujato, accessed on November 8, 2024.

35 *An Arrow* (*Sallasutta*), SN 36.6, translated from the Pali by Bhikkhu Sujato, available at https://suttacentral.net/sn36.6/en/sujato, accessed on November 8, 2024.

36 *The Shorter Discourse on the Mass of Suffering* (*Culadukkhakkhandhasutta*), MN 14, translated from the Pali by Bhikkhu Sujato, available at https://suttacentral.net/mn14/en/sujato, accessed on November 8, 2024. The relevant section is where the Buddha explains the drawbacks of sensual pleasures.

Part II, chapter 8

37 *The Simile of the Boat* (*Nava Sutta*), Snp 2.8, translated from the Pali by John D. Ireland, available at https://www.accesstoinsight.org/tipitaka/kn/snp/snp.2.08.irel.html, accessed on November 8, 2024. (Quotation altered to make it gender-neutral.)

Part II, chapter 9

38 *The Path of Purification*, p.313.
39 *The Path of Purification*, p.312.
40 *Nakula's Father* (*Nakulapitusutta*), SN 22.1, translated from the Pali by Bhikkhu Sujato, available at https://suttacentral.net/sn22.1/en/sujato, accessed on November 8, 2024.

Part II, chapter 10

41 Ram Dass wrote a book with the title *Walking Each Other Home*, but it's not clear that he ever said or wrote the quote that's attributed to him.

Part II, chapter 11

42 I don't want this to sound like it's coming from someone who has all this stuff sorted out. These are just some thoughts about bringing compassion into daily life from someone who struggles with doing that.

Part II, chapter 12

43 He adapted this term from George Gurdjieff, who said there were various kinds of idiot, including the compassionate idiot.

44 *With Prince Abhaya (Abhayarajakumarasutta)*, MN 58, translated from the Pali by Bhikkhu Sujato, available at https://suttacentral.net/mn58/en/sujato, accessed on November 8, 2024.

Part II, chapter 13

45 "Morality," *RadioLab*, WNYC Radio, November 7, 2007, available at https://radiolab.org/podcast/91508-morality/transcript, accessed on November 8, 2024.

46 "Do animals have morals?," *TED Radio Hour*, National Public Radio, September 5, 2014, available at https://www.npr.org/transcripts/338936897, accessed on November 8, 2024.

47 Rob Mitchum, "Helping your fellow rat: Rodents show empathy-driven behavior," *University of Chicago News*, December 8, 2011, available at https://news.uchicago.edu/story/helping-your-fellow-rat-rodents-show-empathy-driven-behavior, accessed on November 8, 2024.

Part II, chapter 15

48 A common myth says that everything is steadily growing worse, although Steven Pinker explains in detail that the opposite is true in *The Better Angels of Our Nature: Why Violence Has Declined*, Viking, New York 2001.

Part II, chapter 16

49 Felix Warneken and Michael Tomasello, "Altruistic helping in human infants and young chimpanzees," *Science* 311, March 3, 2006, pp.1301–3, available at https://www.

eva.mpg.de/documents/AAAS/Warneken_Altruistic_Science_2006_1555118.pdf, accessed on November 8, 2024.
50 David Rand *et al.*, "Spontaneous giving and calculated greed," *Nature* 489, September 19, 2012, pp.427–30, available at https://doi.org/10.1038/nature11467, accessed on November 8, 2024.
51 Kristin Layous *et al.*, "Kindness counts: Prompting prosocial behavior in preadolescents boosts peer acceptance and well-being," *PLOS One* 7:12, December 26, 2012, available at https://doi.org/10.1371/journal.pone.0051380, accessed on November 8, 2024.
52 Thaddeus Pace *et al.*, "Effect of compassion meditation on neuroendocrine, innate immune and behavioral responses to psychosocial stress," *Psychoneuroendocrinology* 34:1, January 2009, pp.87–98, available at https://doi.org/10.1016/j.psyneuen.2008.08.011, accessed on November 8, 2024.
53 Bethany Kok *et al.*, "How positive emotions build physical health: Perceived positive social connections account for the upward spiral between positive emotions and vagal tone," *Psychological Science* 24:7, July 1, 2013, pp.1123–32, available at https://pubmed.ncbi.nlm.nih.gov/23649562, accessed on November 8, 2024.
54 Sofie Isenberg, "Want to feel happier? Science says try being more generous," *WBUR*, July 28 2020, available at https://www.wbur.org/kindworld/2020/07/28/dunn-interview, accessed on November 8, 2024.
55 Lara Aknin *et al.*, "Giving leads to happiness in young children," *PLOS One* 7:6, June 14, 2012, available at https://www.ncbi.nlm.nih.gov/pmc/articles/PMC3375233/, accessed on November 8, 2024.
56 *At Sedaka* (*Sedakasutta*), SN 47.19, translated from the Pali by Bhikku Sujato, available at https://suttacentral.net/sn47.19/en/sujato, accessed on November 8, 2024.

Part II, chapter 17
57 *With Khema* (*Khema Sutta*), AN 6.49, translated from the Pali by Thanissaro Bhikkhu, available at https://www.accesstoinsight.

org/tipitaka/an/an06/an06.049.than.html, accessed on November 8, 2024.

Part II, chapter 18

58 For fascinating insights into the overlap of animal training and human relationships, see Amy Sutherland, *What Shamu Taught Me about Life, Love, and Marriage: Lessons for People from Animals and Their Trainers*, Random House, London 2009.

Part II, chapter 19

59 "Emotions occur when the cognitive eliciting conditions of emotions are satisfied [...] Memory is a cognitive process that allows for the storage and retrieval of eliciting conditions but not of feelings." Gerald L. Clore *et al.*, "Affective feelings as feedback: Some cognitive consequences," in *Theories of Mood and Cognition: A User's Guidebook*, ed. Leonard L. Martin and Gerald L. Clore, Taylor & Francis, London 2001, pp.27–62.

Part II, chapter 21

60 Rolf Dobelli, "News is bad for you – and giving up reading it will make you happier," *The Guardian*, April 12, 2013, available at https://www.theguardian.com/media/2013/apr/12/news-is-bad-rolf-dobelli, accessed on November 8, 2024.

Part II, chapter 22

61 Sean Thomas Dougherty, "Why bother?," in *The Second O of Sorrow*, BOA Editions, Rochester, NY 2018, p.9.

Part II, chapter 23

62 Unlike the modern European convention, the order of the directions is East, South, West, North.
63 *Metta Sutta: Good Will* (2), AN 4.126, translated from the Pali by Thanissaro Bhikkhu, available at https://www.accesstoinsight.org/tipitaka/an/an04/an04.126.than.html, accessed on November 8, 2024.

Notes

64 *A Horn Blower* (*Sankhadhamasutta*), SN 42.8, translated from the Pali by Bhikkhu Sujato, available at https://suttacentral.net/sn42.8/en/sujato, accessed on November 8, 2024.

Part II, chapter 24

65 *A Splinter* (*Sakalikasutta*), SN 4.13, translated from the Pali by Bhikkhu Sujato, available at https://suttacentral.net/sn4.13/en/sujato, accessed on November 8, 2024. (Quotation altered to render *anukampa* as "empathy" rather than "sympathy.")

Part II, chapter 25

66 We encountered this as the concept of "vagal tone" in Part II, Chapter 16.
67 *Inference* (*Anumana Sutta*), MN 15, translated from the Pali by Bhikkhu Bodhi, available at https://www.suttas.com/mn-15-anumana-sutta-inference.html, accessed on November 8, 2024.

Part II, chapter 26

68 This quotation and those following are from "Chapter VIII: the perfection of meditation," in *A Guide to the Bodhisattva Way of Life*, translated from the Sanskrit and Tibetan by Vesna A. Wallace and B. Alan Wallace, Snow Lion Publications, Ithaca, NY 1997.
69 This is the basis of the six-element practice that the Buddha taught. For an extended exploration of this practice, see Bodhipaksa, *Living as a River*, Sounds True, Boulder, CO 2010.
70 *Truths of the Brahmins* (*Brahmanasaccasutta*), AN 4.185, translated from the Pali by Bhikkhu Sujato, available at https://suttacentral.net/an4.185/en/sujato, accessed on November 8, 2024.
71 As we've seen, this practice does not imply experiencing the other person's suffering. It's enough to know that others are suffering, and that this suffering is something they do not want.
72 *A Guide to the Bodhisattva Way of Life*, p.100.

Part II, chapter 27

73 *At Kalaka's Monastery* (*Kalakaramasutta*), AN 4.24, translated from the Pali by Bhikkhu Sujato, available at https://suttacentral.net/an4.24/en/sujato, accessed on November 8, 2024.

74 "Communion" comes from a Proto-Indo-European root meaning "to change together."

Part III, chapter 1

75 *The Path of Freedom*, p.192.

76 In the translation of *The Path of Freedom* I've been referring to, *mudita* is rendered as "appreciative joy." This includes the same two components, joy and appreciation, but the relationship between them is inverted. Mudita is not "joy that is appreciative." It's "appreciation that is joyful."

Part III, chapter 2

77 "You vs. future you, or why we're bad at predicting our own happiness," *Hidden Brain*, National Public Radio, August 23, 2016, available at https://www.npr.org/transcripts/490972873, accessed on November 11, 2024.

78 *Perversions* (*Vipallasasutta*), AN 4.49, translated from the Pali by Bhikkhu Sujato, available at https://suttacentral.net/an4.49/en/sujato, accessed on November 11, 2024.

79 Minda Zetlin, "Stanford and NYU researchers paid 2,844 people to stop using Facebook for a month," *Inc.*, January 31, 2019, available at https://www.inc.com/minda-zetlin/quitting-facebook-research-happiness-stanford-nyu-allcott-braghieri-eichmeyer-gentzkow.html, accessed on November 11, 2024.

Part III, chapter 3

80 To learn more about Bodhipaksa's meditation community, visit https://www.wildmind.org/the-initiative.

Part III, chapter 5

81 *Skillful* (*Kusala Sutta*), AN 2.19, translated from the Pali by Thanissaro Bhikkhu, available at https://www.accesstoinsight.

Notes

org/tipitaka/an/an02/an02.019.than.html, accessed on November 11, 2024.

Part III, chapter 6

82 Jon Kabat-Zinn, *Full Catastrophe Living*, Delacorte, New York 1990, p.2.

83 *To Cunda the Silversmith* (*Cundasutta*), AN 10.176. I have rendered *sukha* as "joyfully" rather than as "with ease," which is Thanissaro's original translation. *Sukha* means "joy" or "happiness" as well as "ease."

Part III, chapter 7

84 From *The Front Page* (1974), directed by Billy Wilder. Screenplay by Billy Wilder and I.A.L. Diamond.

Part III, chapter 8

85 Benjamin Disraeli, *Conningsby*, vol.1, Henry Colburn Publisher, London 1844, p.254.

86 Jonathan Haidt, "Elevation and the positive psychology of morality," May 10, 2001, available at https://pages.stern.nyu.edu/~jhaidt/articles/haidt.2003.elevation-and-positive-psychology.pub026.html, accessed on November 11, 2024.

87 Dacher Keltner, *Born to Be Good: The Science of a Meaningful Life*, W.W. Norton, New York 2009, p.228.

88 I highly recommend all seven volumes of Maya Angelou's autobiography. Her life as a prostitute and pimp is covered in the second volume, *Gather Together in My Name*, Random House, New York 1974.

Part III, chapter 9

89 *The Analysis of the Six Sense Fields* (*Salayatanavibhanghasutta*), MN 137, translated from the Pali by Bhikkhu Sujato, available at https://suttacentral.net/mn137/en/sujato, accessed on November 11, 2024.

Part III, chapter 11

90 Shantideva, *A Guide to the Bodhisattva Way of Life*, p.21.

91 *The Shorter Analysis of Deeds* (*Culakammavibhangasutta*), MN 135, translated from the Pali by Bhikkhu Sujato, available at https://suttacentral.net/mn135/en/sujato, accessed on November 11, 2024.

92 *Dhammapada*, verse 119, translated from the Pali by Bodhipaksa.

Part III, chapter 12

93 *Respect* (*Garavasutta*), SN 6.2, translated from the Pali by Bhikkhu Sujato, available at https://suttacentral.net/sn6.2/en/sujato, accessed on November 11, 2024.

94 *Blessings* (*Mangalasutta*), Kp 5, translated from the Pali by Bhikkhu Sujato, available at https://suttacentral.net/kp5/en/sujato, accessed on November 11, 2024.

Part III, chapter 14

95 *Advice to Sigalaka* (*Singalasutta*), DN 31, translated from the Pali by Bhikkhu Sujato, available at https://suttacentral.net/dn31/en/sujato, accessed on November 11, 2024. I've changed the translation of *anukampa* from "sympathetic" to "empathetic" to maintain consistency with earlier chapters.

96 *The Shorter Discourse at Gosinga* (*Culagosingasutta*), MN 31, translated from the Pali by Bhikkhu Sujato, available at https://suttacentral.net/mn31/en/sujato, accessed on November 11, 2024.

97 *Assemblies* (*Parisasutta*), AN 3.95, translated from the Pali by Bhikkhu Sujato, available at https://suttacentral.net/an3.95/en/sujato, accessed on November 11, 2024.

98 *With Ujjaya* (*Ujjayasutta*), AN 8.55, translated from the Pali by Bhikkhu Sujato, available at https://suttacentral.net/an8.55/en/sujato, accessed on November 11, 2024. (Translation altered to be gender neutral.)

Part III, chapter 16

99 *Advice to Rahula at Ambalatthika* (*Ambalatthikarahulovadasutta*), MN 61, translated from the Pali by Bhikkhu Sujato, available at https://suttacentral.net/mn61/en/sujato, accessed on November 11, 2024.

Notes

100 *Advice to Rahula at Ambalatthika* (*Ambalatthikarahulovadasutta*), MN 61. I've translated two terms differently from Bhikkhu Sujato. I've rendered *vinnu* as "a teacher" rather than "the Teacher" (Pali has no definite or indefinite articles and it seems more likely that "a teacher" was meant). And I've translated *sabrahmacari* as "fellow practitioner" rather than "sensible spiritual companion."
101 Sometimes we'll do both: apologize to the person we've hurt, and also confess to spiritual friends or teachers.

Part III, chapter 17

102 *Matrceta's Hymn to the Buddha*, translated from the Sanskrit by Ven. S. Dhammika, available at https://www.accesstoinsight.org/lib/authors/dhammika/wheel360.html, accessed on November 11, 2024.
103 Jess Cording, "In new book, NYTimes bestselling author Susan Cain explores the value of bittersweetness in a world of toxic positivity," *Forbes*, September 9, 2022, available at https://www.forbes.com/sites/jesscording/2022/09/09/nytimes-bestselling-author-susan-cain-explores-the-value-of-bittersweetness-in-a-world-of-toxic-positivity, accessed on November 11, 2024.
104 Quoted in Susan Moon, *This Is Getting Old Zen: Thoughts on Aging with Humor and Dignity*, Shambhala, Boulder, CO 2010, p.86.

Part III, chapter 19

105 *A Guide to the Bodhisattva Way of Life*, pp.69 and 70.

Part III, chapter 20

106 David Gelles, "She's taking on Elon Musk on solar. And winning," *New York Times*, January 23, 2020, available at https://www.nytimes.com/2020/01/23/business/lynn-jurich-sunrun.html, accessed on November 11, 2024.
107 *Lojong* ("mind training") is a system of practice within Tibetan Buddhism that makes use of lists of slogans, or aphorisms.

Part III, chapter 21

108 It's also what my parents jokingly gave me while I was in the womb, before they finally chose a name for me.

Part III, chapter 22

109 *With Ghatikara* (*Ghatikarasutta*), MN 81, translated from the Pali by Bhikkhu Sujato, available at https://suttacentral.net/mn81/en/sujato, accessed on November 11, 2024.

110 *Dhammapada*, verse 146, translated from the Pali by Acharya Buddharakkhita, available at https://www.accesstoinsight.org/tipitaka/kn/dhp/dhp.11.budd.html, accessed on November 11, 2024.

111 *Quickly* (*Tuvataka Sutta*), Snp 4.14, translated by Thanissaro Bhikkhu, available at https://www.accesstoinsight.org/tipitaka/kn/snp/snp.4.14.than.html, accessed on November 11, 2024.

112 Bodhipaksa, "What the Buddha never said," *Tricycle*, summer 2015, available at https://tricycle.org/magazine/what-buddha-never-said, accessed on November 11, 2024.

113 Juhn Young Ahn, "A malady of meditation: A prolegomenon to the study of illness and Zen," PhD dissertation, University of California, Berkeley 2007, pp.155–6. Square brackets in original.

Part III, chapter 23

114 *Subjects for Regular Reviewing* (*Abhinhapaccavekkhitabbathanasutta*), AN 5.57, translated by Bhikkhu Sujato, available at https://suttacentral.net/an5.57/en/sujato, accessed on November 11, 2024.

115 Bodhipaksa, *Living as a River*, p.xi.

116 Quoted in Susan Shaughnessy, *Walking on Alligators: A Book of Meditations for Writers*, HarperCollins, New York 1993, p.103.

117 *Subjects for Regular Reviewing* (*Abhinhapaccavekkhitabbathanasutta*), AN 5.57.

Notes

Part III, chapter 24

118 *Stand Up*, official lyric video performed by Cynthia Erivo, *Focus Features*, available at https://www.youtube.com/watch?v=sn19xvfoXvk, accessed on November 11, 2024.

Part III, chapter 26

119 Galway Kinnell, "Saint Francis and the sow," in *Three Books*, Houghton Mifflin, New York 2002, p.81.

Part III, chapter 27

120 *The Rod Embraced* (*Attadanda Sutta*), Snp 4.15, translated from the Pali by Thanissaro Bhikkhu, available at https://www.accesstoinsight.org/tipitaka/kn/snp/snp.4.15.than.html, accessed on November 11, 2024.

Part IV, chapter 1

121 *The Path of Purification*, p.319.
122 *The Path of Freedom*, p.193. I've reversed the order of the second and third terms to make it easier to explain what the relationship is between these factors.
123 We need to be wary of what's called "the etymological fallacy," which is the mistaken idea that the etymology of a word reveals its "true" meaning. For example, some people will insist that "to decimate" an army can only mean to kill every tenth soldier, even though it has for a long time meant "to kill or destroy a large part of something." Nevertheless, I think the etymology of *upekkha* tells us something important about it as a practice.
124 *The Path of Freedom*, p.189.
125 A mahasattva (*mahasatta* in Pali) is a bodhisattva at an advanced stage of development.

Part IV, chapter 2

126 Bhikkhu Bodhi, "Toward a threshold of understanding," 5 June 2010, available at https://www.accesstoinsight.org/lib/authors/bodhi/bps-essay_30.html, accessed on November 12, 2024.
127 *The Path of Freedom*, p.194.

128 These connections are laid out in *The Characteristic of Not-Self* (*Anattalakkhanasutta*), SN 22.59, translated from the Pali by Bhikkhu Sujato, available at https://suttacentral.net/sn22.59/en/sujato, accessed on November 12, 2024.

Part IV, chapter 3

129 The Buddha describes three forms of upekkha in the *Niramisa Sutta*, two of which I describe here. I do not discuss the form of upekkha that is the peace of the fourth jhana, since this has nothing directly to do with the brahma viharas. Nevertheless, the later commentarial tradition, with its passion for categorization, insisted – contrary to what the Buddha said – that upekkha bhavana could only be cultivated in third jhana. *Not of the Flesh* (*Niramisasutta*), SN 36.31, available at https://suttacentral.net/sn36.31/en/sujato, translated by Bhikkhu Sujato, accessed on November 12, 2024.
130 In the *Niramisa Sutta* this is "the equanimity of the flesh."
131 Upekkha as a brahma vihara is not mentioned in the *Niramisa Sutta*.
132 In the *Niramisa Sutta* the equanimity of awakening is called "the equanimity that is even-more-not-of-the-flesh."

Part IV, chapter 4

133 "Nous sommes tous pétris de faiblesses et d'erreurs; pardonnons-nous réciproquement nos sottises." Voltaire, "Tolérance," in *Dictionnaire philosophique*, vol.7, Didot, Paris 1822, p.362.
134 *The Path of Freedom*, p.193.

Part IV, chapter 5

135 *The Longer Advice to Rahula* (*Maharahulovadasutta*), MN 62, translated from the Pali by Bhikkhu Sujato, available at https://suttacentral.net/mn62/en/sujato, accessed on November 12, 2024.
136 Shunryu Suzuki, *Zen Mind, Beginner's Mind*, Weatherhill, San Francisco, CA 1999, p.32.

Notes

Part IV, chapter 6

137 *Perversions* (*Vipallasasutta*), AN 4.49, translated from the Pali by Bhikkhu Sujato, available at https://suttacentral.net/an4.49/en/sujato, accessed on November 12, 2024.

138 "Go to the limits of your longing" by Rainer Maria Rilke, from *Rilke's Book of Hours: Love Poems to God*, Riverhead Books, New York 2005, p.119.

Part IV, chapter 7

139 For those interested in etymologies, our verb "create" is from the same Proto-Indo-European root.

Part IV, chapter 8

140 *An Arrow* (*Sallasutta*), SN 36.6.

141 *The Characteristic of Not-Self* (*Anattalakkhanasutta*), SN 22.59.

142 This phrase, *netam mama nesohamasmi na meso atta* in Pali, is found in many of the Buddha's discourses, including in *The Wanderer Susima* (*Susimaparibbajakasutta*), SN 12.70, translated from the Pali by Bhikkhu Sujato, available at https://suttacentral.net/sn12.70/en/sujato, accessed on November 12, 2024.

Part IV, chapter 10

143 "Through upekkha one maintains an even mind towards all beings [...] Equality is its function." *The Path of Freedom*, p.193. Upekkha "is characterized as promoting the aspect of neutrality towards beings. Its function is to see equality in beings." *The Path of Purification*, p.312.

144 *The Appeal of the Divinity* (*Brahmayacanasutta*), SN 6.1, translated from the Pali by Bhikkhu Sujato, available at https://suttacentral.net/sn6.1/en/sujato, accessed on November 12, 2024.

145 C.S. Lewis, *The Weight of Glory and Other Addresses*, Macmillan, New York 1949, p.15. Lewis also notes that we might fear others, as well as worship them!

Notes

Part IV, chapter 11

146 Marian Wright Edelman reports that he said this. Quoted in Paul Rogat Loeb, *Soul of a Citizen: Living with Conviction in a Cynical Time*, St Martin's Press, New York 1999, p.57.

Part IV, chapter 12

147 *A Firebrand* (*Chavalatasutta*), AN 4.95, translated from the Pali by Bhikkhu Sujato, available at https://suttacentral.net/an4.95/en/sujato, accessed on November 12, 2024.

148 Helen Riess MD, "The science of empathy," *Journal of Patient Experience*, May 9, 2017, available at https://journals.sagepub.com/doi/full/10.1177/2374373517699267, accessed on November 12, 2024.

Part IV, chapter 14

149 *Cessation* (*Nirodhasutta*), AN 5.166, translated by Bhikkhu Sujato, available at https://suttacentral.net/an5.166/en/sujato, accessed on November 12, 2024.

150 *Sectarian Tenets* (*Thitthayatanasutta*), AN 3.61, translated from the Pali by Bhikkhu Sujato, available at https://suttacentral.net/an3.61/en/sujato, accessed on November 12, 2024.

Part IV, chapter 15

151 Stephen Batchelor, "A Buddhist Brexit," *Tricycle: The Buddhist Review*, Spring 2017, available at https://tricycle.org/magazine/a-buddhist-brexit/, accessed on January 29, 2025.

152 Ekhart Tolle, *Stillness Speaks*, New World Library, Novato, CA 2003, p.92.

153 For an excellent example of this, see Conor Friedersdorf, "The audacity of talking about race with the Ku Klux Klan," *The Atlantic*, March 27, 2015, available at https://www.theatlantic.com/politics/archive/2015/03/the-audacity-of-talking-about-race-with-the-klu-klux-klan/388733/, accessed on November 12, 2024.

Part IV, chapter 16

154 *The Path of Purification*, p.320.

Part IV, chapter 17

155 From an Instagram post, available at https://www.instagram.com/p/CSoaxJUD677/?img_index=3, accessed on November 12, 2024.

Part IV, chapter 17

156 George Monbiot, "How Britain's oldest animal welfare charity became a byword for cruelty on an industrial scale," *The Guardian*, June 18, 2024, available at https://www.theguardian.com/commentisfree/article/2024/jun/18/rspca-britain-oldest-animal-welfare-charity-cruelty-abuse, accessed on November 12, 2024.

Part IV, chapter 18

157 "Orange" as a fruit is older than "orange" as a color.
158 Nama-rupa has this interpretation in teachings that predate the Buddha, such as the *Chandogya Upanishad*, which he would have been familiar with.
159 The *vi-* in *viññana* and in the word "divide" comes from the same root.
160 "When name and form cease, consciousness ceases. When consciousness ceases, name and form cease." *The Great Discourse on Traces Left Behind* (*Mahapadanasutta*), DN 14, translated from the Pali by Bhikkhu Sujato, available at https://suttacentral.net/dn14/en/sujato, accessed on November 12, 2024.
161 *Bundles of Reeds* (*Nalakalapisutta*), SN 12.67, translated from the Pali by Bhikkhu Sujato, available at https://suttacentral.net/sn12.67/en/sujato, accessed on November 12, 2024.
162 *The Longer Discourse on Arrayed for Battle* (*Mahabyuhasutta*), Snp 4.13, translated from the Pali by Bhikkhu Sujato, available at https://suttacentral.net/snp4.13/en/sujato, accessed on November 12, 2024.
163 *The Roots of Everything* (*Mula Sutta*), AN 10.58, translated from the Pali by Nyanaponika Thera, available at https://www.accesstoinsight.org/lib/authors/nyanaponika/wheel238.html#passage-23, accessed on November 12, 2024.
164 Lynn J. Kelly, "Contempt vs. respect," *The Buddha's Advice to Laypeople*, available at https://buddhasadvice.wordpress.

com/2014/03/02/contempt-vs-respect/, accessed on November 12, 2024.

Part IV, chapter 19

165 *Pairs* (*Yamakavagga*), Dhp 1.5, translated from the Pali by Bhikkhu Sujato, available at https://suttacentral.net/dhp1-20/en/sujato, accessed on November 12, 2024.

Part IV, chapter 20

166 Hakuin, "Song of meditation," in Kerry Brown and Joanne O'Brien, *The Essential Teachings of Buddhism*, Rider, London 1989, p.266.

Part IV, chapter 21

167 Robert A.F. Thurman, *The Holy Teaching of Vimalakirti*, Penn State University Press, University Park, PA 1976, p.54.

Part IV, chapter 23

168 Strictly speaking, the Buddha never said there is no self. He simply stated that nothing we can point to can be considered part of a self. I'd paraphrase his approach as saying that the kind of self you think you have does not exist.
169 David Hume, *Treatise on Human Nature*, Clarendon Press, Oxford 1896, p.252.
170 *Treatise on Human Nature*, pp.251–2. (Spelling modernized.)
171 Alison Gopnik, "How an 18th-century philosopher helped solve my midlife crisis," *The Atlantic*, October 2015, https://www.theatlantic.com/magazine/archive/2015/10/how-david-hume-helped-me-solve-my-midlife-crisis/403195/, accessed on November 12, 2024.
172 *The Path of Purification*, p.319.
173 *Treatise on Human Nature*, p.252.

Part IV, chapter 25

174 *With Kesi* (*Kesisutta*), AN 4.111, translated from the Pali by Bhikkhu Sujato, available at https://suttacentral.net/an4.111/en/sujato, accessed on November 12, 2024.

Notes

Part IV, chapter 26

175 *With Soma* (*Somasutta*), SN 5.2, translated from the Pali by Bhikkhu Sujato, available at https://suttacentral.net/sn5.2/en/sujato, accessed on November 12, 2024.

Part IV, chapter 27

176 *Unskillful Roots* (*Akusalamulasutta*), AN 3.69, translated from the Pali by Bhikkhu Sujato, available at https://suttacentral.net/an3.69/en/sujato, accessed on November 12, 2024.

Conclusion

177 Simone Weil, *Gravity and Grace*, Putnams, New York 1952, p.171.

WINDHORSE PUBLICATIONS

Windhorse Publications is a Buddhist charitable company based in the UK. Our books, which are distributed internationally, champion Buddhism, meditation, and mindfulness. They offer fresh interpretations of Buddhist teachings and their application to contemporary life, with subject matter and authors from across the Buddhist tradition, catering for a broad range of interest and experience. In addition to publishing titles exploring classic texts for modern audiences, we aspire to publish books that offer a Buddhist perspective on today's challenges, including social inequality, the environment and climate, gender, mental health, and more. Established in the 1970s to publish the writing of Urgyen Sangharakshita (1925–2018), the founder of the Triratna Buddhist Order, Windhorse Publications continues to be dedicated to preserving and keeping in print his impressive and influential body of work, making it accessible for future generations. As well as high quality print and eBooks, Windhorse Publications produces accompanying audio, podcast, video, and teaching resources.

Windhorse Publications
38 Newmarket Road
Cambridge CB5 8DT
info@windhorsepublications.com

North America Distributors: Consortium Book Sales & Distribution
210 American Drive
Jackson TN 38301
USA
www.cbsd.com

Australia and New Zealand Distributors: Windhorse Books
PO Box 574
Newtown NSW 2042
Australia
windhorse.com.au/books.html

THE TRIRATNA BUDDHIST COMMUNITY

Windhorse Publications is a part of the Triratna Buddhist Community, an international movement with centres in Europe, India, North and South America, and Australasia. At these centres, members of the Triratna Buddhist Order offer classes in meditation and Buddhism. Activities of the Triratna Community also include retreat centres, residential spiritual communities, ethical Right Livelihood businesses, and the Karuna Trust, a UK fundraising charity that supports social welfare projects in the slums and villages of India.

Through these and other activities, Triratna is developing a unique approach to Buddhism, not simply as a philosophy and a set of techniques, but as a creatively directed way of life for all people living in the conditions of the modern world.

If you would like more information about Triratna please visit thebuddhistcentre.com or write to:

London Buddhist Centre
51 Roman Road
London E2 0HU
UK
contact@lbc.org.uk

Aryaloka
14 Heartwood Circle
Newmarket NH 03857
USA
info@aryaloka.org

Sydney Buddhist Centre
24 Enmore Road
Sydney NSW 2042
Australia
info@sydneybuddhistcentre.org.au

Train Your Mind

Tibetan Exercises in Wisdom and Compassion

Dhirananda and Viryabodhi

The mind training of Tibetan Buddhism (lojong) cultivates wisdom and compassion through 59 slogans. They inspire, challenge, and confront us with life's difficulties and our own limitations, helping develop an enlightened perspective. Dhirananda and Viryabodhi offer commentaries and exercises to bring the slogans to life. With regular practice, our heart-minds can shift from a limited, self-centred view to something more connected and liberated, able to prioritise the welfare of others.

This book is precious. Read it carefully to discover a brilliant map for training your mind and heart that is immediately applicable to all of life's circumstances. If things are going well, be generous and share your good fortune. If things are difficult, use this as an opportunity for empathy for others suffering in similar ways. Dhirananda and Viryabodhi have done a brilliant job of translating the profound and compassionate slogans into immediately accessible and practical teachings for the modern world. – Vidyamala Burch OBE, founder of the Breathworks Foundation and author of *Living Well with Pain and Illness*, *Mindfulness for Health*, and *Mindfulness for Women*

This is a great book for anyone who wants to know how to practise the Dharma in every moment of their life. The authors invite us to change our habitual attitudes to ones in which we treat whatever happens to us as gifts – opportunities to grow spiritually. – Ratnaguna, author of *The Art of Reflection* and *Great Faith, Great Wisdom*

Dhirananda (Kenneth Nolkrantz) is a retired doctor and Triratna Buddhist Order member in Stockholm. He co-founded the Triratna community in Sweden and has taught Buddhism, meditation, and mindfulness.

Viryabodhi has led the Stockholm Buddhist Centre since 1997, translated numerous Buddhist texts into Swedish, and helped establish Dharmagiri Retreat Centre.

ISBN 978 1 915342 51 5
160 pages

Life with Full Attention

A Practical Course in Mindfulness

Maitreyabandhu

In this eight-week course on mindfulness, Maitreyabandhu teaches you how to pay closer attention to experience. Each week he introduces a different aspect of mindfulness – such as awareness of the body, feelings, thoughts, and the environment – and recommends a number of easy practices; from trying out a simple meditation to reading a poem. Featuring personal stories, examples, and suggestions, *Life with Full Attention* is a valuable aid to mindfulness both as a starting point and for the more experienced.

ISBN 9781 899579 98 3
328 pages

For General Product Safety Regulation (EU) queries,
the authorized representative for Windhorse
Publications Ltd is:
Buddhistisches Tor Berlin
Buddhistische Gemeinschaft Triratna (Berlin) E.V.
Grimmstrasse 11B-C
10967 Berlin-Kreuzberg
info@buddhistisches-tor-berlin.de

www.ingramcontent.com/pod-product-compliance
Lightning Source LLC
Chambersburg PA
CBHW072044110526
44590CB00018B/3027